EXPLORATIONS OF VALUE

VIBS

Volume 55

Robert Ginsberg
Executive Editor

Associate Editors

G. John M. Abbarno
Virginia Black
H. G. Callaway
Rem B. Edwards
Rob Fisher
Dane R. Gordon
Heta Häyry
Matti Häyry
Richard T. Hull

Joseph C. Kunkel
Ruth M. Lucier
Alan Milchman
George David Miller
Michael H. Mitias
Samuel M. Natale
Peter A. Redpath
Alan Rosenberg
Arleen Salles

Daniel Statman

EXPLORATIONS OF VALUE

Edited by

Thomas Magnell

Amsterdam - Atlanta, GA 1997

Cover design by Chris Kok based on a photograph, ©1984 by Robert Ginsberg, of statuary by Gustav Vigeland in the Frogner Park, Oslo, Norway.

∞ The paper on which this book is printed meets the requirements of "ISO 9706:1994, Information and documentation - Paper for documents - Requirements for permanence".

ISBN: 90-420-0254-9 (bound)
ISBN: 90-420-0393-6 (paper)
©Editions Rodopi B.V., Amsterdam - Atlanta, GA 1997
Printed in The Netherlands

For
Kim and Albert

CONTENTS

INTRODUCTION	THOMAS MAGNELL	1
ONE	The Value of Value Inquiry for Moral Philosophy THOMAS MAGNELL	7
TWO	Moral Philosophy in Four Tiers JOSEPH MARGOLIS	19
THREE	Objectivity: Wrong Concept for Value Inquiry DON E. MARIETTA, JR.	47
FOUR	Towards a Metaphysics of Practice JAMES B. WILBUR III	61
FIVE	On Intrinsic and Quasi-Intrinsic Value CARLO FILICE	69
SIX	The Postmodern Turn: Plurality of Voice or Cacophony? JAMES S. KELLY	83
SEVEN	The Business of the Ethical Philosopher TOM REGAN	93

EIGHT	The Risks of Advocacy	105
	WILLIAM AIKEN	
NINE	Philosophers and Advocates	111
	ROBERT K. FULLINWIDER	
TEN	The Lost Childhood of *Homo Economicus*	119
	ROGER PADEN	
ELEVEN	Elements of a Naturalistic Realism in Ethics	129
	JONATHAN JACOBS	
TWELVE	The Value of Human Life: An Absolutist Strategy for Attacking Consequentialism	141
	JORAM GRAF HABER	
THIRTEEN	On Benefiting People by Creating Them	155
	JULIAN LAMONT	
FOURTEEN	Forgiveness, Moral Reassessment, and Reconciliation	169
	UMA NARAYAN	
FIFTEEN	The Photograph on My Mind	179
	ROBERT GINSBERG	

SIXTEEN	The Screaming of the Lambs: Philosophical Themes in Demme's *Silence of the Lambs*	189
	SANDER LEE	
SEVENTEEN	Let's Dance with Wolves!	199
	H.P.P. (HENNIE) LÖTTER	
EIGHTEEN	What Is Wrong with Prostitution?	213
	JOSEPH KUPFER	
NINETEEN	Can Love Resolve the Problem of Marriage?	221
	PREDRAG CICOVACKI	
CONTRIBUTORS		235
INDEX		239

Introduction

Thomas Magnell

The essays collected here are drawn from work first presented at the 20th Conference on Value Inquiry, held at Drew University in 1992. They are not mere papers bound in a proceedings. Some of the papers presented at the conference, fine as they were, have not found their way in this volume. As well, the essays that follow are not mere records of conference presentations. The authors have reflected on their initial presentations. They have re-thought arguments in light of discussions at the conference. They have revised their work. All of this has combined to bring fresh ideas on important issues into carefully considered discussions.

The nineteen authors of the essays do not share a common viewpoint on all problems of value inquiry. They are certainly not in agreement in their conclusions. Their concerns, however, cluster around a recognizable body of questions. Several of the authors raise fundamental questions on the nature of values and the possibility of giving them an objective status. Some of the authors raise questions about where value inquiry becomes value advocacy. They are also ready to ask whether or not advocacy is in the legitimate purview of philosophers. A number of authors set out to examine conditions of moral practice and of harming or benefiting people in general. Other authors show a concern for juxtaposing moral values and aesthetic values, in some cases to observe similarities, in some, differences. Finally, a few authors focus on particular notions such as forgiveness, intimacy, and love that are central to our lives.

The first essay, "The Value of Value Inquiry for Moral Philosophy," outlines the boundaries of the work that may come under the designation "value inquiry." After giving expression to the inclusiveness of the subject, I offer a three-way distinction for identifying fields characterized by questions of value, as disciplinary value inquiry, inter-disciplinary value inquiry, and meta-disciplinary value inquiry. I delineate areas of conceptual exploration for meta-disciplinary value inquiry and discuss their importance for normative ethics. I advance reasons for taking moral goodness to be the most general and fundamental moral concern, and point to the need for a general account of the contribution that the term "good" makes in the phrase "morally good." The understanding we gain from meta-disciplinary work may be of service to more specifically meta-ethical work, which in turn may be helpful for work in normative and applied ethics.

Broad conceptual questions are also at the focus of the essay by Joseph Margolis. In "Moral Philosophy in Four Tiers," Margolis presents an overview of contemporary moral theorizing that is wide-ranging and subtle. Central to his discussion is the notion of objectivity with respect to moral values. He maintains that moral philosophers from J. L. Mackie to Thomas Nagel, Bernard Williams, and David Wiggins have kept to three tiers of theorizing. He argues for a fourth tier of thought that offers a new prospect for gauging objectivity. On his view, when we reflect on moral problems, we are left without an agent-neutral perspective, or anything approaching neutrality independently of our place in the world. Margolis suggests that we need to look out through the gates of historicism and radically re-examine our ways of moral theorizing. In doing so, he calls into question our very notion of objectivity in ethics.

The notion of objectivity is also a concern for Don E. Marietta, Jr. In his "Objectivity: Wrong Concept for Value Inquiry," Marietta maintains that values are not objective. He does not deny that values have characteristics which approach an agent-neutral perspective, but takes the position that the notion of objective value can be accounted for in terms of what he calls end value and independent value. He argues that in some respects, end values and independent values may not be as significant as might be supposed. Some important values are not independent of us. In any event, the theoretical issues need not bear on moral problems in practice. He holds that even if we cannot satisfy demands of objectivity for values, that does not undermine rational argument in ethics.

Rational argument over ethics, prudence, and practice in general is the central concern of James B. Wilbur III. In "Towards a Metaphysics of Practice," Wilbur argues that oughts of practice are always hypothetical. He also holds, however, that at least for moral practice, oughts are unconditional. They are presuppositions of moral action. Considerations of a metaphysics of practice may seem far removed from everyday concerns, but for Wilbur they are motivated by questions of moral responsibility in business practice. He finds theory and practice to be tied together tightly and regards the enabling conditions of practice to be the basis of our moral values. Indeed, he takes the enabling conditions of practice to be universal, inasmuch as they are the same for all of us.

Values are sometimes distinguished as intrinsic and instrumental. In "On Intrinsic and Quasi-Intrinsic Value," Carlo Filice argues for a third type of value to lie between intrinsic value and instrumental value. Filice calls values of this third type quasi-intrinsic values. More than mere means, quasi-intrinsic values nonetheless lack characteristics of sentience or pleasure that he considers to be requisite for intrinsic values. Autonomy and excellence, on his view, have quasi-intrinsic value. Aesthetic values too, he maintains, may be quasi-intrinsic. But how are basic values apprehended? After reviewing contemporary discussions of the objectivity of values, James S. Kelly attends to this question in "The Postmodern Turn: Plurality of Voice or Cacophony?" He suggests that we should accord value experiences epistemic weight, much as we do sensory experiences. Indeed, he takes the position that they afford us access to a normative reality. Value experiences themselves, he urges, have grounding in our emotions.

We display our values in our actions. The more strongly we feel about an issue, the more we may do to persuade others to share our views. On some issues we may even believe we are morally compelled to do this. People with a strong sense of values, as may be said, often show a willingness to involve themselves publicly in causes. In what ways and to what extent should moral philosophers act as advocates in the public arena?" Tom Regan raises this fascinating question in "The Business of the Ethical Philosopher." After distinguishing three types of advocacy, logical advocacy, normative advocacy, and political advocacy, he argues that, strictly speaking, only logical and normative advocacy are in the provenance of philosophers. As a philosopher, a philosopher should be engaged in rational argument and criticism. The point is not to still the voice of a philosopher strongly committed to a cause, but to clarify the legitimate role of a philosopher as a philosopher. A moral philosopher may engage in political advocacy *qua* concerned citizen, but not *qua* moral philosopher. The roles need to be kept distinct.

William Aiken and Robert K. Fullinwider also address the matter of political advocacy for moral philosophers. In his "Risks of Advocacy," Aiken dismisses the limits, in principle, to political advocacy that Regan places on moral philosophers. Aiken finds the notion of a neutral philosophical stance suspect, making all talk of roles for philosophers less than clear cut. But even as he argues that philosophers may engage in advocacy irrespective of roles, he holds that moral philosophers should be ready to restrict themselves to rational argument and criticism in order to maximize their effectiveness. Moral philosophers should approach advocacy with caution. Moral philosophers would often be well advised to restrain themselves as a matter of prudence. Like Aiken, Fullinwider is not inclined to limit the role of a philosopher when it comes to political advocacy. In his "Philosophers and Advocates," Fullinwider does find philosophy and advocacy to be distinct and even opposed to one another in some ways. But a philosopher in academia is likely to combine the jobs of an intellectual, a scholar, and a teacher. These jobs may make advocacy obligatory. He suggests that philosophers should even be willing to do more to develop rhetorical skills in order to better discharge their responsibilities. That political advocacy is not excluded from the role of a philosopher, he argues, has historical warrant going back to Plato.

If prudence is a matter of maximizing utility for oneself, a rational utility maximizer should be prudent. We should expect the model of rational utility maximization for economists, *Homo economicus*, to be a prudent individual. In the "Lost Childhood of *Homo Economicus*" Roger Paden points to fundamental problems in the model. Employing ideas of Derek Parfit, Paden examines presuppositions of personal identity which *Homo economicus* does not share with actual people. If prudence is problematic for *Homo economicus*, this presents serious difficulties for other models of practical reasoning, including idealizations in ethics and political theory. Conceptual concerns of practical reasoning are at the heart of the position set out by Jonathan Jacobs in his "Elements of a Naturalistic Realism in Ethics." Jacobs maintains that practical reasoning allows us to recognize the normative significance of facts. He argues that there is a common human nature and that with practical reasoning we may recognize the ethical significance of facts. This provides a basis for a sort of naturalism in ethics that has its roots in Aristotelian thought. Since human needs and interests are various, and the conditions in which people live differ from time to time, and place to place, naturalism in ethics leaves room for much that is found in pluralism today.

In "The Value of Human Life: An Absolutist Strategy for Attacking Consequentialism," Joram Graf Haber offers a defense of moral absolutism, the view that some types of actions cannot be right under any circumstances. Utilitarians and other types of consequentialists do not generally accept moral absolutism. Hard cases may make bad law, but they afford test cases in philosophy. Haber sets out several widely discussed hard cases and considers two theses that moral absolutists might advance to deal with them, the incomparability thesis and the equality thesis. For some hard cases, on the equality thesis, comparisons are odious because there is effectively nothing to choose between alternatives. On the incomparability thesis, comparisons are out of place because the conditions preclude a choice among alternatives. Haber defends the equality thesis on the grounds that life is infinitely valuable and that doing away with a life is infinitely bad.

Julian Lamont is also concerned with the value of life to people, but from the standpoint of their coming into existence. In "On Benefiting People by Creating Them," he raises the question: Does causing someone to exist benefit, in a moral sense, the person brought into existence? In the course of examining arguments of Derek Parfit, Lamont concludes, contrary to Parfit, that there are reasons to think the answer is "no." The problem, he points out, is that no existing person benefits from procreation: no *thing* exists to be benefited prior to coming into existence. Moral injunctions against killing are not similarly problematic, since someone does exist to be harmed by a premature death. The issue of benefiting people by creating them plainly bears on controversies over abortion and population growth. It is of particular importance to some forms of utilitarianism.

Someone who feels wronged, even when justified in feeling so, may nonetheless be morally called on to forgive the wrongdoer. In "Forgiveness, Moral Reassessment, and Reconciliation," Uma Narayan argues that forgiveness is a process that requires the aggrieved party to set aside feelings that have been hurt. Narayan suggests that reasons for forgiveness involve reassessments of wrongdoers, relationships to wrongdoers, wrongs, and reactions to wrongs. She also examines the relation of forgiveness to reconciliation and takes the position that while forgiveness may lead to reconciliation, it is not necessary for reconciliation. The greatest value of forgiveness, she maintains, has to do with the realignment of our reassessments and feelings. Forgiveness is never far removed from the reflections of Robert Ginsberg in "The Photograph on My Mind." He offers a humanistic response to the inhumane image of a nameless man in a Nazi prison who died trying to dig out from under a burning building set on fire just hours before the arrival of American troops. As a reaction to an image, his inner narrative displays the aesthetic power that an image can have. Yet it would be hard to lose sight of the moral overtones of the situation captured in the image. The aesthetic power is largely dependent on the moral values at issue.

Images of death can fascinate. In drawing our attention, they also have the power to entertain. Sander Lee examines the power of film filled with horrific images in "The Screaming of the Lambs: Philosophical Themes in Demme's *Silence of the Lambs*." Lee contrasts the way *Silence of the Lambs* is structured with another film in the horror-suspense genre, *Psycho*. He offers a detailed analysis of *Silence of the Lambs* that probes into the states of mind of the main characters. Nietzscheian themes appear throughout it, among them, the notion of a will to power. Films may also illustrate and promote broad political values. In "Let's Dance with Wolves!", H. P. P. (Hennie) Lötter suggests that the film *Dances with Wolves* exemplifies liberal values that are needed to reconcile differences in pluralistic societies. In particular, the film displays the importance of a complex principle that combines an equal respect for people, with an equal consideration of interests. He finds evidence in the film that acceptance of the complex principle by individuals leads to dialogue. In a broader social context, strengthened dialogue can help to advance a type of consensus that is not easily forged in a pluralistic society.

Respect is central to the issue Joseph Kupfer takes up in "What Is Wrong with Prostitution?". Here, however, it is not so much respect for others, but self-respect that is at issue. He holds that prostitution shows a lack of self-respect requisite for full autonomy. He argues that prostitution precludes intimacy essential for self-development. In the end, prostitution is a bad bargain for the prostitute, with characteristics of high value for a person being tendered for nothing that matters as much. Intimacy is also central to the essay by Predrag Cicovacki. In "Can Love Resolve the Problem of Marriage?", Cicovacki observes that the heights of intimacy can be reached in marriage, though not without difficulty, and that intimacy and constancy are two essential features of marriage relationships. All too often, intimacy and constancy are at odds with one another. Love, of course, is another essential feature of marriage. Cicovacki distinguishes spiritual love from romantic love and argues that while the two types of love are not mutually exclusive, spiritual love in the forms of *eros*, *filia*, *agape*, and *amor* is the main ingredient for easing tensions between intimacy and constancy in marriage. It is as well a key to self-development. Love thus brings together high values for the joint undertaking of marriage and for the individual.

Inquiry is typically spurred by a lack of knowledge or understanding, and value inquiry is no exception. Some question leaves us uneasy; some problem gets under our skin; what someone says rubs us the wrong way—whatever the source of discomfort, we have an itch and feel the need to scratch. But inquiry, at its best, also sets more questions that provoke further thought. It is itself the cause of more itching. The essays that follow are nothing if not thought-provoking. They repay close reading with new questions. Such are the theses, arguments, and conclusions of the authors and the value of their work.

One

THE VALUE OF VALUE INQUIRY FOR MORAL PHILOSOPHY

Thomas Magnell

1. Inter-disciplinary and Meta-disciplinary Value Inquiry

The future of moral philosophy lies in value inquiry. In one sense, that should be uncontroversial: moral philosophy raises moral questions; moral questions are expressions of moral inquiry; and moral inquiry is a type of value inquiry. But there are two more interesting senses in which significant development in moral philosophy will depend on knowledge gained from value inquiry.

What is value inquiry? What do the words "value inquiry" mean? As a designation, "value inquiry" is something of an umbrella term. It covers a broad array of concerns ranging from abstract issues of value theory, ethics, aesthetics, economics, rational decision theory, and social and political theory, to practical issues of applied values discussed by all manner of thinkers from novelists, poets, and playwrights, to anthropologists, psychologists, and historians—indeed to reflective individuals in general. Over the years, questions of value have multiplied and spawned specialized disciplines, even as issues of applied values have stirred all who have had occasion to deliberate.

There are some who deplore specialization. I am not among them. Specialization is a concomitant of intellectual development. What begins as *peri phuseos* becomes physics, chemistry, and biology, not to mention philosophy. The maturation of physics leads to classical mechanics, thermodynamics, quantum mechanics, general relativity theory, and astrophysics. History, at first inquiry in general, matures into a collection of temporally bound and culturally restricted studies of human events—other events being relegated to the altogether different field of natural history. Even the arts grow into areas of specialization. Literature enjoins specialization by language or culture; music by style or period; and the fine arts by medium or school. To some extent, the specialization spawned by questions of value is to be applauded as an index of development.

Where once value inquiry having to do with scarcity was left to moral and political philosophers, since 1776 it has become an activity of specialists. In that year, the author of *The Theory of Moral Sentiments*, who had held a professorship in moral philosophy at the University of Glasgow, wrote *An Inquiry into the Nature and Causes of the Wealth of Nations*. Of course Adam Smith's seminal, specialized inquiry into economic values is not the only reason 1776 stands out as a year to remember. After all, that is the year that Hume died. But his work does much to delimit a field of value inquiry that has developed to a point where some are willing to call it a science. Here, others may be ready to interject, "a dismal science at best." Perhaps because economists are regularly called on to herald the future, they are particularly easy to poke fun at. Who has not heard the old saw: if all the economists were lined up end to end, they still would not reach agreement. Even so, we should be grateful that problems of econometrics are not left to aesthetic intuition alone. If they were, our political leaders might be attracted to policies that mortgage the future by perennially adding to the national debt. Fortunately we may rest easy, since our previous head of state became aware of this possibility long ago and condemned such policies as voodoo economics, and our current head of state sometimes shows a willingness to allow others to balance the Federal budget a decade into the future.

Specialization is nevertheless inherently dangerous. Lessons learned in one area are lost to another. Specialists in the humanities are unprepared to learn from specialists in the hard sciences; specialists in the hard sciences are unwilling to learn from specialists in the humanities; and specialists in both areas care little about the pronouncements of social scientists. The very separation promotes insularity. Specialization can also narrow vision by imposing a limited perspective. Questions that arise in one field or discipline may not be peculiar to that field or discipline alone, but pertinent to many. From a broader perspective it may be apparent that certain questions go beyond the fields that happen to first give rise to them. Questions expressing quantitative relationships that arise in a particular field may, from a more encompassing point of view, be seen to be questions of mathematics.

Moral philosophy is not altogether removed from the dangers of specialization. On the contrary, moral philosophy is subject to dangers of both types. Several distinctions will help to make them clear.

Moral philosophy may be thought of as a field of value inquiry characterized by questions of moral value. Or as may be said, questions of moral value delimit moral philosophy as a field of *disciplinary value inquiry*. Similarly, questions of aesthetic value delimit a field of disciplinary value inquiry, a different field of course, as do questions of economic value and sets of questions directed at narrower sorts of value. Questions of technological value, pedagogical value, ecological value, evolutionary value, and personal value all delimit what may be called fields of disciplinary value inquiry. Yet even if moral philosophers are, as a rule, engaged in disciplinary value inquiry, they need not be. There are two alternatives. In addition to disciplinary value inquiry, moral philosophers may take part in *inter-disciplinary value inquiry* and *meta-disciplinary value inquiry*. I hope no one will be put off by the polysyllabic terms. They are useful, if ugly. Inter-disciplinary value inquiry may be characterized as an activity which has to do with questions of value that bear on two or more fields of disciplinary value inquiry. Inter-disciplinary value inquiry brings together two or more fields of value inquiry, at least by way of contrast. Meta-disciplinary value inquiry may be characterized as an activity that takes in questions that go beyond all fields of disciplinary value inquiry, questions that can be raised for all fields of value inquiry whether disciplinary or inter-disciplinary. Such questions are likely to be conceptual or semantic, if they are to be in place in all fields of value inquiry. They will include questions of value theory. Meta-disciplinary value inquiry is sure to be highly theoretical.

Moral philosophy is sometimes divided into the areas of applied ethics, normative ethics, and meta-ethics. The distinctions make sense, whether or not they are hard and fast. Someone might well spend a lifetime of thought on problems in just one of the areas. The work would be highly specialized. But even someone who worked in all three areas would be a specialist. And that is the common lot of moral philosophers. The driving questions center on one kind of value, moral value. They are questions of a disciplinary value inquiry. Expectably, moral philosophers face the dangers of insularity and limited perspective. How are the dangers to be overcome? The answer is already in view. Moral philosophers with a spirit of adventure must embark on explorations of inter-disciplinary and meta-disciplinary value inquiry.

Inter-disciplinary value inquiry is one of the goals of the Conference on Value Inquiry. The mix of interest, outlook, and expertise on questions of value is designed to promote thought that cuts across fields delimited by disciplinary questions of value. In so far as the goal is met, moral philosophers are sure to benefit. Judging by the wealth of talent found in those who have come together to take part in the annual Conferences on Value Inquiry, there is every reason to be optimistic. If the value of inter-disciplinary value inquiry is not yet evident, it soon will be. I shall say a little more about the importance of inter-disciplinary value inquiry in closing. Let me enter one caveat though: inter-disciplinary value inquiry is no substitute for disciplinary value inquiry. If it is to further our understanding of questions of value, inter-disciplinary value inquiry must supplement but not supplant disciplinary value inquiry. Indeed, strong disciplinary value inquiry, whether in moral philosophy or in some other field, is a prerequisite of worthwhile inter-disciplinary value inquiry.

What of meta-disciplinary value inquiry—beyond broadening the perspective of moral philosophers, can it seriously bring us closer to the ultimate objective of moral philosophy, that of finding rational solutions to the practical, ever-pressing moral problems about us? I believe that it can do at least as much as inter-disciplinary value inquiry to help us realize this end. The lines of inquiry are not entirely independent. Each leads to the other. But the part that meta-disciplinary value inquiry plays in the pursuit of the ultimate objective of moral philosophy is less obvious. Meta-disciplinary value inquiry, as a highly theoretical activity that would have us take up basic conceptual problems found in all fields of value inquiry, seems far removed from practical moral problems. Yet if the practical problems require from us a sound, comprehensive moral theory, and that in turn poses meta-disciplinary questions of value, the importance of meta-disciplinary value inquiry can hardly be exaggerated. As it is, the practical and the highly theoretical are so bound to one another.

2. The Place for Meta-disciplinary Value Inquiry

Nothing more than common sense, or intuition as some philosophers are wont to say, is needed for identifying many problems as moral problems. It is doubtful that common sense or intuition is sufficient for correctly identifying all problems that are moral problems as moral problems. Be that as it may, more than common sense or intuition is needed for determining what it is about a problem that makes it moral. Moreover, common sense or intuition, does not provide us with a reliable means of solving moral problems. Contrary solutions are proffered in the name of common sense. Intuitions conflict. The solutions which are put forward cannot all be correct. Yet we cannot say which are correct and which are not. Thus we must have recourse to a theory of normative ethics.

There are, however, many competing theories of normative ethics. Some are teleologically oriented, others deontologically oriented. For teleological theories, the consequences of actions, for example, are always morally relevant for determining whether they are morally required, permitted, or forbidden. For deontological theories, the consequences of actions are not always morally relevant for making such determinations. Given their fundamental difference, it is not surprising that teleological and deontological theories sometimes diverge in their solutions to moral problems. Normative theories, then, are not enough.

What we need are means of testing theories of normative ethics for adequacy. How are we to gain the means? For a large part of the answer, we may turn to meta-disciplinary value inquiry. The adequacy of a normative theory depends, to a considerable extent, on the functions that the theory assigns to moral concepts in particular, and to evaluative concepts in general. If a theory assigns functions to moral concepts, and more generally to evaluative concepts, which differ greatly from the functions they are given by the conceptual system which we actually employ, the theory must be dismissed. For then the theory will not be to the purpose. It will not bear on the *problems* for which we seek solutions. At the same time, there is no reason to suppose that the functions assigned to moral concepts, and more generally to evaluative concepts, by a normative theory must be precisely the same as those that are given to them by the conceptual system we actually employ.[1] Our actual conceptual system is not sacrosanct. Indeed, we may go further than this. The very unreliability of common sense or intuition as a means of solving moral problems suggests that with regard to moral concepts, the conceptual system we actually employ is neither complete nor entirely consistent. Therefore, the functions assigned to moral concepts by a theory need only resemble those we would ordinarily give them. As long as they have a fair likeness, the problems we face can be given answers in theory. The main conceptual problems which present themselves as soon as an attempt is made to construct an adequate theory of normative ethics are of three types:

(1) problems having to do with the ways in which moral concepts are related to one another and to the world;

(2) problems having to do with the ways in which moral concepts are related to evaluative concepts in general and to the world; and

(3) problems having to do with the ways in which evaluative concepts in general are related to non-evaluative concepts and to the world.

Problems of type (1), which center on moral concepts alone, are classifiable as problems of meta-ethics. Problems of type (2), which fit moral concepts within the broader context of evaluative concepts in general, belong to meta-disciplinary value inquiry, as do problems of type (3), which locate evaluative concepts in general within the full spectrum of our concepts. Problems of type (2) raise issues in value theory or, more generally, what may be called the study of evaluative assessments. They also lead to questions of inter-disciplinary value inquiry. Problems of type (3) have no generally accepted name. They may be said to raise issues in the study of assessments in general. We have, then, something of a hierarchy of conceptual problems, with problems of meta-ethics bridging problems of disciplinary value inquiry in the area of normative ethics on the one side, and problems in two areas of meta-disciplinary value inquiry on the other.

The problems furthest removed from practical moral problems, those of type (3) that contrast evaluative concepts with non-evaluative concepts that come into play in assessments, have been little studied. The reason for this may be that it has seemed that there is little to be said about them. After all, evaluative concepts are markedly different from non-evaluative concepts—and if markedly different, then in a completely distinct category. But this is a mistake. Evaluative concepts and non-evaluative concepts *are* markedly different. But from this it follows that they are different in *some* respects, not that they are different in *all* respects. There may be other reasons as well for the relative neglect of problems of type (3) that have to do with assessments in general. Whatever the reason, there is much to be said about problems of that type. As a requirement for a full understanding of evaluative concepts, the lessons to be learned from them are needed for a full understanding of moral concepts. They are perforce needed for gaining means of testing theories of normative ethics, and so for arriving at one which will help us to settle practical moral problems. Elsewhere, I have done something to deal with problems of type (3) that bear on the concept of goodness.[2] If problems of type (2) are not quite as far removed from practical moral problems as problems of type (3), they are no less difficult. We will briefly take up one problem of type (2), not with the idea of solving it, but to outline the importance of a problem of meta-disciplinary value inquiry. We will consider why the concept of moral goodness needs to be reviewed in the light of what is common to other concepts of goodness, why the use of the word "good" in moral and non-moral contexts alike deserves attention. But before we do so, let us give some thought to a bridging problem of type (1), a meta-ethical problem about the nature of the concept of moral goodness.

3. The Most General and Fundamental Moral Concern and Moral Concept

Moral problems are problems of evaluation. Like all evaluative problems, they have two components: a matter under evaluative consideration, the subject of some moral concern, and an evaluative consideration of some matter, the moral concern at issue. A wide variety of things may become subjects of moral concern. Among the most concrete subjects are people, their actions, their motives, and their intentions. Less concrete subjects are social policies and laws. Fully abstract subjects of moral concern are concepts such as liberty, equality, and fraternity, and properties such as charity, honesty, and happiness. There are several common moral concerns. The broadest of them involve considerations of matters as morally good or bad or indifferent, morally right or wrong, morally required or forbidden or permitted, or simply just or unjust. The first of these types of considerations, those of moral goodness, form what is at once the most general and the most fundamental moral concern.

Considerations of moral goodness make up the most general moral concern because its domain is no less than the class of all subjects of moral concern. If a given matter can become a subject of any moral concern at all, it can be made a subject of the concern of moral goodness. If we can sensibly consider whether a certain matter is morally right or morally required or just, we can also sensibly consider whether that matter is morally good. No other moral concern has so broad a domain.

Matters which cannot become subjects of a concern of moral rightness or moral obligation or justice, are, nevertheless, sensible subjects of the concern of moral goodness. When a person is compelled to do something, when he cannot but do what he does, it makes no sense to consider whether his action is morally right. If a spy who has been unwittingly drugged reveals classified information due to the influence of the drug alone, it makes no sense to consider whether it is morally right for him to say what he says. It does make sense, however, to consider whether his action under these circumstances is morally good: perhaps it will shorten a likely war. An action may become a subject of the concern of moral goodness even if the action is somehow compelled. Likewise, when a person is prevented from doing something, when he cannot perform a certain action, it makes no sense to consider whether he is morally required to perform that action. If I am unable to identify Bernard J. Ortcutt as a double agent, it makes no sense to consider whether I am morally required to expose him. Nevertheless, we can consider whether an identification of him by me would be morally good: perhaps this would diminish the likelihood of war. Neither does it make sense to consider whether a person is morally required to perform a supererogatory action. If Bernice M. Ortcutt can save my life only by performing an extraordinary deed that would cut short her no doubt already exemplary life, then she cannot be morally *required* to do so. Yet if an action cannot be morally required because it is literally beyond the call of duty, it certainly may become a subject of the concern of moral goodness. For it cannot be a supererogatory action unless it is a morally good action to perform. Finally, it is plain that the domain of the concern of justice is narrower than that of moral goodness. Some considerations of justice can only arise over matters that occur within a stable, orderly society. There is no sense in considering whether the self-directed actions of people living in a Hobbesian state of nature are, in general, just or unjust. It is arguable that outside the confines of society, even killing is not a sensible subject of the concern of justice. Nevertheless, all the things that people would do, or might do, in a Hobbesian state of nature would be sensible subjects of the concern of moral goodness. Considerations of whether killing is morally good or morally bad or morally indifferent are called for even where, or especially where, the lives of people are "solitary, poore, nasty, brutish and short."[3]

It is not so easy to show that considerations of moral goodness form the most fundamental moral concern. To hold that they do is to hold that considerations of moral goodness have theoretical primacy. In saying that they have theoretical primacy, I mean that all moral concerns could be accounted for on the basis of considerations of moral goodness alone. In this regard two other views are possible. One would be to hold that some other moral concern is more fundamental than the concern of moral goodness. The other would be to hold that no single moral concern has theoretical primacy. Deontologists and Intuitionists have held these views. The first view was held by Kant, the second by David Ross.[4] If there is no short way to show that these views must be rejected, still there are conditional grounds for not accepting them.

The second view allows that there are moral problems which, in principle, have no rational solution. If no single moral concern has theoretical primacy, then two evaluations of a certain matter that present different moral concerns can come into irreconcilable conflict. Of two proposed actions, only one of which can be performed, it may be that one of them is unjust, though on the whole morally good, while the other is on the whole morally bad, though just. We may be faced with the problem of choosing between the proposed actions—no other action being possible under the circumstances. Our problem would be a moral one. If the concern of justice and the concern of moral goodness were equally fundamental and no other moral concern were more fundamental than either of them, our problem would present an irreconcilable moral conflict, an irresolvable moral dilemma. It would be a problem which, in principle, lacked a rational solution. Some philosophers contend that such moral problems abound, arguing that irreconcilable moral conflicts reflect distinctive aspects of the human condition. Existentialists have taken this position as have Bernard Williams and Alasdair MacIntyre.[5] Yet there is no compelling evidence in its favor.

The contention that some moral problems have no rational solutions in principle needs to be distinguished from the similar but more moderate contention that we are unable to give some moral problems, or more generally some evaluative problems, rational solutions. The less extreme contention does not imply that there are irreconcilable moral conflicts or irresolvable moral dilemmas. Problems may have solutions even though we are unable to say what they are.

It goes without saying that there are unsolved moral problems. But no one has shown that any coherent moral problems are unsolvable. Nor is anyone likely to do so, since any evidence that might be offered in support of the contention that some moral problems do not have rational solutions may be regarded instead as evidence for the more moderate contention that we are unable to give some moral problems rational solutions. Until the extreme contention is supported by compelling evidence, it is not unreasonable for a moral philosopher to accept the more moderate contention. We may conditionally hold that no two moral concerns of the same matter will come into irreconcilable moral conflict. On this basis we may conditionally hold that one moral concern is more fundamental than all others, being comprised of moral considerations having theoretical primacy.

Two points count against the first view that there is a more fundamental moral concern than that of moral goodness. One of them is simply that the domains of other moral concerns are more limited than that of moral goodness. As we have seen, there are sensible subjects of the concern of moral goodness which are not sensible subjects of other moral concerns. Some matters which can come under considerations of moral goodness cannot come under considerations of moral rightness, moral obligation, or justice. The second point is that the concern of moral goodness has a domain which is fully general with respect to moral matters. It takes in, or comprehends, the domains of all other moral concerns. For, as we have also seen, if a matter can come under moral consideration at all, it can come under considerations of moral goodness. Among moral considerations, those of moral goodness are the only ones which are never out of place. Together, the two points make considerations of moral goodness the only moral considerations that are suited to theoretical primacy. If one moral concern is more fundamental than the rest, it is that of moral goodness.

When we express a moral concern we put a moral concept to use. To say of some matter that it is morally good or morally required or just is to bring the concept of moral goodness or moral obligation or justice to bear on the matter. The domain of each moral concern is the class of things on which the moral concept that it puts to use can be brought to bear. If the concern of moral goodness has a broader domain than any other moral concern, the concept of moral goodness has a wider bearing on matters than any other moral concept. It is the most general moral concept. And if one moral concern is more fundamental than the rest, then the moral concept that it puts to use is the most fundamental moral concept. Plainly then, the grounds for supposing that considerations of moral goodness form the most fundamental moral concern are grounds for supposing that the concept of moral goodness is the most fundamental moral concept.

A long line of teleologists have supposed that the concept of moral goodness is the most general and fundamental moral concept. There are fundamental reasons to stand with them.

4. A Problem for Exploration

If the most general and fundamental moral concept is that of moral goodness, the penultimate objective of moral philosophy, the construction of an adequate theory of normative ethics, calls for an answer to the question: What is it for some matter to be morally good? This is a conceptual question. Like many conceptual questions, it may be represented as a semantic question. For we represent our conceptual system with language. By investigating the meanings of words as we do use them, how they fit together, and how they are related to the world, we may recognize how concepts which we regularly bring to mind are tied to one another and to the world.[6] This we need to do if we are to go on to modify our concepts and revise our conceptual system. Thus with the aim of constructing an adequate theory of normative ethics, we may ask: What is the meaning of the term "morally good?"

Unfortunately we cannot set about explaining the meaning of "morally good" directly as we would many general terms. If we wished to explain the meaning of the word "horse," we could start by listing characteristics or properties that are common to horses. Some of them, such as those having to do with size or color might be accidental properties of horses; others, such as those of being herbivorous or mammalian, might be regarded as properties which beings must have if the word "horse" is to apply truly to them. These would be among the defining characteristics or properties of members of the genus *Equus*. It would be difficult to come up with anything like a complete list of equine properties. We might have to settle on a partially disjunctive list if the word "horse" represents what is sometimes called a cluster concept. But with a list of equine properties in hand, we should be well on our way towards explaining the meaning of the word "horse." There is, however, a precondition for employing this method of explanation. The meaning of a general term can only be explained in this way if there is some consensus as to what are the things to which the term applies truly. We can proceed to list equine properties because there is widespread agreement about what things belong to the genus *Equus*. If we could not say from the outset which things are members of the genus *Equus* and which are not, we could not begin to list the properties that members of the genus *Equus* have in common. When it comes to explaining the meaning of the term "morally good," it is plain that the precondition is not met. Not only is there no consensus as to what are the things to which the term "morally good" applies truly, there is, in fact, widespread disagreement about what belongs to the class of morally good things—hence the broad appeal of moral relativism which trades on the disagreement. Nor is a consensus to be found even among philosophers. Some philosophers go so far as to hold that there is *nothing* to which the term "morally good" applies *truly*. Those who do so, non-cognitivists and anti-realists, are usually among the philosophers who contend that some moral problems in principle lack rational solutions.

The widespread disagreement has two sources: limited understandings of the contributions that the adverb and the adjective make to the meaning of the term "morally good." Neither is well understood. To know what it is for something to be morally good as opposed to aesthetically good, or economically good, or prudentially good, or good in some other fairly broad respect requires an understanding of the criteria that set apart moral evaluative assessments from evaluative assessments belonging to other fields of disciplinary value inquiry. The criteria have proven to be notoriously difficult to pin down. But in the main, discussions of the criteria of moral evaluative assessments have been conducted within ethics as a field of disciplinary value inquiry. The difficulties have reflected the danger of insularity. Explorations of inter-disciplinary value inquiry will allow moral philosophers to contrast alternative criteria of moral evaluative assessments with proposed criteria of evaluative assessments in other fields of disciplinary value inquiry. The comparative work will be a large undertaking. Indeed, it will be encyclopedic in scope.

We are left with a need to account for the contribution of the word "good" in the term "morally good." Whatever its contribution, we may take it that the word makes the same contribution in moral and non-moral contexts alike. Consider other adjectival terms that are used in moral and non-moral contexts. A given matter may be morally repugnant or aesthetically repugnant; it may be morally objectionable or legally objectionable. There is, not to put too fine a point on it, no shortage of ways for matters to be repugnant or objectionable. Alternatively, a given matter may be morally uplifting or personally uplifting; it may be morally admirable or pedagogically admirable. We may take some consolation in the variety of respects in which matters may be uplifting or admirable. Yet while the ways or respects that the matters are evaluated differ, the adjectival terms "repugnant," "objectionable," "uplifting," and "admirable" are not employed equivocally. Their contributions to the evaluative assessments are unambiguous. The word "good" is, of course, more general than any of these words. But that does not keep it from making the same contribution in all manner of contexts. If the word "good" is employed unequivocally, then its contribution in the term "morally good" is the same as its contributions in the terms "aesthetically good," "economically good," "prudentially good," and in other terms that are used to make evaluative assessments. The word re-presents the common evaluative element found in evaluative assessments that pertain to all fields of disciplinary value inquiry. Discussions of the common element belong to meta-disciplinary value inquiry. Explorations of meta-disciplinary value inquiry will allow moral philosophers to come to grips with the evaluative component of evaluative assessments that are specifically moral. The combined knowledge gained from inter-disciplinary and meta-disciplinary value inquiry will help us to find the answer to the conceptual question that we need in order to construct an adequate theory of normative ethics: What is it for some matter to be morally good? It will help to bring rational solutions to inescapable moral problems into view. If moral goodness is indeed the most general and fundamental moral concept, then explorations of value inquiry are sure to be explorations of value.

Notes

1. For a contrary view see R. M. Hare, "The Argument from Received Opinion," in his *Essays on Philosophical Method* (London: Macmillan, 1971).

2. See Thomas Magnell, "Evaluations as Assessments, Part I: Properties and Their Signifiers," *Journal of Value Inquiry*, 27:1 (1993), and "Evaluations as Assessments, Part II: Classifying Adjectives, Distinguishing Assertions, and Instancing Good of a Kind," *Journal of Value Inquiry*, 27:2 (1993). Both papers have been reprinted in Richard T. Hull, ed., *A Quarter Century of Value Inquiry: Presidential Addresses of the American Society for Value Inquiry* (Amsterdam: Rodopi, 1994).

3. Hobbes, *Leviathan*, ed. C. B. Macpherson (Harmondsworth, England: Penguin Books, 1977), Part I, ch. 13, p. 186.

4. For Kant, moral considerations of obligation with regard to the categorical imperative make up the only fundamental moral concern. See Kant, *Groundwork of the Metaphysic of Morals*, trans. H. J. Paton (New York: Harper & Row, 1964). For Ross, there are two fundamental moral concerns, one being made up of moral considerations of rightness, the other of moral goodness. See Ross, *The Right and the Good* (Oxford: Oxford University Press, 1930) and *Foundations of Ethics* (Oxford: Oxford University Press, 1939).

5. See Jean-Paul Sartre, *Existentialism*, trans. Bernard Frechtman (New York: Philosophical Library, 1947), pp. 28-34, and Bernard Williams, "Ethical Consistency," reprinted in his *Problems of the Self* (Cambridge, England: Cambridge University Press, 1976), p. 179. Williams there neatly sums up his position by saying: "Moral conflicts are neither systematically avoidable, nor all soluble without remainder." See also Alasdair MacIntyre, *After Virtue*, 2nd ed. (Notre Dame, Ind.: University of Notre Dame Press, 1984), *passim*.

6. See Moritz Schlick, *General Theory of Knowledge*, trans. A. E. Blumberg (Vienna and New York: Springer-Verlag, 1974), § 2 & 3.

Two

MORAL PHILOSOPHY IN FOUR TIERS

Joseph Margolis

"Objectivity," Thomas Nagel affirms, "is the central problem of ethics. Not just in theory, but in life."[1] Brave words.

Beginning thus, I begin in the middle of things. I shall track what Nagel has to say about this important matter, but chiefly as a specimen or sample. Nagel's speculation as well as that of others affords a great economy in understanding the current impasse in moral philosophy. Nagel does not resolve the impasse. Nor does anyone else, as far as I can see. I mean to strip the philosophical paper from the moral plaster, but the plaster, of course, is hardly virgin wood. Recent moral theorizing—of what I call the "third-tier" sort—has been circling for some time on the essential problematic of moral objectivity, but it has missed its mark. That is what I mean by the housekeeping image. It has taken the entire history of moral theory to bring us in an unblinking way to the still-unanswered question on which all responsible moral practice depends. The importance of that question justifies, I feel sure, a continued measure of tolerance for the philosophically picayune. The grander possibilities seem to lie in that direction. But you will have to judge how well the paint and paper have been removed.

In any case, I contend that inquiries of what I call the third-tier sort, which represent the most sustained effort of standard Anglo-American moral philosophy in our generation to come to terms with the troubling problem of objectivity, have utterly failed. Their failure can be tracked only by a certain painstaking detail that might otherwise put readers off. I justify this scrutiny by its benefit, if that is the right word, because, if the charge holds, it signifies that the entire set of strategies I call first-, second-, and third-tier—in effect, the entire resource of analytic moral philosophy—cannot possibly supply the legitimating arguments needed. We must look elsewhere. I do not say moral objectivity is impossible to secure, but the failing anticipated suggests a search for a fourth-tier change of direction. Analytic philosophy, I say, is opposed to what that indicates. There is the distant lesson I have in mind. But, for the time being, we must look to our specimens and earn the verdict. I must leave the full prospects of what I am calling fourth-tier efforts for a fresh beginning. As promised, I shall keep entirely to the housekeeping task.

1.

Nagel had opened *The View from Nowhere* by advising us that his was a book "about a single problem: how to combine the perspective of a particular person inside the world with an objective view of that same world, the person and his viewpoint included."[2] What was the point of beginning in that way? How might Nagel have succeeded or know that he had? "Objectivity," he tells us, "is a method of understanding." Yet, a few pages later, in the same forthright way, he blithely confesses: "I believe that the methods needed to understand ourselves do not yet exist."[3] You may read this as a piece of becoming modesty, but it is also seriously intended. "There is," he explains, reviewing the objectivity of values and practical judgment, "no present method of carrying out a normative investigation, though the aim of achieving integration between the subjective and objective standpoints gives the process direction and sets conditions of success and failure."[4] The inquiry is a strenuous one: not impossible but distinctly difficult. Mention is made of "the subjective and objective standpoints"; but *what are they*?

Nagel promises to lay before us the grounds for the objectivity with which morality and practical life can be managed—in a way that compares favorably, we must believe, with the objectivity of the sciences but also preserves their distinction. "The standpoint of morality," he warns in the introductory chapter, "is more objective than that of private life, but less objective than the standpoint of physics." Examining this matter with due care, Nagel warns us also of an opposing worry: "I have argued against skepticism," he says, "and in favor of realism and the pursuit of objectivity in the domain of practical reason. But if realism is admitted as a possibility, one is quickly faced with the opposite of the problem of skepticism, namely the problem of overobjectification: the temptation to interpret the objectivity of reason in too strong a way."[5] So the tables have been turned: Nagel has evidently discovered part of the method wanted. What it is, is not yet clear. But it emboldens him to advise us. He is ready to help us elude both a skepticism about practical values and an overzealous objectivism that fails to preserve the critical difference between the objectivity of science and the appropriate objectivity of morality. One might easily have missed the need for such assistance. Evidently, its explanation is not entirely necessary.

If you read Nagel's discussion with the close attention it invites, you will see, first, that Nagel supposes there is no way to explicate the realism and objectivity due moral matters, and other matters of practical reason as well, without explaining the relationship between them and the forms realism and objectivity take in the natural sciences; and, second, you will guess correctly that Nagel himself is motivated to answer in the way he does because of the compelling but inexplicit presence, in the two chapters devoted to the issue, of the well-known answers offered by John Mackie and Immanuel Kant. The reference to skepticism implicates Mackie, though Mackie is nowhere relevantly mentioned; and the appeal to (practical reason) suggests the influence of Kant, though Kant is not discussed in the setting offered.

It is clear that Nagel believes he has indeed answered Mackie's challenge—and that he had to if he was to vindicate moral objectivity. It is also clear that he opposes Aristotle, though chiefly through Bernard Williams's critique. Nagel does not actually take up Williams's strong objection to Aristotle and Kant, which had appeared a year before *The View from Nowhere*.[6] His own solution is more Kantian than Aristotelian. It is spared Kant's conceptual business and departs from Kant by way of reconciling the subjective and objective standpoints, somewhat in Rawls's way perhaps: it combines "a view from nowhere," a paraphrase of Kant's thesis in the *Foundations of the Metaphysics of Morals*, and an accommodation of our subjective or egoistic interests, which are, as such, incapable of vindicating moral objectivity in the Kantian sense.

Nagel's thesis is worth a moment in its own right, and I shall have something to say about it. But it is far more instructive for its argumentative strategy than for its substantive moral claims. You have to appreciate that Nagel's argument belongs to what I am calling the third tier of contemporary efforts to recover moral realism and moral objectivism. Realism and objectivism need not be the same—in the sense that Kant is plainly an objectivist about moral matters but not a realist in the exemplary sense that Aristotle or the moral intuitionist is. The first tier of the would-be recovery is simply the reaffirmation of the Aristotelian and Kantian positions, or the positions of weaker neighbors. The contemporary attack on Aristotle and Kant had been memorably fixed, though certainly not formulated for the first time, for Anglo-American philosophy, in 1977, in J. L. Mackie's *Ethics: Inventing Right and Wrong*.[7] The operative word of the title is "inventing," which was meant to undercut any Aristotelian-like normative essentialism as well as any Kantian-like universalism of rational interests. Bernard Williams's *Ethics and the Limits of Philosophy*, which appeared in 1985, confirms the continuing dissatisfaction with such first-tier views over more than two decades among English-language philosophers, though on different grounds from Mackie's. Mackie's book became the litmus for testing the threshold plausibility of any attempt at recovering moral realism or moral objectivism.

The second tier belongs to various ingenious arguments that overlap the efforts of the third tier: notably, in Alasdair MacIntyre and Martha Nussbaum, as Aristotelians, and in John Rawls and catching up Continental Kantianism, Jürgen Habermas, whose work—I mean the work of all four—is marked by a studied avoidance of the explicit strategies of Aristotle and Kant *and* by the seeming recovery of realism or objectivism in spite of that.[8]

Efforts of the second tier have had a reasonably strong inning, but *not*, in the opinion of many, in the way of actually putting to rest our pointed doubts about first-tier realism and objectivism or of supporting the conceptual prospects of a suitable replacement. Thinkers of the second tier do not directly confirm the philosophical viability *of* realism or objectivism; they assume instead a satisfactory argument and offer a congenial moral ideology—liberal, in somewhat different ways, in Rawls and Habermas; conservative, again in different ways, in MacIntyre and Nussbaum—only loosely congruent with the original strategies of Aristotle and Kant. They insinuate a sense of having met third-tier queries, but they never address them frontally. The objectivity that results is something of an illusion cast by an attractive ideology more or less in accord with the objectivism of one or the other of our master thinkers, Aristotle, Kant, or indeed some lesser master.

Authors of the third tier—Mackie, Williams, Nagel, David Wiggins—are more concerned to retrace the prospects of *ever* generating a realism or objectivism than to provide a compelling moral ideology of the second-tier kind. That is where we are today in moral philosophy—largely though not exclusively of the analytic sort. There are excellent reasons for rehearsing this bit of history. The first tier is no longer compelling on the essential issue, though our admiration for Aristotle and Kant remains unmatched and though their substantive views are entirely open to recovery. The second tier is respected, but its best representatives fail at the point of explicit moral legitimation. They are remarkably successful in muffling the frontal evidence of failure. The third tier robustly insists on the legitimative question; although, as I shall show, the memory of Aristotle and Kant—perhaps more Kant than Aristotle—has, till now, hopelessly deformed the essential question, so that it cannot be resolved, it seems, without invoking Kant or Aristotle again. We tend to shuttle endlessly between second-tier and third-tier efforts—and even to unite them. There is the irony that needs to be explained. Third-tier questions are transparently partisan and self-defeating. Their correction is a strenuous affair that requires the picayune that leads us to admit the need for a fourth-tier effort. But you would be right to insist on the supporting evidence.

2.

I offer three third-tier figures to consider: Mackie and Nagel, because they insist on Kant's condition of legitimation but draw utterly opposed verdicts regarding the possibility of an objective morality; Wiggins, because he insists more on a somewhat if distinctly altered Aristotelian rationale, though he comes to it indirectly and only with a settled awareness of the impossibility of recovering any functional naturalism of the eudaimonistic sort; and all three together because their common lack of success is due to interlocking considerations and exaggerated expectations of what is legitimatively possible or necessary, and to their jointly having ignored certain conceptual resources that, at a price, *might* still bring legitimation within acceptable reach.

They play a riskier game than the second-tier thinkers, but they offer relatively little in the way of substantive moralities. Their speculations confirm, I believe, that any and every seriously recovered Kantian or Aristotelian legitimative strategy is utterly misguided: that moral philosophy has been led up the garden path by first- and second-tier maneuvers; that the absurdities of third-tier strategies are plain enough, symptoms of a profound mistake—insuperable once made but easily avoided nonetheless; and that there remains before us a perfectly straightforward line of reasoning by which to recover an objective form of legitimation.

If that were all there were to the argument, the promise of an easy victory might rightly deserve the ridicule it would be bound to invite—particularly from analytic philosophers. But there is a soberer lesson in the offing: that the conceptual space for recovering an objective morality is *never* enough to satisfy Kantian or Aristotelian legitimative demands *or ever* enough to retire the legitimative question altogether. The ground on which this finding rests I shall hold for the right moment of disclosure. It may serve to mark the theme of what I am calling the fourth tier: it suggests the systematic similarity between legitimating knowledge in general and legitimating moral objectivity in particular. The fates of science and morality go hand in hand, I say, though why that is so is hardly obvious and though science and moral judgment are very different fish.

There is the challenge. Now the argument.

Mackie's claim has drawn the greatest fire. The first sentence of his *Ethics* affirms without ceremony: "There are no objective values."[9] What could Mackie possibly have meant by that? He goes on—forthrightly:

> The claim that values are not objective, are not part of the fabric of the world is meant [he says] to include not only moral goodness, which might be most naturally equated with moral value, but also other things that could be more loosely called moral values or disvalues—rightness and wrongness, duty, obligation, an action's being rotten and contemptible, and so on. It also

includes non-moral values, notably aesthetic ones, beauty and various kinds of artistic merit.[10]

It is too easy to misunderstand Mackie, as he himself observes. He does *not* mean to deny that people in general regularly make judgments of the sorts mentioned, and do so in an orderly way. *No*: making moral judgments one way or another, even affirming or denying that there are moral values, counts as "first order moral views, positive or negative; the person who adopts either of them is taking a certain practical, normative stand."[11] Doing that *is* part of "the fabric of the world." Mackie insists on that. For his own part, he opposes only "a second order view, a view about the status of moral values, about where and how they fit into the world." First order and second order views address entirely separate and independent matters. Moral skepticism, on Mackie's reading, views his original charge, already mentioned, only as a second order claim: "The kinds of behavior to which moral values and disvalues are ascribed are indeed part of the furniture of the world, and so are the natural, descriptive, differences between them; but not, perhaps, their difference in value."[12]

Mackie may be too familiar by this time, so that the reminder of what he actually says may seem unnecessary. I want to say, however, that he is right, on *both* first and second order grounds, but that *that* does not confirm that, in the second order sense, values are *not* objective, and demonstrably not part of the fabric of the world! On the contrary, the first order admission confirms— *when rightly understood*—that there *is* a second order sense in which values *are* part of the fabric of the world: that Mackie's reading of what a second order view requires is entirely arbitrary, unnecessarily severe on internal grounds, much too Kantian in any case and therefore flawed, *and easily* replaced by an alternative second order reading that, trivially, defeats the moral skeptic out of his own mouth. You may not believe all that, but that at least is the claim I make. Moreover, similar arguments, I hold, can be convincingly mounted against Nagel and Wiggins, although they are already sanguine about recovering an objective morality. Their errors take another turn. Nagel, for instance, is too confident that a legitimative maneuver of a Kantian-like sort can be satisfactorily recovered: but it cannot be, of course. And Wiggins relies too heavily on dredging up a supposed necessary connection between the meaning of life and a pared-down Aristotelian-like legitimative maneuver in order to ground satisfactorily an adjusted morality; but either there is no such connection or it presupposes a deeper answer, and is demonstrably question-begging for that reason. In any case, my third-tier specimens are paradigms of the tribe: their failure is the tribe's failure.

Mackie's mistake lies in not recognizing that what *he* admits in the first order sense is already too strong to disallow *every* second order claim about the objective standing of moral norms and values; hence, the reason his argument seems compelling lies entirely with the easy acceptance of a *first-tier* sense of *what* legitimation should require without adopting any particular first-tier vision. Deny the credentials of the Kantian line and Mackie is defeated. Odd though it may seem, Nagel shares the same Kantian impulse that Mackie favors: the difference is that Nagel is a self-styled realist and Mackie, a self-styled skeptic. Nagel's realism, however, cannot be sustained, and Mackie's skepticism is too extreme: both are defeated by their own words. Wiggins is more careful than either of them; in any case, he examines the legitimative matter in Aristotelian rather than Kantian terms. But Wiggins attenuates in too extreme a way the necessary premiss on which legitimation is thought to be secured by avoiding both first-tier and second-tier devices. He is right to do so but mistaken in what he unearths. A double disaster ensues: first, because none of the tortured strategies any of the specimen theorists offer is tenable or necessary; and second, because there is a perfectly straightforward, even trivial, way to secure the objective standing of moral values and norms both Nagel and Wiggins want and Mackie denies. This explains the sense in which I say we need a fourth-tier strategy.

3.

The argument against Mackie is the easiest to mount. Remember: Mackie holds that "moral skepticism [is] the denial of objective moral values," where that doctrine is not to be "confused with any one of several first order normative views, or with any linguistic or conceptual analysis." It is said to be "an ontological thesis."[13] This in itself fails to offset the fact that *if* first order moral behavior *is* part of the fabric of the world, as Mackie concedes, then *that* too is an ontological thesis: and then, there must be a further sense in which moral values *are* objective and some diminished form of legitimation is possible.

At this point, Mackie distinguishes between "descriptivism" and "objectivism." Descriptivism he says is:

> A doctrine about the meanings of ethical terms and statements, namely that their meanings are purely descriptive rather than even partly prescriptive or emotive or evaluative, or that it is not an essential feature of the conventional meaning of moral statements that they have some special illocutionary force, say of commending rather than asserting. It contrasts with the view that commendation is in principle distinguishable from description ... and that moral statements have it as at least part of their meaning that they are commendatory and hence in some uses intrinsically action-guiding. But descriptive meaning neither entails nor is entailed by objectivity.[14]

This is not a felicitous view, though its correction still leaves intact Mackie's skeptical intent. For surely *if*, as Mackie also says, "first order moral views" *do* involve "taking a certain practical, normative stand," then either first order views are *not* "descriptive" merely in the sense given or else, contrary to what Mackie says, descriptivism at the "first order level" *is* ontologically robust, "objective" in *some* first order sense, leaving aside the intended second order sense, *and therefore already prescriptive, commendatory, and action-guiding*. I cannot see how that can be denied: I take Mackie to have contradicted himself; but I do not mean by that that *his claim against the objectivity of values fails for that reason alone!* But it sets the stage.

A closer reading shows that the formulation is an inadvertence of sorts: it is more telling than Mackie realizes. Mackie's intention is clear enough. For example, he says:

> The subjectivist [that is, the skeptic] about values . . . is not denying that there can be objective evaluations relative to standards, and these are as possible in the aesthetic and moral fields as in [any field that calls for expertise and invokes standards]. But the statement that a certain decision is thus just or unjust will not be objectively prescriptive: insofar as it can be simply true it leaves open the question whether there is any objective requirement to do what is just and to refrain from what is unjust, and equally leaves open the practical decision to act in other ways.[15]

Notice, please, that judgments of what is just or unjust *might* well occur *in* first order discourse, which is to say, again, that they may be prescriptive *in a first-order sense even if not in a second-order sense*. There *is* an objective requirement but *not* one *that is also categorical in Kant's sense*. Mackie says as much: "we may make [the] issue clearer by referring to Kant's distinction between hypothetical and categorical imperatives." You may object that Mackie is no Kantian. You would be right of course: he says that "the objective values which I am denying would be action-directing absolutely, not contingently . . . upon the agent's desires and inclinations":

> A categorical imperative [he adds] would express a reason for acting which was unconditional in the sense of not being contingent upon any present desire of the agent to whose satisfaction the recommended action would contribute as a means.[16]

But, of course, although Mackie is not a Kantian, he does believe that genuinely *objective* moral values *are* values only if they can support a Kantian-like categorical obligation, or something of comparable strength. When, therefore, he says there are no "objective values," he means that there are none that could support *that* kind of truth and legitimation. *If* there are any objective values at all, they meet the Kantian test at least; but there are none. *That* is what Mackie means by "the argument from queerness":

> If there were objective values, then they would be entities or qualities or relations of a very strange sort, utterly different from anything else in the universe. Correspondingly, if we were aware of them, it would have to be by some special faculty of moral perception or intuition, utterly different from our ordinary ways of knowing everything else.[17]

About this notorious remark, it must be said: first, that it is not a serious argument, in the plain sense that, in the *Foundations of the Metaphysics of Morals*, Kant advances objective values but not by way of any of the objectionable devices Mackie opposes; second, that Kant's own argument is, as it happens, fatally defective in its moral presumption;[18] third, that Mackie nowhere shows that *any and every* attempt to recover something like objective values *must* adhere to the Kantian-like claim, that nothing conceptually or ontologically slimmer could possibly do the requisite legitimative work; and, fourth, that there are in fact strategies for securing objective legitimation that might be reasonable *if only we abandoned Kantian objectivism and Aristotelian essentialism as ideal models and looked to the full import of Mackie's concessions.* The irony is that Mackie's boldness is completely undercut by his appeal to a first-tier vision of moral objectivity that he himself opposes. Also, of course, there is no need to remind us that the real world does indeed *include* first order moral behavior. Mackie never denies the fact.[19]

I conclude, therefore, that, conditionally, Mackie's argument is a failure—on internal grounds. Mackie nowhere shows the propriety of invoking the Kantian or, indeed, any counterpart Aristotelian legitimative test, and he nowhere shows that no diminished second-order claim could never recover moral objectivity. His inquiry does serve as a warning of the difficulty of the task before us. I acknowledge the fact, but it is much overblown. For, on the argument supplied, there *is* a first order objectivity and a *prima facie* legitimation of objectivity of first order action-directing imperatives, if that is what they are. Nothing that Mackie says gainsays that.

4.

Turn back to Nagel.

I mentioned, you remember, the odd quality of Nagel's running remarks: on the one hand, it seems, we first discover how to pursue the objectivity of morality and practical life, as if for the first time, for there is evidently no method in place; on the other hand, Nagel has surely found an effective way to begin. All that within the space of twenty-five pages!

What is the key? Consider this:

> In theoretical reasoning objectivity is advanced when we form a new conception of reality that includes ourselves as components. This includes an alteration or at least an extension of our beliefs. In the sphere of values or practical reasoning, the problem is different. As in the theoretical case, we must take up a new comprehensive viewpoint after stepping back and including our former perspective in what is to be understood. But there the new viewpoint will be not a new set of beliefs, but a new or extended set of values. We try to arrive at normative judgments with motivational content, from an impersonal standpoint. We cannot use a nonnormative criterion of objectivity, for if values are objective, they must be so on their own right and not through reducibility to some other kind of objective fact. They have to be objective *values*, not objective anything else . . . . Normative realism is the view that propositions about what gives us reasons for action can be true or false independently of how things appear to us, and that we can hope to discover the truth by transcending the appearances and subjecting them to critical assessment. What we aim to discover by this method is not a new aspect of the external world, called value, but rather just the truth about what we and others should do and want.[20]

I risk citing the full passage because it shows that it would not be unreasonable to say that Nagel has simply recast Kant's notion of the *Foundations* by an economy that sets aside Kant's very doubtful metaphysical baggage. We are left, however, with the same sort of dualism as with Kant: theoretical reason aspires to a truth about the world—said to rest on experience but to be not confined to experience, that embodies the epistemic neutrality of "the view from nowhere"; practical reason, building on that supposed achievement, is said to *add* to it—to reconcile it with—a motivational vision, a view from nowhere as well, that catches up what we and others should do and want. One might go the extra mile and suggest that either Nagel has in mind Rawls's model of a "naturalized" Kantian-like proposal, or else he means to offer just such a proposal of his own.[21]

That is not my concern, however. To pursue it would be to construe Nagel as a second-tier thinker. I am interested in him more as a third-tier thinker; but you must already see how natural it is to suppose that second- and third-tier questions go hand in hand. By parity of reasoning, it would not be difficult to suppose that Rawls or Habermas or MacIntyre or Nussbaum *do* pretend to have addressed the third-tier issue. But they invariably withdraw from the riskier, more frontal second-order questions now before us. That is just what I mean by "second tier." *At* the third tier—in my view, at the more courageous front—Nagel admits that if "a richer metaphysics of morals" were wanted, he cannot guess what it would be or would be like. He summarizes matters in a pared-down Kantian-like lingo: regarding science, we must ask, he says, "What can we see that the world contains, considered from [the, or an] impersonal standpoint?" Regarding morality, we ask: "What is there reason to do or want considered from this [same] impersonal standpoint?"[22] This now begins to clarify the sense in which, as I originally remarked, Nagel thinks the standpoint of morality combines and reconciles the subjective and objective standpoints.[23]

How can it do that *if* we abandon the first-tier recovery of Kant's proposal but still cleave to its general intent? There is the daring question. Nagel sees his project as one of resisting skepticism, solipsism, "Humean subjectivism," reduction to "materialistic psychology," and, of course, Mackie's thesis.[24] Fine. But what is the strategy? "The first type of [counter] argument," he says, "depends on the unwarranted assumption that if values are real, they must be real objects of some . . . kind [other than what is found in the first order world of science; they must be 'queer', as Mackie says]."[25] What Nagel means is: (1) that values are not "real occult entities or properties" in the "first order" world of science; (2) that the answer to questions of moral or practical values are validated by offering justificatory reasons; (3) that "reasons play no role in causal explanations" in first order science; (4) that the worlds of theory and practice are disjointed in this respect though conceptually reconcilable; and (5) that "normative realism" is focused on supplying valid reasons—"claims about values and about what people have reason to do [that are] true or false independently of our beliefs and inclinations."[26] Science concerns truth and fact; morality, what it is rationally right to do.

Nothing could be more Kantian, except that Nagel's third-tier answer is not, finally, Kantian at all. It does not fail for that reason, but it fails nonetheless, which, joined to Mackie's failure, goes a long way to closing down an enormous legitimative industry that, rightly pursued, would reach to Rawls and Habermas—and beyond, by analogy, to the Aristotelian wing of the reigning philosophical conglomerate. So a great deal is at stake.

It is at his second step that Nagel's ingenuity shows itself:

> If we push the claims of objective detachment to their logical conclusion, and survey the world from a standpoint completely detached from all interests, we discover that there is *nothing*—no values left of any kind: things can be said to matter at all only to individuals within the world. The result is objective nihilism.[27]

This again is Kantian, but it prepares the ground for a new maneuver. I shall come to it in a moment. But notice that what Nagel offers signifies: (1) that it *is* possible to form a science "detached from all interests"—which I deny and the denial of which entails the denial of *any* principled disjunction between theoretical and practical reason; and (2) that normative objectivity requires some deep analogy between the possible disinterestedness of motivation and the detachment from all interests of perceptual and theorizing inquiries of the sort science favors. Since Nagel is *not* a full-fledged Kantian—since he does not argue that we *must* begin from a *concept* of practical reason capable of constructing a certain universality and necessity, in fact, just the categorical force Mackie was so keen to invoke and then dismiss, Nagel is bound to supply a heterodox rationale. Otherwise, he would simply have had to fall back to a first-tier thesis, which would have been uninteresting. The plain fact is that he never shows that *there is* a view from nowhere—in science or in morality.

It is hard to *appear* to do full justice to Nagel's third—Nagel's decisive—step. Quite frankly, the third step is a disaster; but I should like you to draw that conclusion from what Nagel actually says. He is canny about acknowledging the difficulty of his own proposal. For instance, he says: "no completely general argument about reasons can show that we must move from the admission that pleasure and pain have relative value to the conclusion that they have neutral value as well."[28] That is: although it is true that "we have reason to seek/avoid sensations we immediately and strongly like/ dislike," we cannot be sure that this is a sufficient ground for claiming "neutral value"—the "agent-neutral" perspective.[29] He is right, of course. Nevertheless, he insists—after making the concession—(3) that "it is conceivable, but false, that pleasure and pain provide only agent-relative reasons for action."[30] He falls back to a thin essentialism. There is no advantage in a quarrel here. The question remains whether all that is needed for full moral objectivity *can* be reasonably drawn from a Kantian-like beginning or from such a beginning plus the thin essentialism now appended. The matter was always doubtful; on Nagel's argument, it is impossible.

Here is the clue. In the introductory chapter of *The View from Nowhere*, after having introduced the *two* standpoints, Nagel neatly observes—I cite the entire remark:

> The distinction between more subjective and more objective views is really a matter of degree, and it covers a wide spectrum. A view or form of thought is more objective than another if it relies less on the specifics of the individual's makeup and position in the world, or on the character of the particular type of creature he is. The wider the range of subjective types to which a form of understanding is accessible—the less it depends on specific subjective capacities—the more objective it is. A standpoint that is objective by comparison with the personal view of one individual may be subjective by comparison with a theoretical standpoint still farther out . . . . An objective standpoint is created by leaving a more subjective, individual, or even just

human perspective behind; but there are things about the world and life and ourselves that cannot be adequately understood from a maximally objective standpoint.[31]

It takes a moment to grasp the peculiarity of what Nagel is saying. First of all, it departs from Kant's view, in *The Foundations of the Metaphysics of Morals*, by making the distinction between the subjective and the objective a matter of degree. That is not fatal in itself, though it is plainly incompatible with Kant's thesis; for Kant's notion is a purely formal one. Secondly, Kant does not pretend to determine moral or practical objectivity on the basis of *any* true substantive view of actual human interests; Kant's claim invokes only a universalized formal constraint to be imposed on whatever, contingently, answers to actual human interests. Nagel relies on some inchoate reading of normative human nature itself. Thirdly, there can be no approximation to the universality Kant requires; *any* generality that fails to take a universalized form would be instantly inadmissible. Nagel endorses approximations.

For Nagel, objectivity is continuous with subjectivity, a matter that presupposes some initial sorting of the substantive interests and purported human needs relative to which *increased generality is then judged to be equivalent to increased objectivity.* Suppose, for instance, one had to decide whether the Marxist notion of the dictatorship of the proletariat was objectively more valid than global capitalism, or whether a conversion to Catholicism was more valid than an informal respect for private religious conscience, or whether a benignly intended public instruction along the lines explored by the Marquis de Sade was more liberating than the unmonitored hit-and-miss discoveries of naive children. *How* should we apply Nagel's doctrine? I see no prospect of ever doing so convincingly; and I see no way of distinguishing, on Nagel's grounds, between increased generality with respect to doubtful interests and lesser generality with respect to interests inherently less agent-relative than others. Surely, *any* ramified provision along such competing lines could not fail to reflect abstract *but* partisan interests as much as putatively neutral concerns abstracted *from* all partisan interests. The failing of Nagel's formula, it should be noted, affects Aristotelian-like objectivity as much as Kantian-like objectivity, consequentialism as much as intentionalism. The short characterization of Nagel's project is progressivist, a thesis or project essentially indistinguishable from Rawls's and Habermas's and Mill's progressivisms—which betray, reflexively, a conflating of second- and third-tier inquiries.

Certainly, Nagel cannot succeed in meeting Mackie's challenge—which he initially accepts—either in the first-tier Kantian way or in the diminished and eclectic way he favors. He fails, but in failing he reinforces our sense of the excessive demands of first and second-presumptions. Fourth-tier legitimation will have to be more modest.

5.

Turn, finally, to Wiggins, who is by far the subtlest of the three—hardly more compelling but certainly subtler. I warn you of the danger of losing our way in the details of Wiggins's argument. Here, the picayune features of my complaint are at their worst. It is a kind of compliment to Wiggins's subtlety.

Let me collect my findings a little more trimly first.

My argument against Mackie rests with the fact that Mackie believes that *if* moral objectivity may be saved it must be saved by meeting some strong first-tier condition like Kant's that ensures categorical, absolute, or unconditional obligation. There is no such argument, Mackie claims. He is surely right. Nothing follows from that, however, that bears on the final prospects of objectivity. But why should Mackie fall back to a Kantian requirement, if *he* rejects the relevance of the Kantian thesis? It is, as he says, "queer." My argument against Nagel rests with the fact that, taking up Mackie's challenge, Nagel believes he can supply a second-tier answer that abstracts moral objectivity from obviously partisan or subjective interests by some policy of increasing generality. But he cannot show that *any* merely formal generality abstracted *from* admittedly partisan or egoistic interests, or any seemingly altruistic interests thought to be opposed to egoistic interests, can rightly count *as* progressively objective in any pertinent sense at all. *That* strategy has no way of distinguishing moral ideology from moral objectivity. To the extent it pretends to make the case, it intrudes a form of moral essentialism, which Nagel means to avoid.

Wiggins begins at a greater remove; but he eventually brings his answer back to the question of objectivity. He anticipates the unlikelihood of ever recovering objectivity by way of any of the usual first- or second- or third-tier strategies. Hence the inventive extravagance of first invoking the question of the meaning of life and then of presuming to demonstrate how *that* is linked to resolving the question of objective moral truths. I cannot hide the fact that I find the argument utterly uncompelling. I offer it as a specimen, because it rounds out our sense of the lengths to which third-tier thinkers are prepared to go in order to recover moral objectivity without inviting the resources of first- and second-tier thinkers, because Wiggins has a very clear sense of the limited effectiveness of third-tier thinkers like Mackie and Nagel, and because he may be the most admired of the entire raft of third-tier thinkers. Also, Wiggins leads us back to a point at which, implicitly, the excessive demands of Kantian-like requirements may be set aside and replaced by other marks of objectivity—which is to say, his own effort affords a footing for a fourth-tier innovation.

Wiggins's own argument is more hospitable to an Aristotelian-like approach, though its treatment of *eudaimonia* is critical of Aristotle and marks the most original part of Wiggins's effort. There is the theme of Wiggins's strategy at least.

In the first section of his paper "Truth, Invention, and the Meaning of Life," his inaugural lecture at Oxford in 1976, Wiggins says very plainly:

> In what follows, I try to explore the possibility that the question of truth and the question of life's meaning are among the most fundamental questions of moral philosophy .... My finding will be that the question of life's meaning does, as the untheoretical suppose, lead into the question of truth—and conversely. Towards the end I shall also claim to uncover the possibility that philosophy has put happiness in the place that should have been occupied in moral philosophy by meaning.[32]

This is an extremely condensed announcement. I read it by way of a loose association with the difference between Freud's and Jung's psychoanalytic conceptions: the one, emphasizing libidinal gratification; the other, a meaningful life. It explains, as I read it, Wiggins's astute criticism of Aristotle and of Spinoza's reversal of Aristotle's formula, and the point of his own replacement of "happiness" by "meaning." Wiggins cites Aristotle's remark from the Metaphysics at 1072a29, itself a variant of the question posed in Plato's *Euthyphro*, bearing on the objectivity issue:

> We desire the object because it seems good to us, rather than the object's seeming good to us because we desire it.

Wiggins counts this an "error." It is not, he thinks, as serious an error as the one that may be drawn from Bentham's *An Introduction to the Principles of Morals and Legislation,* which, recalls Nagel:

> Strictly speaking, nothing can be said to be good or bad, but either in itself, which is the case only with pain or pleasure, or on account of its effects, which is the case only with things that are the causes or preventives of pain and pleasure.

Wiggins's subtle objection, if I understand it rightly, is that: (1) Bentham's formula is false to the facts, since "many ... conscious states" have intentional objects, are states of striving for "objects" that are not themselves conscious states, and include states that assign "a non-instrumental value" to their intentional objects;[33] and (2), even more significantly—now, against Bentham, Aristotle, and Spinoza—any version of the strategy that disjoins or merely conjoins, by some addition, conscious states and their "valued" objects will fail to account for "the meaning of life" which more fully recalls Nagel's union of the "subjective" and "objective."[34]

It is at this point that Wiggins provisionally concludes:

But maybe it is the beginning of real wisdom to see that we may have to side against both Aristotle and Spinoza [*Ethics*, part III, proposition 9, note] here and ask: 'Why should the *because* [of Aristotle's remark, cited] not hold both ways round?' Surely an adequate account of these matters will have to treat psychological states and their objects as equal and reciprocal partners, and is likely to need to see the identification of the states and of the properties under which the states subsume their objects as interdependent.[35]

Remember, we are reviewing Wiggins as a third-tier thinker, not as a second-tier thinker. I am prepared to concede that Wiggins's objection to Bentham and the others is quite reasonable and shows a reasonable way of linking the question of moral values and the meaning of life. But I do not believe the link Wiggins provides has strategic importance for moral legitimation.

Nearly half the essay pursues a pointed attack on a clever discussion by Richard Taylor of the Sisyphus myth, in which Taylor tries to explain how Sisyphus's meaningless life *might* be converted into a meaningful life.[36] Let me say straight out that Taylor *does* show that Sisyphus might, for reasons we should probably think monstrous or preposterous, come to believe his life to be meaningful; Wiggins *fails* to show that that is unlikely, false, or impossible. But Taylor's case is marginal at best and does not really touch on the central question Wiggins raises about the link between the meaning of life and the objectivity of moral values. Furthermore, *Wiggins* misperceives the irrelevance of Taylor's case—*and,* therefore, allows himself to be deflected into a blind alley. Here, my interest is not to demolish Wiggins's argument, though it invites the strongest objection. I mean rather to show that Wiggins has missed the important lesson of his own argument; that it explains the pointlessness as well of both Mackie's and Nagel's third-tier strategies; that the corrective that may be drawn from rightly understanding Wiggins's argument leads us in the direction of what I am calling a fourth-tier approach and, by way of anticipation, a clue to the second-order excesses of an entire tribe of thinkers who have sought to apply the benefit of Wiggins's ingenious argument and have produced instead an odd mixture of second-tier and third-tier strategies now known as moral realism.[37] I bring the argument to the doorstep of moral realism, but I do not cross the threshold—unless, of course, Wiggins and Nagel are, as the second-tier thinkers they are, moral realists as well.

6.

Wiggins's attack on Taylor is an attack on non-cognitivist views of morality and meaning, both of meaning *in* life and of the meaning *of* life. But in defending a form of moral cognitivism, Wiggins explicitly distances himself from both Kant and Aristotle: hence, from all first- and second-tier theories. That is the technical intent of the recent school of moral realism. In this sense, Wiggins combats Mackie on the one hand and, on the other, finds Nagel too obscure or too concessive regarding the role of the meaning of life in slipping back to Kant or Aristotle or both.

Let me cite, therefore, Wiggins's explicit rejection of the Kantian and Aristotelian themes. Against the Kantian, he straightforwardly affirms:

> There is no such thing as a pure *a priori* theory of rationality conceived in isolation from what it is for us as we are to have a reason; and that even if there were such a thing, it would always have been irrelevant to finding a meaning in life, or seeing anything as worth while.[38]

Wiggins's local reason for pressing the charge was to disallow a non-cognitivist such as Taylor any Kantian-like resource for recouping the meaning of life. But if, as I believe, Wiggins's overly elaborate treatment of the meaning question is entirely unnecessary, inadequate, irrelevant, corrective only of a puzzle of its own making, then we may as well salvage the evidence of Wiggins's having also distanced himself from Kant. Similarly, reviewing the well-known line in Aristotle's *Nicomachean Ethics* at 1094a23: "Will not knowledge of the good have a great influence on life? Shall we not, like archers who have a mark to aim at, be more likely to hit upon that right thing?", Wiggins adds:

> But in reality there is no such thing as *The Good*, no such thing as knowledge of it, and nothing fixed independently of ourselves to aim at. Or that is what is implied by the thesis of cognitive underdetermination.[39]

Here, too, Wiggins has a local reason for mentioning his stand against Aristotle: namely, he supports a strong disjunction between *matters of fact* and *matters of practice*—or practical matters—which clearly recalls Mackie. He presses his objections against Kant and Aristotle in the service of defeating Taylor, but the issue of linking meaning and value is more difficult than Wiggins admits. For, although the intended disjunction seems reasonable on its face, Wiggins wants to contrast that disjunction with a favorable continuum between *matters of fact* and *evaluative matters*. As I have already suggested, in reviewing Mackie's reading of the same matter, the continuum between the *factual* and the *evaluative* ineluctably supplies a ground for admitting a continuum between the *factual*, the *evaluative*, and the *action-guiding*. Once you grasp that, there is no longer any point to intruding the question of the meaning of life, as if the answer to that were needed to bridge the divide between the factual and the evaluative *and* to ensure the disjunction between that continuum and the practical or action-guiding.

The first continuum, Wiggins thinks, subverts Taylor's strategy for recovering meaningful life. There, Wiggins's theory goes badly awry. Believing he has caught the essential connection, he skews the rest of his argument to service a pointless attack. It does not work against Taylor; Taylor's strategy is heroically relevant only in the most marginal sense; and, by the exhaustion of his own effort, Wiggins misses *the clear link between the meaning of life and moral objectivity* that readily supports a fourth-tier strategy. What his failing along these lines shows is why nearly all analytic moral philosophers fail to answer Mackie's question, fail to press beyond first- and second-tier strategies and the various third-tier strategies that merely service, as with moral realism, failed second-tier options.

We are near the nerve of Wiggins's theory. Wiggins is a moral cognitivist: make no mistake about that. He means us to understand that value judgments address the real world, take truth-values, enter into explanatory discourse, and are no different in these respects from scientific statements.[40] Moral realists are cognitivists in at least this sense. As a realist, Wiggins is also specifically committed to treating moral values as non-natural in G. E. Moore's sense, but *not* as necessarily supervenient on natural properties in the dubious sense advanced by Donald Davidson and in a different way by Jaegwon Kim.[41] When, however, Wiggins explains the sense in which *he* takes values to have a realist import, he retreats to the model of a very strong objectivism regarding facts. Apparently, he believes that if he were to weaken his objectivism, in either science and morality, say, in the direction of relativism, he would not be able to defend moral realism at all and perhaps would not even be able to distinguish his cognitivism from something close to Taylor's non-cognitivism. These topics are not sufficiently pursued, though they belong to the context of Mackie's third-tier question.

There is a great lacuna in Wiggins's argument; worse still, Wiggins cannot defend his account except by retreating to some first- or second-tier doctrine possibly neither Kantian nor Aristotelian: perhaps Humean. He brings his entire strategy before us in remarks like the following:

> The cognitivist will see nothing in modern evolutionary theory, or in any other branch of modern science, that forbids us to allow to thoughts themselves and the standards to which these thoughts are answerable the explanatory role that he himself attributes to them when he endorses as explanatory such claims as: "Everyone thinks that $7 + 5 = 12$, because, in the end, there is nothing else to think" or "We converge in the belief that the slaughter of the innocent is wrong because, in the end, there is nothing else to think on this question." If the cognitivist sticks his neck out anywhere, it is here. What he refuses to allow is that non-natural properties are explanatorily inert.[42]

We must consider how cannily crafted and lean these remarks are. The operative phrase is "there is nothing else to think." In the same vein, Wiggins speaks of "the passion to get the answer to this or that moral or political question *right*"; or of moral explanation that fastens finally on "the only opinion that would survive reflection."[43] I cannot see that such a confidence can ever be counted on in the sciences. Why should one suppose it might be possible in moral matters? Surely there is an unexplained second-tier optimism here, something close to intuitionism. What if that optimism were not invoked *and* what if Wiggins's continuum and disjunction claims *remained in play* and were brought to center stage?

Wiggins takes the non-cognitivist such as Taylor, R. M. Hare, the emotivists, and Mackie to deny moral realism—hence, to deny the continuum of facts and values or matters of fact and evaluative matters. *That* denial, Wiggins claims to show, makes it impossible for Taylor to make provision for the meaning of life. I have suggested that the argument against Taylor fails because it is misguided as a general strategy. That is hardly to endorse Taylor's gymnastic solution, which is itself irrelevant, or only marginally relevant, to the central matter of the meaning of life. The trouble is, it is also irrelevant, or marginally relevant, in the same sense in which Wiggins's countermove against it is irrelevant, or marginally relevant. Hence, although I concede the continuum—even insist on it—*its* relevance to the meaning-of-life issue depends on considerations Wiggins nowhere develops; rightly understood, the continuum *cannot* secure the kind of claim Wiggins makes in the passage just cited: it goes no further than what Mackie means by a first order view of morality. Wiggins apparently does not see the difficulty; but *if his proposal* fails, as I suggest it must, then we may claim to have good evidence that the general run of *third*-tier theories cannot succeed in answering the objectivity question its own champions have posed for themselves and us. In that case, my brief for a fourth-tier conception will seem stronger, possibly unavoidable.

I urge a stronger claim, in fact. I claim that the solution to the meaning of life question is conceptually trivial: that Wiggins had no need to pursue it by the detour involving Taylor's detour regarding Sisyphus; and that grasping *that* brings us back, in an ampler space, to the finding I pressed against Mackie earlier but did not pursue: namely, that Mackie's admission of first order morality *already* sets the stage for the objectivity of second order morality *if* only we abandon the untenable reliance on first- and second-tier legitimative strategies Mackie, Nagel, and Wiggins favor. There is the nerve of my fourth-tier proposal.

All right. Wiggins combines two notions: first, that the continuum ensures a *cognitivist* solution to the meaning of life question; second, that, once granted, evaluative claims may then be seen to match the objectivity accorded factual claims: so that the moral cognitivist may "reach the state of mind where one thinks that *p* because there is nothing else to think but that *p*."[44] The trouble with this picture is this: first, the question about the meaning of life is *not* a cognitivist question at all, and could not be such but at the price of cognitive privilege. It is always and everywhere trivially answered—except, derivatively, by way of idiosyncratic convictions within the conceptual space in which it is answered: second, factual matters *never* reach that state of mind that Wiggins favors and *never* need to; third, evaluative matters *cannot* reach any such state of mind except by cognitive privilege and *can never* claim the explanatory power of factual, causal matters, though they are not altogether without explanatory or justificatory resources; fourthly, the mere admission of the continuum is too abstract to validate or legitimate any particular morality. Wiggins completely fails to probe beyond these slim concessions.

Wiggins defends a very strong disjunction between "pure valuations" and "pure directives": that is, he insists, that "the fact-value distinction and the is-ought or is-must distinction" are not the same; that evaluative discourse is continuous with factual discourse in the way of taking truth-values but that directive discourse is not similarly continuous because it does not take truth-values.[45] As I say, this permits Wiggins to defeat the non-cognitivist, since on Wiggins's reading, "life is *objectively* meaningless" for the non-cognitivist, and meaning is supposed to be infused *only* by a subjective *addition* of values to what is objectively meaningless.[46]

This will not do at all—that is, Wiggins's resolution, *not* Taylor's extravagance. For, *if* obligation belongs to the evaluative side of discourse as much as to the directive, then particles like "ought" and "must" must themselves belong *to* the evaluative as much as to the directive *and* the practical force of directive discourse *may* itself be logically entailed *by* the evaluative force of what is being affirmed.[47] Wiggins opposes such an argument but fails to say why. He needs the disjunction in order to make the case that the non-cognitivist cannot by any means reclaim the meaning of life. The trouble is, the issue is largely vacuous, though hardly unimportant for that reason. At one stroke, we can resolve the meaning question *and* provide a basis for a pared-down, second-order legitimation that escapes all first-, second-, and now the usual third-tier presumptions. In doing that, we should have met Mackie's challenge, answered Nagel's question, and explained more satisfactorily the close linkage between meaning and truth that Wiggins insists on. For the moment, I say only that that is the theme of the fourth-tier maneuver I have been promising.

"In matters of practice" as opposed to "matters of fact," Wiggins says, "we are grateful for the existence of alternative answers." "If there were practical truth it would have to violate [what Wiggins had earlier offered as] the third and fifth truisms of truth [namely, 'the independence of truth both from our will and from our own limited means of recognizing the presence or absence of the property in a statement' and the fact 'that every plain truth is compatible with every other plain truth']."[48] But, of course, this is simply to endorse a first- or second-tier confidence without benefit of supporting argument. It is also to entrench a bivalent logic, where the threat of relativism remains undischarged, by the device of subsuming evaluative discourse under factual discourse, by refusing to do the same for directive discourse, *and* by assuming too easily that a bivalent logic is the only logic that rightly services factual discourse whether it includes evaluative discourse or not. There would *be* no need for the strong disjunction between the evaluative and the practical *if* it were seen that evaluative discourse *already* challenges the adequacy of a bivalent logic.[49] This goes to Wiggins's extravagant wording: "nothing else to think"—which ignores the challenge from Mackie that Wiggins plainly is addressing. But if what I have already said about "ought" and "must" holds, then Wiggins has landed himself in an insoluble and self-inflicted dilemma. He endorses bivalence explicitly, by the way.[50]

7.

I must bring the argument to a close; but you may perhaps see that its being closed is nothing but a new beginning—tethered to what I am calling the fourth-tier conception. I must take advantage of Wiggins again, to bind up all the loose ends of my account. I draw your attention therefore to what is both the best part of Wiggins's lecture and what I take to be its essential mistake: perhaps it is the *ur-*clue to all the failings I have been tracking and to the need for a turn into the fourth tier. Here is what Wiggins says, as he begins to close his own lecture and as he deliberately and effectively defeats the Aristotelian thesis, that "happiness is the end":

> Inasmuch as invention [Mackie's term] and discovery [the term Wiggins shares with Nagel] are distinguishable, and insofar as either of these ideas properly belongs here, life's having a point may depend as much upon something *contributed* by the person whose life it is as it depends upon something discovered. Or it may depend upon what the owner of the life brings to the world in order to see the world in such a way as to discover meaning. This cannot happen unless world and person are to some great extent reciprocally suited. And unluckily, all claims of human adaptability notwithstanding, those things are often not well suited to one another.[51]

A little further on, returning to adjust his charge that Aristotle's view that the "point of human existence" that "*eudaimonia* [is] not exactly happiness but a certain kind of success"—"is absurd," Wiggins explains:

> This is not to deny that Aristotle's doctrine can be restored to plausibility if

we allow the meaning of the particular life that accommodates the activity [in question, the activity (say) of ditch-digging to help a neighbor] to *confer* intrinsic worth upon the activity. But this is to reverse Aristotle's procedure (which is the only procedure available to a pure cognitivist). And I doubt we have to choose. At its modest and most plausible best the doctrine of cognitive underdetermination can say that we need to be able to think in both directions, down from point to the human activities that answer to it, and up from activities whose intrinsic worth can be demonstrated by Aristotle's consensual method to forms of life in which we are capable by nature of finding point.[52]

Here you have Wiggins's splendid effort: first, to redeem Aristotle against himself; second, to read Aristotle along Wittgensteinian lines; third, to recover the very point of Nagel's later and lamer marriage of the objective and the subjective; fourth, to satisfy Mackie's challenge; fifth, to launch thereby an entirely new form of objectivism—what has come to be known as moral realism. I say Wiggins's effort fails, but, in failing, provides the clue to a fourth-tier recovery. The trick is this—or at least one way of recovering the essential clue is this: Wittgenstein's *Lebensformen* may be read either along *individualistic* lines, as *per* Hume or Moore, doubtless also as per Aristotle or Kant, or *per* Wittgenstein himself; or, along *collectivist* lines, as *per* Hegel preeminently, or *per* Marx or Foucault or Bourdieu, with the inevitable admission that Wittgenstein had no particular interest in the historicity of the forms of life or the import of their being collective on the matter of the meaning of life.

In a word, I claim that *all* of Wiggins's strenuous labor against Taylor's effort to reclaim the meaning of life within an empiricism or noncognitivism seemed necessary to Wiggins *only because he treated the question of the meaning of life, as did Taylor, as a matter of an individual person's contributing to or conferring upon his activity an intrinsic meaning that he autonomously discovers in living in the world.* But that is an enormous extravagance. If Wiggins believed that *that* would work, then he could never preclude Taylor's own extravagant solution. But both maneuvers are otiose *if we but concede that life is already meaningful: in the perfectly trivial sense that, having internalized the Lebensformen that make us the apt individual agents (persons) we are, we internalize the norms and values that make life meaningful;* or, *derivatively*, within those terms, *we confer some further idiosyncratic meaning that suits an individual life within the collective possibilities of the other.*

The question of historicity is extremely important here, but I must waive its discussion. It would complicate matters unnecessarily.[53] The point is, *if* both science and morality take their characteristics form as objective disciplines only within the collective terms of one cultural *Lebensform* or another—which is certainly not *added*, subjectively, to our living in the world, but signifies a lifelong engagement with a world *already* intelligible and meaningful within the encompassing terms of a collective form of life—then any additional contributing and conferring obtain *only within the internal space* of that *Lebensformlich* experience. Kant and Aristotle would never agree to that—would never consider it. Neither would Wittgenstein, actually. Neither does Wiggins or any of the first-, second-, or third-tier thinkers I have been tracking.

Here are its advantages. First of all, it makes the question of the meaning of life conceptually trivial: life, in the collective sense in which human societies sustain a viable "form of life," cannot but be meaningful collectively; *every* individual person discovers or invents a variant of the meaningful structure of the world he shares. Second, that advantage can be sustained only if individual perception, thought, understanding, knowledge, interpretation, theory, practical commitment, and judgment are *already* collectively informed by the language, customs, institutions, traditions of the *Lebensform* that resolves the meaning question. That explains why, *if* Mackie cannot make a principled cognitive distinction between first- and second-order queries, his own acknowledgment that first order views *are* part of the fabric of the world prepares the ground for admitting that second order views are also part of the fabric. Admittedly, the question remains: How? But the verdict ramifies through the larger quarrels regarding facts and values. Third, the upshot of the first two gains is that there is no principled distinction, in terms of second-order legitimation, between scientific knowledge and moral or practical knowledge, although there is a difference between the inquiries of science and the inquiries of morality. That cuts against the excessively labile sense in which Nagel treats the subjective and the objective as both disjunctive and in some respect a matter of degree. Finally, if we grant the foregoing, then we cannot claim *a priori* that science or morality *requires* a bivalent logic. Relativism may be unavoidable in the space of either. If so, then we need not fall back, as Wiggins does, to any perhaps inexplicit first- or second-tier theory.

All I dare, or need, add here is this. In the English-language literature of moral philosophy—of the third-tier sort, of the moral realist sort, of the sort influenced by the queries of Mackie, Nagel, and Wiggins at least—there seems to be only one reasonably sustained account that comes at all to grips with the collective reading of Wittgenstein's *Lebensformen*. That is Sabina Lovibond's account in *Realism and Imagination in Ethics*.[54] I believe Lovibond's argument fails, for reasons that have the widest conceivable implications for the entire tradition of Anglo-American moral philosophy.[55] I was hinting at this in the tally I have just supplied. But, for my present purpose, I merely note that Lovibond construes Wittgenstein's *Lebensformen* in terms of Hegel's magisterial notion of collective *Sitten*.[56] This, of course, brings us to the matter of historicity, though Lovibond makes no particular use of it. Generally speaking, Lovibond prepares the way for a fourth-tier effort but herself falls back to a third-tier position that integrates all the themes I have been tracking as well as the strongest analytic views regarding the possible linkage between understanding language, objective factual knowledge, and objective moral and practical judgment—that is, all that is essential to Wiggins's concern. We must go on to see what more may be gained from Lovibond's advance and what needs still to be supplied beyond it. But it is enough, for the time being, to have vindicated a fourth-tier speculation by supporting it dialectically against the demonstrable limitations of the best third-tier thinking. I have no illusions of having answered Mackie's question fully. But we are well on our way.

Notes

1. Thomas Nagel, *The View from Nowhere* (New York: Oxford University Press, 1986), p. 138.

2. *Ibid.*, p. 3.

3. *Ibid.*, pp. 4, 10.

4. *Ibid.*, p. 149.

5. *Ibid.*, pp. 5, 162.

6. See Bernard Williams, *Ethics and the Limits of Philosophy* (Cambridge, Mass.: Harvard University Press, 1985).

7. See J. L. Mackie, *Ethics: Inventing Right and Wrong* (Harmondsworth, England: Penguin Books, 1977).

8. I have discussed the basic lines of argument of both tiers in "A Reckoning of Sorts on the Prospects of Moral Philosophy," *Philosophic Exchange,* forthcoming; and "Moral Optimism," forthcoming.

9. Mackie, *Ethics: Inventing Right and Wrong*, p. 15.

10. *Ibid.*

11. *Ibid.*, p. 16.

12. *Ibid.*, pp. 16-17.

13. *Ibid.*, pp. 48, 18.

14. *Ibid.*, p. 22.

15. *Ibid.*, pp. 26-27.

16. *Ibid.*, pp. 27, 29.

17. *Ibid.*, p. 38.

18. I provide the evidence in "A Reckoning of Sorts on the Prospect of Moral Philosophy."

19. See, for instance, the argument in Mark Platts, "Moral Reality and the End of Reason," in Mark Platts, ed., *Reference, Truth, and Reality: Essays on the Philosophy of Language* (London: Routledge and Kegan Paul., 1980).

20. Nagel, *The View from Nowhere*, pp. 138 - 139.

21. As in John Rawls, *A Theory of Justice* (Cambridge, Mass.: Harvard University Press, 1970).

22. Nagel, *The View from Nowhere*, p. 140.

23. *Ibid.*, p. 142.

24. *Ibid.*, p. 145.

25. *Ibid.*, p. 144.

26. *Ibid.*

27. *Ibid.*, p. 146.

28. *Ibid.*, p. 159.

29. *Ibid.*, p. 158.

30. *Ibid.*, p. 159.

31. *Ibid.*, pp. 5, 7.

32. David Wiggins, "Truth, Invention, and the Meaning of Life," *Needs, Values, Truth*, 2nd ed. (Oxford: Basil Blackwell, 1991), p. 88.

33. *Ibid.*, pp. 104-105. The citations from Aristotle and Bentham are given by Wiggins.

34. *Ibid.*, p. 107.

35. *Ibid.*, p. 106.

36. See Richard Taylor, *Good and Evil* (New York: Macmillan, 1970).

37. For a sample of moral realism, see Geoffrey Sayre-McCord, ed., *Essays on Moral Realism* (Ithaca, N.Y.: Cornell University Press, 1988). Wiggins's paper, somewhat altered, is reprinted in this collection.

38. Wiggins, "Truth, Invention, and the Meaning of Life," pp. 122-123.

39. *Ibid.*, p. 126. Wiggins cites Aristotle's line.

40. See Wiggins, "Postscript," *Needs, Values, Truth,* pp. 354-356.

41. I take Davidson and Kim to have fundamentally misunderstood Moore. Moore holds that non-natural properties depend on natural properties; but he does not hold and in context he would undoubtedly deny that specific non-natural predications are necessarily entailed by specific natural are necessarily entailed by specific natural predictions: there is said to be a one-on-one correlation that holds in a modally necessary way. Moore's holism clearly goes against supervenience; but in any case Moore nowhere espouses the doctrine. See *The Philosophy of G. E. Moore*, ed. Paul Arthur Schilpp (Chicago: Open Court, 1942), p. 488. See, also, Donald Davidson, "Mental Events," *Essays on Actions and Events* (Oxford: Clarendon Press, 1980); and Jaegwon Kim, *Supervenience and Mind: Selected Philosophical Essays* (Cambridge, England: Cambridge University Press, 1993). I have examined Davidson's and Kim's view in greater detail in "A Biopsy of Recent American Philosophy," forthcoming.

42. Wiggins, "Postscript," pp. 354-355.

43. *Ibid.*, p. 354.

44. *Ibid.*

45. Wiggins, "Truth, Invention, and the Meaning of Life," pp. 95-96; see p. 126.

46. *Ibid.*, p. 99.

47. I have, in *Values and Conduct* (Oxford: Clarendon, 1971), shown that "ought" is often not a copula but a predicate reasonably rendered by "oughtful." This is conveniently in accord with Wiggins's continuum but is opposed to his strong disjunction between evaluative and directive discourse.

48. Wiggins, "Truth, Invention, and the Meaning of Life," pp. 115, 126.

49. See Joseph Margolis, *The Truth About Relativism* (Oxford: Basil Blackwell, 1991).

50. Wiggins, "Truth, Invention, and the Meaning of Life," p. 126.

51. *Ibid.*, p. 132. I have italicized the word, "contributed."

52. *Ibid.*, pp. 133-134. Wiggins himself has italicized "confers."

53. I have pursued the issue in many places, mostly recently in *The Flux of History and the Flux of Science* (Berkeley: University of California Press, 1993) and *Interpretation Radical but Not Unruly* (Berkeley: University of California Press, 1995).

54. See Sabina Loribond, *Realism and Imagination in Ethics* (Minneapolis: University of Minnesota Press, 1983).

55. I have explored the matter in "Moral Realism and the Meaning of Life," *Philosophical Forum*, 22 (1990).

56. See G. W. F. Hegel, *Philosophy of Right*, trans. T. M. Knox (Oxford: Clarendon Press, 1952).

Three

OBJECTIVITY: WRONG CONCEPT FOR VALUE INQUIRY

Don E. Marietta, Jr.

1.

A frequent concern when philosophers talk about value is whether values can be objective. This is the wrong way to approach what may be a legitimate concern.

Two developments in modern fields of thought indicate that we are simplistic in referring to values as either objective or subjective. They are contemporary physics and phenomenology. They show that the distinction between subjective and objective ideas or values is not tenable. In contemporary physics, we have relativity theory, the principle of complementarity, and the uncertainty principle. The old way of thinking about the knower and the known simply does not fit what is happening in quantum mechanics.

The objection that what applies at the micro-level of quantum mechanics is not relevant to ordinary experience is answered by the other development in a modern field of thought, phenomenology. The traditional dichotomy between subject and object, with its separation between representations in the knowing subject and external objects known, at the macro-level of experience, is not supported by phenomenological analysis. Phenomenology leads to a rejection, or complete reinterpretation, of the notions of pure subjectivity and objectivity. There is no factual knowledge which simply reflects the world, without activity of the knowing subject; there are no mental activities which are not correlated in some way with the extra-mental world.

Phenomenological analysis of perception shows that awareness of objects in the world is an activity of consciousness. By a process known technically as constitution, consciousness places a thesis on the object to which it is attending, giving it natural and cultural characteristics that make it an object of such and such a kind for the observer. When I see an apple, my consciousness has made it an apple for me. The apple which I see in the dish on my table only became an apple in my lived world when it was constituted as an apple. The table and the dish were constituted as well. It is unlikely that the apple would be constituted as a watermelon, but I might have ignored the apple or constituted it as an undistinguished part of a table decoration.

Our lived worlds are what we are talking about when we speak of the real world of experience. Except for the constituting consciousness, we would not have a real world. This talk of the role of consciousness in constituting our lived worlds might make us draw the mistaken conclusion that everything of which we are conscious is simply subjective. There is a personal aspect of constituting objects, but this is only half the story. The objects constituted by consciousness are not whimsical imaginings, without relation to an extra-mental world. Our consciousness does not create objects out of nothing; the things themselves have a part in their constitution.

A number of years ago, before the later writings of Edmund Husserl were available to scholars, some interpreters thought that phenomenology was a kind of subjective idealism. It is now obvious that phenomenology should not be understood that way. Husserl and other phenomenologists realized that the only access we can have to the world is through our consciousness of the world, but that does not mean that the world is just consciousness. Phenomenologists are leery of theoretical explanations of the world which get far away from actual experience, so they urge repeated returns to conscious experience. Husserl called this returning "to the things [*Sachen*] themselves."[1]

Let us be clear about this: checking up on consciousness is not meant to reduce everything to consciousness, and it does not imply that all our constituted objects are simply subjective. This is clearer when we see that individual consciousness alone is not the point of focus. Phenomenological analysis is concerned with what is commonly experienced. Some constitutions of worldly objects and events seem to be the same for all people, or at least for people in a broad cultural group. The commonality in perception is called intersubjectivity, and it serves as an important check against certain sorts of subjectivism. Phenomenologists are not picking up the argument of Theaetetus which Plato thoroughly demolished.[2] The common world of intersubjectivity is very important to phenomenologists, and it is not considered to be a world of ideas, as Berkeley argued, or a world of spirit, as Hegel argued, or even an ideal world as Royce and Croce explained it in this century.

Why do phenomenologists reject the subjective idealist concept of the world? How do we know that the constituted objects in the world are not just ideas in our minds? Phenomenological analysis gives us strong reasons to believe that the objects we experience are not wholly subjective. To some extent we can identify the function of the objects themselves in our constitution of them. In his work on art theory, Rudolf Arnheim explains how people see lines and colors on a flat surface as pictures, showing connections between the way a picture is constituted and the plastic features themselves. We can see how they make a difference in our perception of lines and colors as three-dimensional pictures. The lines and colors are seen as a picture instead of being seen only as lines and colors. Shapes with unbroken contour lines, textured surfaces, smaller surfaces, and the bottoms of pictures tend to be seen as figures with other parts of the picture seen as background. Simple and symmetrical shapes also tend to be seen as figures.[3]

Eugene Kaelin calls these plastic features of the art work surface counters.[4] We do not understand the constitution of a picture very well if we ignore the function of the surface counters. Other easily described aspects of a picture play an important role in depth perception. Seeing a picture involves mental activities and is affected by the viewer's interests and previous knowledge. But seeing a picture cannot be explained completely in terms of personal elements. The actual shapes and colors of a picture limit the appropriate constitutions of the picture. One of the most convincing indications that the objects in our lived worlds are not just ideas is found in the spatial location of the consciousness of objects. Objects in the world always stand apart from us in a definite direction and distance. When I see my cat, it is always somewhere in relation to me. It often seems that it is usually underfoot, but I might see my cat in the chair six feet in front of me or in a sunny spot by the window to my left. Ideas are not like this. If I think about a mathematical problem, it is not in a place in a certain direction from me. When I remember a pleasant walk in Florence, my thought is not located spatially in relation to my body.

Another indication that objects in the world are not thoughts is that objects in the world only present to us that part of the object which faces us. If I sit down on a dirty seat in the cafeteria, you will not know about the catsup on my trousers until I turn and walk away. When we constitute an object we see it as having parts which we do not actually see, parts which are not presented to us. You constitute me as having clothes on my back, even though you do not see them and do not see the catsup stains. Our knowledge of the world enables us to enter a strange building with no fear of dropping off into space just beyond the door. When we think about this experience, however, we can notice the limitations in the way perceived objects are presented to us. When we are thinking about objects, we discover no such limitations in our thoughts. Thoughts do not need to be positioned, and we can think about all sides of an object. When you think about a flower pot for your new begonias, there is no one side presented to you at a time. There is such a great difference between experiencing objects and thinking about objects, that we realize that we have no reason to worry about everything in the world being purely subjective.

We do judge that some awareness of objects is more real than others, in the sense that it gives us less ground for doubting the existence of the object. We feel sure that it can be seen by other people. We base this sense of reality on a high level of intersubjectivity. Even though there is a subjective aspect to all perception, there are some things which most of the people we know see as we see them. Many objects are invariably constituted the same way, at least by the people who share a common culture. The common way of seeing the world is still partly subjective; each of us constitutes the objects, but my subjectivity does not clash with yours. We expect all our friends to agree that this is a chair, this a table. The intersubjective agreement breaks down so seldom for familiar objects that we think we are dealing with objective things. Since the intersubjective support breaks down more often with values, we tend to consider values to be subjective, but this is a mistake. It is a matter of degrees of intersubjective agreement. Intersubjectivity is the nearest thing we have to objectivity, but we should not confuse a high level of intersubjective agreement with the notion that we have access to objects which is totally independent of consciousness. It is also important that we not assume, in the face of disagreement over values, that values are subjective while factual knowledge is not.

The terms "subjective" and "objective" tend to mislead us, especially when we think in terms of objective facts and subjective values. We continue to be confused when we ask whether values can be objective. Our awareness of facts and valuings of objects are alike in being constitutions of the world. They are also alike in not being completely independent of an extra-mental world. We do well to study the part the world plays in our perception of fact and of value, but we do not facilitate understanding when we label things as simply objective or subjective.

When we consider something to be a fact, we are constituting it as a fact. When we call something a value, we are constituting it as a value. We are separating something from our original awareness of the world and giving it the significance for us of being a fact or being a value. In our original awareness there are no pure facts or pure values, but there are things which we constitute as facts and things which we constitute as values. By a kind of extraction or abstraction we can look upon this or that as a value or as a fact. Another way of saying this is that fact and value are united in our original turning to the world. In much of our constitution of the world, even after reflection, fact and value continue to be joined. One of the clearest explanations of this union of fact and value is in Abraham Maslow's paper, "Fusions of Facts and Values."[5] It is commonly believed that values are supervenient upon facts, but phenomenological analysis shows that facts have no priority. Judgments of fact and judgments of value can be constituted independently of each other. Realization of value is as primitive as the constitution of factual information. We do not need to start with cognition of the height and color of a mountain to experience it as awesome, beautiful, or threatening. A mountain might first strike us as awesome. Later, we might realize that certain natural features of the mountain can be correlated with our feeling toward it. We might not observe a correlation between physical features of the mountain and our feeling of awe, however, because the feeling of awe does not need to be supported with factual observations about the mountain. Our feeling toward the mountain might be the most important thing about the mountain, while other matters are left unattended. In confronting something else, it might be different. We might pay most attention to physical aspects of what we confront or what we want to do about it. All the aspects of confronting a mountain, a chair cover to fit the chair in the hall, or a lost child are combined in our original coming upon the thing. We need not follow a pattern of first getting the facts, then making an evaluation, then deciding what we want to do. Fact, value, and volition are imbedded in our original constitution of the world.[6]

To think about factual aspects of a thing, or to contemplate values, or to ponder what to do, we must extract these factual, valuational, and volitional aspects from the common ground in which they stand as equals. We must constitute aspects of the common ground of our most primitive encounter with the world as cognitive, evaluational, or volitional reflection. No one aspect of that primitive experience has temporal or logical priority over the others. We cannot look upon part of it as objective and other parts of it as subjective. These categories do not reflect what we have encountered, and they do not help us sort things out. What we find in our lived world are characteristics which we can identify as naturalistic and characteristics which have their signification in the social and intellectual aspects of our lives. Some of the sense which we give objects and events is personal, while other aspects of our lived worlds are intersubjective. To speak of all this in terms of what is objective and what is subjective does not further understanding.

2.

Asking whether values are objective or subjective does not help us. How can the real issues be stated? Two aspects of value are indicated by talk about objectivity. One is valuing something because it is valuable in itself, not as a means for achieving something else which is valuable. The other aspect is valuing something which ought to be valued. This is often seen as value which is in the valued object itself and cannot be reduced to an act of evaluation. In treating these aspects of value, philosophers often talk about values being intrinsic or inherent. There are problems with this because the terms "intrinsic value" and "inherent value" are not clear. The dictionary definitions of these terms are of little help; the distinction between the concepts is not clear, and some dictionaries employ one of the terms in defining the other. Philosophers have used the terms in various ways, without agreement.

To be as clear as possible about value, I will use some new terms to which specific meanings can be assigned. These words may sound awkward, but they have the advantage of not carrying the associations which readers have with words like "intrinsic" and "inherent."[7]

What kinds of value have philosophers been seeking when they talked about objectivity? One aspect of value which we need to consider is the value of things valued for themselves and not as means to something else. This is often spoken of as valuing something as an end in itself. I will refer to value as an end in itself as end-value. What is meant by "X has end-value" is "some subject (S) values an object (X) as an end in itself."

Being valued as an end in itself may not be very important. Virtually anything can be valued as an end in itself. All that is required to give something end-value is its being valued. Attributing end-value to an object does not describe characteristics of the object. I can value something just for itself, and you might see no value in it; I might be unable to tell you anything about the object which would make you see it as valuable. I might not know myself why my old fountain pen is valuable to me, but I take good care of it and provide it a special place of storage. For me it has end-value.

To say that an object has end-value is a loose use of language. The semantics of this is clear: referring to end-value is referring to the act of valuation. It is sometimes simpler and easier to refer to value than it is to speak of someone's act of valuing. Nothing is wrong with this handy linguistic device as long as we realize that the noun form "end-value" does not refer to some quality in the thing itself.

Many philosophers believe that all value is really evaluation. This popular view might be true, but it is not obviously true, and the matter is still under discussion in this paper. I will explore the possibility that some values might be more than a person's act of valuing.

My term for values which are not simply acts of valuation will be "independent value." If there are any independent values, they will be independent of human ascription of value. What I will mean by "X has independent value" is "X has value independently of being valued by some S."

Consider things which we now value but were once not valued. Some writers call values which will come to be values in the future, virtual value; the idea is that the object that is not now valuable may be valuable at some later time. The term "virtual value," however, does not do anything but save the speaker from talking about independent value. It saves us from admitting that something can be valuable without anyone knowing about it. Having denied that there can be value without valuation, it seems that the object cannot be valuable while unknown; when we start with the evidence, however, and not with the belief about value, it is easier to believe that an object which is now valued was valuable even when we were ignorant of its worth. The term "virtual value" begs the question and closes the discussion prematurely.

When we look at actual examples of valued object which were once unrecognized, what do we see? What sorts of things have value in this way? Holmes Rolston III writes about values in nature and cites myoglobin, which evolved into hemoglobin, and the natural processes of photosynthesis and glycolysis, along with other things in the working of ecosystems.[8]

When we look at valuable things we now know about which were once unknown, we recognize things on which all life depends. Is it not strange to insist that these things were not valuable when they first began serving their purposes? The ozone layer did not become valuable only in recent times. Some things have independent value. When we examine more carefully things which have independent value, do they reward our quest for "objective" value? We need to consider carefully the significance of having independent value.

All the things we can point to as independent values seem to be things which are valuable as parts of, or processes within, larger systems. Their value is instrumental, but in a particular manner. There are a number of ways for a thing to have value as a means, and our examples of independent value form a special case. They are not valuable the way a tool is valuable as a means, but as parts of a system.

I will use a new term, "functional value," to refer to the role of a valuable part in a system. "X has functional value" will mean "X has value as a significant part of a valued system."

3.

The notion of objective value, often expressed by the terms "inherent" or "intrinsic," is a combination of end-value and independent value. This combination provides an object which is valued for itself independently of any human ascription of value. It would be a real value, which ought to be valued.

What is the connection between the combination of end-value with independent value and the notion of objective value? What are people looking for when they seek objective value? That they are asking for something which is not instrumentally valuable is clear from the repeated contrasting of instrumental value with intrinsic and inherent value. The disjunction of intrinsic and instrumental value indicates that objective value is end-value. Being an end-value is all that objectivity, found in intrinsic value, requires for some thinkers. My examination of end-value, a thing which is valued as an end in itself, indicates that this kind of value is not as significant as some people have tried to make it, since it can be quite arbitrary. But objective value must not be arbitrary. What might save objective value from being arbitrary is independent value.

Putting the matter in such awkward terms as end-value and independent value might seem needlessly complicated, but we gain a clearer way of talking about the concern over objective value. The taxonomy I suggest avoids the conceptual confusion over the term "objective." If the combination of end-value and independent value is possible would it have the significance which is associated with the concept of objective value?

An object can be valued in several ways at the same time. Dad's old fly rod can be valued as a fishing instrument, as a keepsake because it was Dad's, and just for itself for no special reason. His fly rod could continue being valued even if I lost interest in fishing. An object can be valued in several ways, but this might not have much importance. The different sorts of value do not augment each other or create any additional value. My keepsake would not be any less valuable to me as a keepsake, if it were not in usable condition. When it comes to fishing, a new rod with no sentimental value would be better if it were a better fishing tool. Thus, two kinds of value are independent of each other.

One entity can have independent value and end-value. We can discover actual unproblematic examples of things being valued in both ways and think of possible examples which are not strange or farfetched. I can value photosynthesis for itself, independently of the fact that my life depends upon it. Would this be of any importance, or would it be a fortuitous conjunction of no real significance? Instead of looking for examples of things with both types of value in order to assess their importance, let us be sure that we are clear about the nature of the types of value involved.

In examining the significance of an object having end-value and independent value, we first need to see that end-value does not give the object much axiological status except for the valuer. To say that something has end-value is not to say anything about the valued object, except that someone values it. This is a weak footing on which to rest our ethical or aesthetic claims. Surprisingly perhaps, being valued as an end in itself turns out to be one of the least impressive kinds of value.

Since much has been made of virtues, beauty, health, and a good disposition as ends in themselves, perhaps I should re-examine my statements about end-value. But if we looked for more significance in the notion of end-value, what would we look for? Little would be gained from citing something which virtually everyone values as an end in itself. This might teach us something about human psychology, but it would not teach us anything else. The fact that nearly everyone values something gives us some ground for giving it consideration as an object of value, but we would have little reason for adopting the value if everyone values it for no discoverable reason. The bare fact that an object is valued is a weak reason for valuing it. Members of some nonhuman animal species can be attracted to something which is detrimental to them, such as alcohol. This happens among members of our species too. If we want a justifying reason for valuing something, we need to look for something about the valued object which explains its being valued. Some of the objects most often cited as valuable in themselves can be more intelligibly understood as means to valuable experiences or states of affairs, and these in turn seem to be valued as means to even other things, or to be valued only under certain conditions. Only "the dread of something after death, the undiscovered country from whose bourn no traveler returns" could make a reasonable person value life under all conditions.[9] The wide use of living wills indicates that many thoughtful people realize that there are conditions under which they would not value life. To value beauty one must be not only in the right state of mind but free from other urgencies and indispositions. Life and beauty are valued because, under the right conditions, they give us good experiences. I doubt that health is really an end in itself. Some people make good use of their ailments, and it seems to me that most of us value health for what it enables us to do and what it allows us to escape. The pious praise of virtue for its own sake often signals hypocrisy or confusion. When we look at valuing virtue for its own sake, we find that some honest people value virtue without being able to give a reason for valuing it.

The very notion of having reasons for valuing an object as an end in itself seems self-contradictory. If there is a reason for valuing the object, that reason itself must be a value. So how can we escape the implication that the object is valued as a means? Of course the second value could be incidental to our valuing the first object, but then it is not the reason why we value the first object. I cannot consistently claim that I value my father's fly rod for itself for the reason that it casts flies better than any other rod I have used.

The demand for objectivity requires that values be end-values and not instrumental values. It also requires that values not be idiosyncratic or whimsical. In short, objectivity requires reasons for holding end values, which we have found to be problematic.

In ethics especially, there is a felt need for values which are not just instrumental and which are well founded in some way. This may be a frail support for an ethical claim, since valuing as an end in itself something which also has independent value is not a significant thing to do. There appears to be no logical connection between these two kinds of value; valuing as an end in itself something which has independent value does not satisfy the demand for objectivity.

4.

We have seen that end-value and independent value are not as significant as we might expect. The sorts of things we can recognize as having independent value have functional value as parts of a valued larger system. This calls into question our classifying them as independent values. They are not entirely independent of human ascription of value if their worth lies in being part of a good system, one which is valued by human beings. The independence of these values is compromised.

If we drop the requirement that functional value consist of playing a role in a good system, we escape the problem of making functional value dependent upon human ascription of value to the larger system. We could define as independently valuable the parts of any system, even an evil one from a human perspective. This way of solving our problem runs into a new difficulty. To call such functions valuable does violence to the word "valuable." Is the nutrient which enables eutrophication of a lake valuable? Value is a normative concept, not a merely descriptive one. To call valuable something which cannot be valued by responsible people is odd indeed. To say it is valuable to the evil system is to use the language of value when descriptive language would be more appropriate.

We must either acknowledge that independent values are not entirely independent of human valuing or insist that they are entirely independent by using a dubious notion of value. We must maintain a meaningful normative concept of value by holding that the value of a part must lie in its contribution to a valued system. We can still make a limited sense of the notion of independent value by showing that there are larger wholes which we ought to value. The parts which contribute to such a whole would have a sort of independent value, since our valuing the whole would not be a matter of taste, but a moral obligation. Before we snort at this suggestion, let us look at it seriously. It would not apply to every whole favored by people, and certainly not to relatively small and unimportant wholes. There are, however, some wholes on which a great deal depends. Let us consider the biosphere, the whole system of nature on which all life depends. To value the essential parts of this system is not like attributing independent value to part of a pipe organ or to the sidewalk before one's house. The things which have essential functional value in the biosphere are not valuable because we happen to like life. To refuse to value what all life and all human ascription of value rest on is not just bad taste or bad judgment, but ultimately irrational. Valuing the biosphere is reasonable, and hardly anything affords more good reasons for attributing value.

We have found at least one thing for which we can give undeniable good reasons for valuing. Someone's denying that the biosphere is valuable is hard to comprehend and impossible to condone. But is the value of the biosphere entirely independent of human evaluation? I cannot claim that we have found something equivalent to what people have sought when they wanted objectivity. We might be right in saying that everyone should value the biosphere, but I do not think we can show that its value is entirely independent of human evaluation.

5.

Quantum mechanics and phenomenology have not destroyed the foundations of knowledge and value. They have undone the kind of absolutism which gave comfort to moralists, religionists, and natural scientists in past times, but this does not mean that no knowledge is worth having and no values are worth seeking. We may not be able to claim a kind of certainty which has always been spurious, but we can have adequate reasons for believing and valuing. When intersubjectivity must be made to serve instead of objectivity, we need not fear that everything will come tumbling down. We live with uncertainty in important areas of our lives. We usually take our medicine even though the doctor is not certain that it will cure us. We make financial investments when we are not certain that they will be successful. We drive over long bridges when we are not absolutely certain that we will not make local history by driving the first car to go down with a faulty bridge. This does not make our decisions regarding health and finances whimsical. It does not mean that one medical treatment or one investment is as good as any other. If the bridge shakes too much, we might go around the long way next time. Uncertainty does not make us fools. We learn to be thoughtful and make careful decisions in the face of uncertainty.

Our pursuit of certainty in morality has done us more harm than good. It has lead philosophers to be excessively critical of ethical approaches which can contribute to moral understanding and to intelligent decisions. Rather than rejecting entirely an approach which does not offer moral certainty, we should emphasize the contributions which it makes to our understanding. Moral philosophers have contributed to subjectivism and skepticism about moral knowledge. We have helped teach people that moral philosophers spend most of their time disagreeing with each other and that no significant contributions can be made. No wonder few people understand the nature of progress in the philosophical enterprise.

It would be silly of us to give up the pursuit of knowledge on the grounds that all our scientific theories depend upon an element of uncertainty that invades all our factual knowledge claims. We would be just as silly to give up on values on the ground that they cannot be purely objective. We know that there are ways to check knowledge claims; there are also ways to check our value judgments. We do not need absolute certainty or objectivity in the realms of fact or of values.

We are familiar with the ways we check knowledge claims. Experience can teach us much about values. Personal experience helps us check the fittingness of our values with the actualities of life. A rich intersubjectivity allows us to learn from our contemporaries, and a knowledge of other cultures and of people's lives in the past gives us perspective on our values. We should remember that values are related to other values. An atomistic approach to values is as unsound as an atomistic approach to facts. Values are hard to defend when we examine them in isolation. An isolated value, like an uprooted plant, is bound to fail.

To think of facts as objective and values as subjective is to create needless problems. When we see that values can be examined in ways which are similar to the ways we examine factual claims, we can face the uncertainty and the need to act upon probability. Understanding that values are not objective does not destroy rational ethics. It does not take away our ability to judge works of art. It does not make whimsical our decisions about daily life. When we see that facts and values are not entirely objective or subjective, we can deal more fittingly with both aspects of our lives. We do not lose our values. Since they become less mysterious, we have a more secure grasp of them and know more clearly how to make them a part of our lives.

Notes

1. Herbert Spiegelberg, *The Phenomenological Movement: A Historical Introduction*, 2nd ed., vol. 1 (The Hague: Martinus Nijhoff, 1971), p. 82.

2. Plato, *Theaetetus*.

3. Rudolf Arnheim, *Art and Visual Perception: A Psychology of the Creative Eye, The New Version* (Berkeley: The University of California Press, 1974), pp. 219-312.

4. Eugene F. Kaelin, *Art and Existence: A Phenomenological Aesthetics* (Lewisburg, Pa.: Bucknell University Press, 1970), pp. 82, 87.

5. Abraham H. Maslow, "Fusion of Facts and Values," *American Journal of Psychoanalysis*, 23 (1963): pp. 127-129.

6. Lester Embree, "Some Noetico-Noematic Analyses of Action and Practical Life," J. J. Drummond and L. Embree, eds., *The Phenomenology of the Noema* (Dordrecht: Kluwer Academic Publishers, 1992).

7. Don E. Marietta, Jr. "Thoughts on the Taxonomy and Semantic of Value Terms," *Journal of Value Inquiry*, 25:1 (1991), pp. 43-53.

8. Holmes Rolston, "Are Values in Nature Subjective or Objective?", *Environmental Ethics*, 4:2, p. 131f.

9. Shakespeare, *Hamlet*, Act 3, Scene 1, lines 78-80.

Four

TOWARDS A METAPHYSICS OF PRACTICE

James B. Wilbur III

I suspect that the choice of the phrase, "Value Inquiry," in the titles of both *The Journal of Value Inquiry* and the Conferences on Value Inquiry marked out opposition to value-free science and the emphasis on epistemology as well as the then current reductive naturalism that seemed to undercut much of what is essentially human. American philosophy has always been naturalistic in attitude under the dominance of science and I consider myself to be of the same bent, though unhappy with mechanistic and behavioristic accounts of human nature.

My reflections will be based on the conclusions and unfinished business in my *The Moral Foundations for Business Practice*. My point of departure will be Kantian not only for some of his conclusions, but, even more, for some of his suggestions.

One such is that practical reason is prior to theoretical reason. It is prior in an existential sense. It is in response to the fundamental fact of being-in-the-world that practical reason arises. Thinking is a form of practice. All theoretical truth of which I am aware is hypothetical only, and not certain. Theoretical reason is either deductive where, given certain premises, a certain conclusion is seen to follow validly, or inductive where, given certain relations in past instances, a certain probability or expectation is seen. Criticisms of both are embodied in Hume's critique. I would agree that the certainty of any of our ideas is a function of the system of ideas or the meanings of the words employed to communicate them and not indicative of anything metaphysical in the traditional sense. Also, there are no theoretical grounds to argue inductively from past to future.

The point of view of theoretical reason is often characterized as a disinterested one. While that way of speaking emphasizes the unbiased as opposed to the biased, it nevertheless presupposes things that are questionable and overlooks the more basic form of reason, practical reason. Theoretical reason takes a spectator or God's eye view on the part of the rational knower and brings up problems of universals, realism, and the problem of induction, as well as difficulties with the individualism underlying our political system. From that point of view, knowledge looks like a very special sort of revelation vouchsafed to the rational, a direct contact with the way things are. I am not casting aspersions upon our ability to grasp rational conclusions, as in if a>b, and b>c, then a>c. But questions arise concerning the context in which our ability arises, is exercised, and understood. Practical reason is prior to theoretical reason in so far as it can be claimed that thinking is a practice. Aristotle's three, so-called laws of thought, Identity, Excluded Middle, and Non-Contradiction, should not be thought of as laws but as necessary conditions, imperatives and limitations on the practice of thinking: if you would think, then you ought to follow them. C. I. Lewis called them "the morality of thinking."[1] You do not have to follow them, but if you do not, then you are not thinking. Practice requires thinking.

Kant speaks about three presuppositions of practical reason: freedom, immortality, and God. They constitute the conditions without which there would be no practical reason. In his little book, *The Self in Philosophy*, Alburey Castell distinguishes between a process and an activity, as, for instance, between astronomy and astronomizing.[2] Astronomy is the scientific system of planetary motions. Astronomizing is the discipline that studies planetary motions, a form of human practice embodying the scientific method.

Several years ago I began to wonder, if there are oughts for the practice of thinking, could there be a morality of practice as well? At the time I was teaching a required business course, Ethics and Management, and had realized that unless I had a good answer to the question "Why ought anyone be moral?" I really did not have anything important to say to students of business. Castell lays out the characteristics of activity or practice as being purposive, critical, fallible, corrigible, meaningful, a locus of choice, and a locus of responsibility, involving the distinction between the real and the ideal, and having presuppositions.[3]

Every end has certain conditions connected with it such that if you want that end, then you ought to fulfill those conditions. The oughts are hypothetical. Deny the end and the ought is undercut. That would not have been an adequate answer for my students because the moral ought is traditionally supposed to be binding no matter what. From the point of view of theoretical reason, there are no binding oughts unless they are the conditions of an accepted end. But whatever made anyone think that the moral ought was unconditionally binding? We are able to arrive at the necessary conditions of thinking by reflecting upon thinking and the conditions without which thinking could not be. Aristotle's so-called laws of thought are unconditionally necessary for the practice of thinking. Are there any unconditionally necessary conditions of all practice, of practice in general? This takes us back to Kant's presuppositions of practical reason: freedom, immortality, and God. Most commentators on Kant have seen the importance of freedom for human practice, but question the requirements of immortality, and God as only peculiar to Kant's religious beliefs. However, if we generalize his requirements of immortality, and God, something important comes into view. Immortality is really a condition of continuity for the realization of Kant's notion of a good will. Of course, "ought" implies "can" and the good will cannot be attained in this world. With regard to practice, a world in which there is continuity is necessary for purposive activity. Newtonian and Humean atomistic impressionism leaves a world of bits and pieces, and cannot handle the carry-over, the push of practice. Continuity is needed in the world and concern is needed on the part of anyone acting in that world. Kant's God assures that individuals with a good will will be happy. In the end, virtue is rewarded. But structure is required for practice. Choice would be meaningless without structure through time. Also, choice would be pointless without multiple alternatives from which to choose. If we organize these conditions, the result is two sets of three. We have choice, concern, and consistency on the part of the practicing self, and multiplicity, continuity, and structure on the part of the world in which practice occurs.

But where does the moral ought come in? Let us borrow a distinction from Aristotle between the actualization of a potential and the exercise of a capacity. Kant saw that in making choices to actualize an end, we can undercut and destroy our capacities to practice. Drug taking is a clear example: one choice may be the last choice. Lying is another example, since the right choice is the one that is consistent with its own possibility. I believe that all of the usual moral norms can be understood in this fashion. Whatever else may be accomplished in practice, the enabling conditions ought to be maintained. But what makes these oughts of practice unconditional?

From a theoretical point of view, the oughts of practice are all hypothetical. But what I am doing now presupposes them and continuing to act requires them. Being in the middle of practice and reflecting upon my being so, I see that they are required in the same way that I see that norms of thought are required in my thinking. Someone may ask if the moral ought is conditional upon wanting to practice. The answer is no. The enabling conditions are necessary presuppositions of action. There is no conditional here. I do not become a liar as a consequence of telling a lie, I am one in the telling. Putting it as a conditional, "If I want to act, then I ought to maintain the enabling conditions of the action," and then denying the antecedent with "I do not want to act," puts me in the same position as the skeptic who wants to deny we have knowledge. My denial undercuts what I would deny. Here, we have a pragmatic contradiction, a condition relegated to the fringe of the logic of theory and referred to as a paradox of self-reference. But self-reference becomes central to the logic of practice.[4] The paradox renders practice meaningless and impossible. Right choices avoid this by being consistent with their own possibility. Although any norm or imperative can be rendered hypothetical by being made an object of practice, all imperatives cannot be hypothetical because the imperatives of practice are unconditioned in the context of practice. Kant called them "categorical" and he was dead right from the perspective of practice as basic.

Kant completely separates moral judgment from prudential judgment. But for a morality of practice, this will not do. Concern with the outer world and its consequences upon the enabling conditions is just as categorically imperative as the concern for the inner conditions of the self. It covers both aspects of practice.

Practice is purposive and reaches beyond itself. So does a categorical imperative of practice. If a categorical imperative of practice did not do so, it would be empty. The domain of morality constitutes a set of limitations within which a range of possibilities reside. Practice that falls within that range will have its appropriate hypothetical imperatives, depending upon the ends involved, and be consistent with its own possibility.

From this point of view, Adam Smith's much chided saying that if everyone pursued their own self-interest, then the good of the community would follow, would be quite reasonable provided that everyone possessed an adequate idea of self-interest, one that included the conditions of its own possibility. Without an adequate idea of self-interest, one that includes its enabling conditions, we are limited to our modern instrumental use of reason, and that can be vicious.

Our modern, much stressed appeal to experience has been one-sided. To fully understand our experience we need to consider more than just the consequences of practice. We should also take into account the pre-conditions necessary to practice. This is accomplished by the reflective use of reason exemplified above. I think an appeal to the pre-conditions or enabling conditions of our experience through reflective reason is just as empirically oriented as an appeal to the post-conditions or consequences of our experience. This is the only way to understand our human experience as a type of practicing. There is no human experience outside of the context of practice. What we know about our world, including ourselves, comes from practice, either reflectively or consequentially.

But are not these reflections on practice just as much without justification for what they say about the world and the self as any other theoretical product? There are two responses that need to be made to this question.

In the first place, both practical and theoretical activities involve ideas as well as the self-referential character of consciousness, being aware you are aware. This element of self-reference brings about the paradoxes of self-reference previously referred to. From the point of view of practice, however, there is another element of reference involved. Following Dewey and Whitehead, let us understand "feeling" as descriptive of our generic relation to any and all experience. Along with my sense that such feelings are mine, that is, the element of self-reference, there is also my sense that they are feelings about something other than themselves or even myself. This reference beyond is evidenced in our common sense belief in an external world and seconded in the way our language is structured.[5] We are aware of both of these elements of reference in our practicing. They allow us to control our practice, in so far as we are able, and make possible its successes and failures. Practice occurs in *medias res* and is more in touch than theory. But what feeling has reference to will remain meaningless until interpretation occurs. This, of course, involves more than just naming which may objectify for purposes of reference but conveys no meaning. Some form of classification is required at every level of experience for meaningful reference.

Secondly, if what I have been saying about the standpoint of practice makes sense, then there are some necessary conditions of practice discoverable, as the realists would have it, and not only constructed as conceptualists would have it. They comprise the categories of a metaphysics of practice, are thoroughly objective, as the *sine qua non* of practice, necessary, for anyone practicing, and ultimately contingent, because practice itself is not necessary unless there are persons to do it.

The enabling conditions of practice have significance for us in that they can be destroyed by choice and without them practice is not possible. I can discover them through reflection on the nature of practice while I am practicing. And while I am practicing, they function unconditionally and are the basis for our moral values. In fact, moral concern only arises in the context of practice. It is not unusual for our metaphysical concern for reality and our moral concern for rightness to be closely connected. I happen to have approached reality from my concern for the nature of the moral ought, but the morality of practice rests on the metaphysics of practice that tells us about what is real in our experience of the world that includes our practice. Only to the degree that we are able to live within a context of practice and maintain it are we responsible individuals. Being a person in the full sense is a social condition as well as an individual one. When achieved, something comes into being that would not otherwise be. The nature of reason is social, especially in practice. The consequences of my telling the truth to a would-be assassin of my friend, not only to my friend's enabling conditions and those of everyone else but to his very existence, are so momentous compared to those occasioned by my telling him a lie as to be insignificant. This does not make lying any more acceptable, but it does show that, given the bi-polarity of practice, just what we ought to do is always a matter of individual responsibility. In time of war we are faced with the same conditions, and we restrict freedom of speech as necessary for the maintenance of our practice. When the social conditions enabling reasonable practice are obviously down, as they are in the case of war or a would-be assassin, telling a lie may well maintain the conditions of the possibility of practice far more readily than would the truth.

Even if a bi-polar view of practice is adequate for human behavior, is it compatible with our scientific views? Science does not conceive of nature, of which humans are a part, in any such fashion at all. As I said at the beginning, I have been bothered about this problem. Even with evolutionary development, how do we arrive at a complicated double-aspect view of practice out of atoms or particles in motion, or even stimulus and response? I had nothing by way of an answer until I read about Chaos theory and the influence of computer modeling on a wide range of sciences and disciplines, from basic physics and weather prediction, to understandings of the circulatory system, insect population control, and free-way traffic flow. Classic models of forces of motion, such as the pendulum, have been found to be inadequate. Motion in nature is not just linear or serial so that, given the initial conditions, the results are determined and predictable. There is a non-linear element functioning in motion as well. For example, a maple leaf will respond to changes in its environment according to its range of possible accommodations including dying, but throughout it remains a maple leaf, even if a dead one. James Gleick's book, *Chaos*, tells of the development of Chaos theory. It is guardedly speculative, but very suggestive to someone with a background in Western philosophy and science. This bears on my concern about reductive naturalism. Human motion is now no longer regarded as alien to natural motion. The new mathematics of fractile geometry measures the differing, non-linear aspects of differing motions in terms of dimensions of flexibility. There has been some talk of correlating dimensions of flexibility with the problem of freedom, but, while the categories of practice involve flexibility in the sense of alternatives for choice, flexibility alone is not an adequate substitute for choice. However, recognition of the dual aspects of practice, and the linear and non-linear elements of motion puts human nature into a closer relationship with nature than it has enjoyed since prior to early, modern history.

I have been concerned with a metaphysics of practice because I was searching for a ground for moral responsibility in business practice. I was also bothered by the imbalance between rights and duties that characterize so much of our social and political thinking. Rights should have to do with the furtherance and protection of our human potential and our capacities to practice, to be of use to ourselves as well as to one another. Duties arise from our being able, through choice, to affirm or destroy the capacities for others as well as for ourselves. With regard to these enabling conditions, there are no conflicts between egoism and altruism.

The enabling conditions of practice are the same for everyone. One of the reasons why theory must be tied in with practice is that practice includes the outside within its concern. This is made clear in the major difference between a logical contradiction and a pragmatic contradiction. In a logical contradiction the destroying opposition lies within the context of ideas, while in a pragmatic contradiction, the opposition lies in the incompatability of the context of ideas with the assertion of that context in practice. The difference between the two is largely ignored in the traditionally rationalistic view of things that takes theoretical reason as fundamental, but it seems to me that, in the light of the things pointed out herein, it is practical reason that is fundamental. Both are important to practice, however, and the relationship between them needs further reflection.

Notes

1. Classroom remark, 1948.

2. Alburey Castell, *The Self in Philosophy* (New York: The Macmillan Co., 1965), pp. 21-25.

3. *Ibid.*, chs. 2 and 3.

4. For further thought on this cf., my "Reason and the Individual: Some Parameters of Practice," *A Quarter Century of Value Inquiry: Presidential Addresses of the American Society for Value Inquiry,* Richard T. Hull, ed. (Amsterdam: Rodopi, 1994), pp. 63-76, and *The Moral Foundations of Business Practice* (Lanham, Md.: University Press of America, 1992), pp. 93-101.

5. For further thought on this cf., "The Value of a Liberal Education: An Essay on the Power of Knowing," *The Journal of Value Inquiry,* 2:2-3 (1968), pp. 187-195.

Five

ON INTRINSIC AND QUASI-INTRINSIC VALUE

Carlo Filice

Is there a single type of intrinsic value from which all other value derives? A number of philosophers have been tempted to answer "Yes," and have proposed pleasure as the basic value. Among them are Epicurus, Bentham, Mill, and Sidgwick. Others, including Plato, Aristotle, and Kant have vehemently opposed this. I would like to argue for a middle ground position. My twofold contention is (1) that pleasure, or at least its enabling trait, sentience, may be absolutely necessary for value; and (2) that even so, pleasure or sentience would not exhaust all value. There are phenomena which may be value-activated by sentience and pleasure without deriving their value from sentience or pleasure. These I will call phenomena of quasi-intrinsic value.

1.

Most of us proceed practically and philosophically on the assumption that most people have intrinsic value. Perhaps other living beings also have intrinsic value; and perhaps even some non-living things do. But surely we take most people to have such value. We speak of human life as sacred, as having absolute worth. We react with horror at unjustified violence against people. Prophets and philosophers alike have called for respect, compassion, and love for other people.

If such pronouncements were correct, what would endow people with intrinsic value? On the most general ontological level, which aspects are the potential sources of value? Consider the example of a substance-attribute ontology. On such an ontology a person is a particular *individual* endowed with multiple attributes. If so, then a person's worth must derive either from the substance pole or from the attribute pole. It is difficult to see how the substance component could be the source of intrinsic value, since that component is shared by non-valuable individuals like pebbles. A substance is that which bears properties, individuates, and may account for identity through time and change. This last function may require substances to be necessarily of a this such variety. But even then, it would be the such as a sortal attribute that would account for the difference between pebble, table, and human substances. Thus, if people have intrinsic worth and pebbles do not, their worth must derive from some special *attributive* aspect of people.

This conclusion has not always been accepted. For example, recently Tom Regan, in arguing for animal rights, has proposed a distinction between inherent and intrinsic value. Only intrinsic value, according to Regan, derives from attributes, in particular attributes of sentient consciousness and correlative pleasures and satisfactions. Inherent value, he argues, derives from an individual's status as a subject-of-a-life. He explains that as follows:

> To be a subject-of-a-life . . . involves more than merely being alive and more than merely being conscious. To be the subject-of-a-life is to be an individual whose life is characterized by . . . [having] beliefs and desires; perception, memory, and a sense of the future, including their own future; an emotional life together with feelings of pleasure and pain; preference and welfare interests; the ability to initiate action in pursuit of their desires and goals; a psychological identity over time; and an individual welfare in the sense that their experiential life fares well or ill for them, logically independently of their being the object of anyone's interests. Those who satisfy the subject of a life criterion themselves have a distinctive kind of value—inherent value—and are not to be viewed or treated as mere receptacles [of intrinsic value].[1]

Regan maintains that inherent value is incommensurable with value based on pleasant experiences of intrinsic value. Inherent value endows those individuals having it with rights, and precludes such individuals from being ever used as means only.

The distinction between inherent and intrinsic value, between value as an *individual* and value derived from conscious experiences, is not tenable. What ultimately makes subjects-of-a-life different from non-subjects-of-a-life is their having special attributes. Regan himself lists consciousness, feelings, and desires as the special attributes necessary and sufficient for acquiring the special status of subject of a life. Thus, I find his notion of inherent value to be just as much an attribute-based value as is his notion of intrinsic value.

A general lesson is that a similar fate would befall related propositions, such as that the soul is the source of the unique value of people. Upon analysis we would find that what makes soul individuals, unlike non-soul individuals, endowed with special value is the presence of special qualities like consciousness, free will, and rationality. Value must derive from the attributive aspect of individuals, not from their substance aspect.

2.

If most people possess intrinsic value, what attributes endow them with it? Many philosophers have answered that ultimately only sentience plays this magical role through the countless variety of pleasant, satisfying, stimulating, and interesting states of consciousness it enables. Hence pebbles and tables have no intrinsic value, while cats, people, and angels and gods, if there are any, do. J. S. Mill is perhaps the strongest proponent of this view. Plato, Aristotle, and Kant, though perhaps granting intrinsic value to sentience and pleasure, have held that rationality or autonomy are the highest sources of intrinsic worth. That is how they explain the generally accepted fact that people and angels and gods are of much greater value than subhuman, sentient beings devoid of reason and autonomy.

Sentience and pleasure are intrinsic goods. Or, in any case, enjoyment of pleasure is an intrinsic good, even if the unexercised ability to enjoy is not. The value of the actual enjoyment of a bowl of chocolate ice cream does not lie primarily in the benefits derived from having ice cream, but in the quality of the experience of eating ice cream. The taste of ice cream is of positive value for those who enjoy it because it is enjoyable. And it is enjoyable because it tastes good! Similarly with all other pleasures. Pleasure is its own reward, though some pleasures carry a high risk, or require the pain of others, or produce other forms of harm, and are thus consequentially evil.

To people who do not see pleasure as being *per se* a good, I can offer no decisive argument to change their minds. If they were to persist in denying that the pleasure they feel adds anything to the experience or activity of, say, eating ice cream, I would have to admit that we have reached a conflict of basic intuitions. Nor is it plausible to maintain that pleasure has value, but that its value is derived. Even if there are other *sui generis* and irreducible types of intrinsic values such as life, health, and knowledge, it is doubtful that they can explain the value of pleasure. For instance, the view that pleasure is of value *only* as a sign of organismic health, which has been suggested by radical environmentalists such as J. Baird Callicott, can be taken seriously only by those willing illicitly to ignore pleasure's desirable phenomenology.[2]

A related position which can be shown to be untenable affirms the intrinsic value of our own pleasures while denying the intrinsic value of the pleasures of others. The metaphysically and ethically interesting form of this position is one which, though allowing for the reality of the pleasant experiences of others, would declare such experiences to lack any intrinsic value.

Insofar as I can understand this position, I see it as based on the assumption that what makes my pleasant experiences intrinsically valuable is that they are *mine*—*not* that such experiences are pleasant. For if we granted that the source of value is the pleasant character of the experience, then we could not consistently deny the intrinsic value of the *pleasant* experiences of others.

However, the *mineness* aspect cannot be the basis of value for two reasons. First, on such a view we would have to claim that prior to determining the intrinsic value of a pleasant experience, we have to know that the experience is ours. But this is implausible. A Siamese twin would presumably affirm the value of a pleasant bodily sensation *even if* the joined twin is uncertain about the primary ownership of the sensation.[3] Second, and more importantly, if the mineness aspect were the basis for the value of a pleasure, the value would have to apply to all the other experiences that are *mine*, including my pains. My other experiences presumably share the same mineness as my pleasures. But it is surely false that my painful experiences possess intrinsic value. Insofar as we affirm the intrinsic value of our own pleasures, we must do so on the basis of the pleasant character of such experiences. And if so, we must extend this affirmation of value to *anyone's* pleasures.

Suppose that my opponent were to grant the intrinsic value of pleasure, if only for the sake of argument. We could then ask: Is pleasure the only intrinsic good? Those who say that it is maintain that all other goods are good because they permit and enhance pleasant states of consciousness in ourself and others. Even knowledge, virtue, rationality, free will, and beauty are of value only as pleasure promoting instruments.

Proponents of this kind of hedonistic outlook must deal with obvious counter examples. If there were a machine that would guarantee us a future consisting of a succession of pleasant conscious states including the delusion of the higher satisfactions normally linked with intellectual and aesthetic activities, with friendships, and with free will, most of us would recoil from being hooked up to such a passive experience machine. For similar reasons most of us would refuse the option of living in a happy Brave New World society. Does this not show that there is some value associated with *genuine* rationality, free will, intellectual and aesthetic activities, and friendships, which does not derive from the pleasures and satisfactions attending and resulting from them?

Mill, of course, would have to deny this. Perhaps he might respond that if we make the experience machine world rich enough, subjectively indistinguishable from our real world, and, in addition, much more pleasant for ourself and others, *then* most of us *would* opt for such a world. Certainly if being hooked up to the machine would guarantee maximization of the total good, including in the total the good of those not hooked up, we would have to go for it. We know that Mill maintains that the difficult but noble and virtuous life *is* preferable to the pleasant but limited life of a Philistine. But he thinks that this is due to the higher-quality pleasures "of the intellect, of the feelings and imagination, and of the moral sentiments."[4] These pleasures are what render the higher but quantitatively less pleasant life more valuable, not the *activities* linked with them.

For Mill, nothing determines the higher quality status of certain pleasures beyond *hedonistic grounds*. Those who have experienced different kinds of pleasure, and are thus *competent* to judge, simply prefer intellectual and social pleasures to bodily pleasures.[5] Their preferences are what endows intellectual and social pleasures with their higher-quality status.

But it is legitimate to ask Mill if this is the whole story. Do we really prefer the so-called higher activities merely on hedonistic grounds?

One phenomenological datum is clear: we do *not* derive more intense enjoyment from so-called higher-quality pleasures, in the sense in which we find sexual orgasm more intensely enjoyable than eating ice cream. Our supposedly higher-quality preference is not sensation based, as any superficial phenomenological comparison of sex and poetry attests. Mill, of course, was well aware of this.[6]

Might the preference for so-called higher pleasures derive from their being more intensely enjoyable in *non-sensation* terms? What could this mean? Is there a way in which visual, auditory, social, and intellectual pleasures are intense but non-sensation based? We undoubtedly enjoy works of art, sunsets, films, symphonies, and chess games. The activities involved in these enjoyments can even be exhilarating. Yet the supposedly higher enjoyments at issue here do not consist primarily of bodily sensations. Do they consist of pleasant mental stimulations, pleasant feelings, sentiments, or emotions? Even if such a hedonistic, yet non-sensation based, analysis of such experiences were possible, the hedonist would still have to explain our preference for mental stimulations and feelings over bodily sensations. Is this to remain a brute, unanalyzable fact? Or is the hedonist forced to appeal to a sense of pleasure intensity common to both kinds of enjoyment, but present to a higher degree in mental stimulations? Both options are less than satisfactory. Before embarking on a track promising little explanatory light, we should look for possible non-hedonistic explanations of our preference for so-called higher pleasures over so-called lower pleasures. Perhaps, as Aristotle and Kant maintained, our preference is based on non-hedonistic factors, such as a genuine sense of dignity and nobility which attaches to certain activities and traits. Mill's talk of higher quality pleasures, I believe, masks that intuition.

3.

Aristotle, as is well known, viewed the pleasures attending rational activities to merely complete the activities.[7] The main intrinsic value for Aristotle lies in the *activities* themselves. Kant, no doubt, agreed, since he argued that the good will is the true glory of human beings. Happiness, in Kant's view, is a separate good. It is a good which produces the *Summum Bonum* for an individual when divinely conjoined with virtue.

Panayot Butchvarov argues along Aristotelian and Kantian lines that so-called higher goods such as intellectual understanding, aesthetic appreciation, friendship, and fortitude owe their higher status not to the quality of pleasure they may promote, but to values independent of pleasure.[8] Butchvarov goes so far as to propose that we restrict the application of the term "pleasure" to enjoyable bodily *sensations*. Such enjoyments have no object. In contrast, so called higher pleasures are distinguished by their intentionality. According to Butchvarov, the latter pleasures should be analyzed in terms of the *consciousness of some independent* good. Just as musical enjoyments must be understood in terms other than physical sensations, so too, for Butchvarov, a virtue like fortitude must be understood as the disposition to follow reason's preference for things of excellence, like fine poems and brilliant chess games, over things like bodily pleasures. Genuine friendship, too, he views as built on perceiving a friend as worthy *qua* volitional and intellectual being. In short, Butchvarov finds higher satisfactions and traits to involve the awareness "of the goodness of certain objects, conditions, or activities."[9] Actual or only apparent, the goodness is independent of pleasure. It may at times be attended by some bodily pleasure. But a bodily pleasure would be incidental to the goodness of the objects in question.

Butchvarov's Aristotelian position, in its criticism of hedonism, is quite compelling. Clearly the higher status of chess playing and poem reading, when compared to eating ice cream, derives from their involving the pursuit and appreciation of *quality* or *excellence*. The successful search for brilliant moves is what truly satisfies the chess player. Similar things can be said of all activities involving arts and crafts. Even sports, work, and pastimes often involve the pursuit of excellence. The best achievements of human civilizations can only be understood in terms of our hankering after the good and the beautiful.

A hedonist could try to respond that quality or excellence is simply the pleasure-inducing *power* possessed by some things, conditions, or activities. A similar position has been held, though only with respect to beauty, by W. D. Ross. He argued that beauty is simply "the *power* of producing a certain sort of experience in minds, the sort of experience which we are familiar with under such names as aesthetic enjoyment or aesthetic thrill."[10] Suppose that we were to apply Ross's analysis not just to beauty, but to all forms of excellence, and indeed to virtue, rationality, autonomy, and justice. Can a hedonistic analysis appealing to the power to produce enjoyment on the part of various objects, traits, conditions, and activities succeed?

I must answer no. For ice cream also has the power to produce enjoyment. This line of analysis would be unequipped to explain the original datum—namely, that poetry enjoyment is of *higher* status than ice cream enjoyment. It would also be unable to explain our preference for, and hence the higher status of, real-world experiences when compared to experience machine world-duplicate experiences. Both worlds have the power to produce experience and enjoyment. But, for instance, the autonomy experienced in the machine world is no match from the subjectively similar autonomy experienced in the real world.

Additionally, even if pleasant feelings and pleasant mental stimulations are always involved in our pursuit and attainment of quality or excellence, we would still want to know what in certain patterns or arrangements induces the pleasures. The power to produce certain effects must be due to non-relational properties of the object having power. Hence, Platonic arguments would force us back to some shared general property or cluster of properties ontologically independent of pleasure. Moreover, the property of excellence in rhythm, sound, logic, and morality, is precisely the main objective of poets, chess players, and others. Excellence, when captured by the poet, musician, or policy maker, will induce approval and satisfaction *in the informed appreciator. Often induced satisfaction may be* the way of picking out items of excellence. But there may well be other and *formal* methods of picking out items of excellence. The availability of formal methods would explain our being able to learn to recognize items of excellence including great poems, paintings, and our own autonomy, even items of excellence which produce an aggregate effect of disturbance and grief, instead of pleasure or satisfaction. We may appreciate an opponent's brilliant chess-move, or the justice of a social policy, even when we are devastated by it.

4.

However, even if hedonism is untenable, it does not follow that goods involved in the higher satisfaction, whether novels, symphonies, chess games, friendships, or autonomy, exist as goods independent of sentient consciousness. Would these goods retain their value status in a universe without sentience? There is a case to be made for answering no.

Admittedly, symphonies and poems in a universe without sentience would remain products with certain distinctive formal symmetries. Right actions might remain actions in accord with the dictates of reason. Noble acquaintances might remain beings excelling in rationality and will. A just system might remain an arrangement promoting the continuing proper functioning of all the non-sentient inhabitants. Would these products, traits, and arrangements have any intrinsic value in the absence of sentience? I am not sure, for there is a sustainable, though not decisive, line of thought according to which *genuinely* cognitive, moral, artistic activity is inseparable from the sentient.

Consider the case of cognition, which on the surface appears to be the most abstract and non-sentient phenomenon. Genuine cognition, as opposed to mere input and output correlational and parroting skills, seems to require consciousness of meanings, or understanding. The example of advanced chess playing machines illustrates this. Their operation may be complex and functionally similar to the operation of human chess players, yet they can hardly be viewed as engaged in genuine cognitive processes. The machines would not understand that they are playing chess.

Can the consciousness of meanings necessary for genuine cognition be analyzed merely in terms of some set of rule-governed computational behavior dealing with uninterpreted symbol sequences? Thought experiments of the type made famous by John Searle appear to prove otherwise.[11] Though the issue is far from settled, a robot's passing the Turing test does not seem enough to show that the robot engages in cognitive activities. If what the robot does is to receive uninterpreted data, which it then processes with other uninterpreted data in order to produce the right correlative output, then it is hard to fault AI skeptics like Searle for rejecting attributions of cognition to such robots.

But is this not what our brain does, at some level of operation, when we engage in cognitive activities? Perhaps, but surely it is not all *we* do. We transform our data processing into cognition by employing some non-behavioral, non-formal, sentient element. This would not require that the sentient element *be* the cognition or understanding, only that it be a prerequisite for understanding. Wittgenstein has shown that one can have a feeling of understanding without the understanding.[12] Understanding has an undoubtedly objective and publicly testable aspect. On the other hand, it also has a subjective and what-it-is-like aspect, as reflection on various imagined intelligent machines shows. If so, then cognition in its *genuine* form must only be possible for sentient beings.

Is there independent ground for believing that cognition requires a sentient what-it-is-like element? Ultimately there is not. We could try to appeal to the intuition shared by the Cartesian tradition that all mental phenomena, including cognitive states, have consciousness in common. Though opponents have argued that there are plenty of non-conscious mental states, their arguments probably only persuade the converts.

Take belief, often proposed as an example of a mental state that can commonly remain unconscious. Is a belief of mine, of which I am not presently aware, one of my current *mental* states? Or does it become a mental state only upon its becoming conscious? We could consistently opt for the latter option. For if a non-conscious belief were mental, then it ought to be possible to have a complete mental system in which every state is non-conscious. But this latter possibility is absurd to those of us attracted by Cartesian intuitions. Precisely on the basis of the assumption that our smart computers lack consciousness, many of us are unwilling to attribute mentality to computers.

Unfortunately this line of thinking is question begging. For ultimately it is supposed to show that in order for what would otherwise be a cognitive state to be *genuinely* cognitive it must be accompanied by sentience. But it tries to show this by assuming that for a super-smart robot to have *genuinely* cognitive states it must be conscious and thereby sentient.

This long excursion is not for naught, however. It shows that there is a respectable tradition for whom the value of cognitive phenomena cannot survive the complete loss of sentience. For this tradition, the purely formal aspects of cognitive phenomena have no intrinsic value. Cognition would not preserve its intrinsic value in a universe without sentience.

What goes for cognition and its cousins, rationality and autonomy, surely goes, *ceteris paribus*, for the more phenomenologically infused items in the moral and aesthetic arenas. Aesthetic awareness, for instance, is intimately bound with the sensuous in the areas of sight, sound, and taste. The aesthetic elements of poetry, mathematics, and chess, when not derived from hedonistic or imaginative factors, derive from allied cognitive factors that might require a sentient element. The moral realm is likewise bound up with intentionality at the motivational pole. It is also bound up with preventing harm at the consequential pole. There is thus no question of its independence from the sentient.

In short, it appears that all of the phenomena which appear endowed with forms of intrinsic value *separate* from sentience have intrinsic value *in part* because they are somehow linked with sentient elements. This explains why we do not regard chess-playing machines, whatever level of skill they may display, to be intrinsically valuable. For instance, I doubt that we would attribute intrinsic value to a self-improving autonomous chess computer *so long as* we held it to lack sentience.

In the absence of sentience, intrinsic value might well disappear from what is formally and functionally a moral, rational, and symmetry-producing universe. The universe might be devoid of *genuine* rational, moral, and aesthetic agents, products, and arrangements. As hinted at earlier, a delusory experience-machine world would lack true nobility and autonomy, since it would possess only the subjective pole of such traits. We now may have found, in a world without sentience, the other extreme. We may have found a world endowed *only* with the objective pole of traits like nobility and autonomy. Each extreme is incomplete.

Both poles may be necessary to produce genuinely cognitive, moral, or aesthetic traits of intrinsic value.

5.

Must those of us still hooked to a Cartesian view of the mind conclude, then, that philosophers like Butchvarov, Plato, and Aristotle are mistaken in postulating intrinsic goods other than sentient consciousness? My answer is yes. Insofar as philosophers construe traits like rationality, autonomy, virtue, justice, and so forth, to be independent and separable from sentience, they focus on the purely formal aspect of these traits. And if they then attribute intrinsic value to the formal aspect, they may make a mistake. For, as we have seen, there may be nothing intrinsically valuable in what is, for example, only formally rational and cognitive.

On the other hand, formal symmetries, rationality, autonomy, and so forth, *add* value to sentient and pleasant animal existence.[13] These formal capacities, traits, and products catapult sentient animal life to a new level. Again, most of us would not exchange a life open to the pursuit of excellence but with much pain, for one free of pain but also devoid of excellence. Most of us would also reject a pleasant and exciting experience-machine world. If formal capacities, traits, and products add value to sentience and subjectivity, must they not have value in their own right? Yet, how can traits possibly lacking intrinsic value have value in their own right?

I suggest that the powers of rationality and autonomy, as well as the excellence endowing features of superior symphonies, poems, and chess games, are intrinsically valuable *in potential*. Their value, however, needs to be activated by sentient consciousness. Sentience is not the source of their value. Yet without sentience and feeling, features like excellence and autonomy remain dead, formal aspects of phenomena.

Analogies from the general areas of semiotics and semantics may help here. Think, for example, of the film *Casablanca* being run through a projector, but with no screen to receive its images. The film's very status as a film, and thus its beauty, would be suspended in a limbo state. Sentience and feeling are to an advanced mind what a screen is to a film. A great film would be a mere organized stream of complex radiation, unless translated by the proper receiver into images. Without any such receiver the *formal* excellence of the film might still be there. The pattern of projected radiation might even be capturable mathematically. But its status and beauty as a film would remain suspended. The formal features of autonomy, of great poems, and symphonies would likewise persist in a universe without sentience. But their *value* in such a universe would remain suspended, dormant, waiting to be vivified. Sentient consciousness, I claim, is the screen that translates excellence and autonomy into value.

This position has the virtue of enlisting the correct insights of hedonists and Aristotelians. It grants hedonists the *sine qua non* status of sentience and pleasure with regard to all value. But it also preserves for Aristotelians the pleasure-independent basis of the value of excellence, autonomy, and rationality.

The drawback of this syncretic position is its reliance on the notion of existence in potential. To say that formal excellence and rationality are potentially, but not actually, of intrinsic value is contradictory. The intrinsic value of any phenomenon should not depend on conditions outside itself. A pleasant experience, *as such* for instance, has intrinsic value. In contrast, if a phenomenon has only potential value, then its value must depend on factors outside the phenomenon. The value cannot be intrinsic. Hence, if formal excellence, for example, depends for its value on sentience, then formal excellence cannot be intrinsically valuable.

However, the value of excellence or autonomy is not merely instrumental like the value of money. A stream of radiation impulses in a sense *contains* the film and its beauty, though it *is not* by itself the film and its beauty. Similarly, a sequence of undeciphered symbols of a dead language may contain a story without being by itself the story. The stream of radiation impulses, and the sequence of symbols, are not simply means for the production of something quite different—the film, the story, and their respective beauty and value. Or perhaps we should say that the stream and the sequence are means, but very special means. They carry their end implicit within them. This differs strikingly from the way money is a means to the end of, say, pleasure. Dollar bills do not carry pleasure within them. No matter how unpacked and reconstituted, there is no structural correspondence between dollar bills and the pleasure they may bring about. A structural correspondence does exist between stream or sequence, and film or story. An analogous correspondence exists between great poems or great chess games, or autonomy, or virtue, *and* value. Poems, chess games, autonomy, and virtue *contain* value without being, by themselves, of intrinsic value. Perhaps we can call the value they contain *quasi intrinsic*.[14]

6.

The notion of containing needs to be explicated. Consider the cases of a projected, but screenless, would-be film, and of a would-be story on a tablet of undeciphered Linear X. There is surely a sequential, *structural* correspondence between the stream of photons and the would-be succession of visual images constituting the film *Casablanca*; and a like correspondence exists between Linear X marks and the succession of concepts constituting the story. But a film or a story is more than a sequence of neutral items mirroring the *structure* of a photon stream of a sequence of marks. The syntactical *structure* of the appropriate Linear X marks, for example, could be transferred onto a sequence of meaningless logical symbols, say, p's, q's, and r's, without conveying the story. Similar things could be done with the light stream without resulting in the film.

The items structured in the right way must themselves be meaningful units for the sequence to be a story or a film. Going from photon stream on screen to *Casablanca* is more than a jump from form to form or structure to structure. The jump is from form to content. Content has to do with meaning and understanding. Even the sequence of color patterns on the screen is not itself *Casablanca*. Each color-pattern element has to be an image *of something*. A lower consciousness may see the color pattern on the screen, and yet not see it as an image of, say, Bogart. This point is much more evident in the case of a sequence of marks of imaginary Linear X. This latter sequence will be a story only when each unit of marks is seen as a unit of meaning. This can only happen through the interpretive action of a cognitively advanced consciousness.

Consciousness cannot simply endow any sequence of physical items with whatever meanings it pleases. To produce a symbolic rendition of a story, the physical items endowed with the story meaning must possess the same logical structure as that of the Linear X marks. The usual arrangement of desks in a school room, for example, cannot generally come to represent or contain a story. Likewise, most color-pattern sequences cannot come to be seen as *Casablanca*. In short, even if consciousness were necessary for meaning, it might still be the case that certain physical vehicles contribute necessary ingredients for meaning. This might apply not only to written marks and visual images, but also to sounds and thoughts. Perhaps *all* meaning requires a combination of consciousness plus some appropriate physical elements.

In at least some cases, properly structured physical items do contribute in a special structural way, to meaning gestalts. The physical items contain a story, a film, or a piece of music. I do not pretend to have given a complete explanation of the containing relation. Nonetheless it seems undeniable that stories, films, and songs are generally contained in rightly arranged physical items.

In a parallel fashion, formal excellence and rationality contain quasi-intrinsic value. A formally rational being, for example, has value in its own right, yet the value remains suspended, like the meaning of screenless projected film, until activated by sentience. The parallel may extend to the *structural* preconditions for quasi-intrinsic meaning and quasi-intrinsic value. Certainly works of excellence must have distinctive structures. In subtler ways autonomy, rationality, and virtue also exhibit definite structures and regularities. Take autonomy, which on the surface conveys unpredictability and non-lawfulness. In the final analysis it too must display a structure. For instance, autonomy logically requires a multi-level awareness that would permit second-level consideration of first-level desires and beliefs. Similar things could be said of rationality and of virtue.

7.

If the preceding discussion is sound, phenomena of quasi-intrinsic value and of quasi-intrinsic meaning may shed light on each other. Their respective value status and meaning status is not intrinsic. It is latent and open to activation by consciousness through its respective aspects of sentience and intentionality. Perhaps a further parallel can be found in the realm of intentional action. Some bodily movements, for instance, hand movements, may have the structural prerequisites for action status. Yet even if highly complex, the movements would not ascend to the level of intentional actions unless causally-intentionally linked in the right way to a conscious will. Without a link, the movements would remain mere events. Pursuing the parallel, we could call the complex movements quasi-intrinsic actions, given their rule-governed nature. On a larger scale, the movements of the universe may be sufficiently structured, at least according to defenders of the Design Argument, to constitute quasi-intrinsic actions pointing at a divine will.

Perhaps this is going too far. But it would be fitting if in the marriage between consciousness and physicality the three main powers of consciousness, sentience, intentionality, and will would each produce a unique good out of latent physical quasi-goods.

Notes

1. Tom Regan, *The Case for Animal Rights* (Berkeley: University of California Press, 1983), p.243.

2. J. Baird Callicott, "Animal Liberation: A Triangular Affair," *Environmental Ethics*, 2 (Winter, 1980). Reprinted in C. Van DeVeer and C. Pierce, *People, Penguins, and Plastic Trees* (Belmont, Cal.: Wadsworth, 1986), pp. 194-195.

3. See Thomas Nagel, *The View from Nowhere* (New York: Oxford University Press, 1986), p. 161.

4. J. S. Mill, *Utilitarianism* (Indianapolis: Bobbs-Merrill, 1957), p. 11.

5. *Ibid.*, pp. 14-15.

6. *Ibid.*, p. 15.

7. Aristotle, *Nicomachean Ethics*, Book 10, chs. 6-8.

8. Panayot Butchvarov, *Skepticism in Ethics* (Bloomington, Ind.: Indiana University Press, 1989).

9. *Ibid.*, p. 92.

10. W. D. Ross, *The Right and the Good* (Oxford: Clarendon, 1930), p.127.

11. John Searle, "Minds, Brains, and Programs," from *The Behavioral and Brain Sciences*, Vol. 3 (Cambridge, England: Cambridge University Press, 1980).

12. See Ludwig Wittgenstein, *Philosophical Investigations*, ed. G. E. M. Anscombe, (New York: Macmillan, 1958), sections 131-155 and 269-323.

13. William Frankena says much the same thing. See his *Ethics*, 2nd ed. (Englewood Cliffs, N.J.: Prentice-Hall, 1973), pp. 91-92.

14. C. I. Lewis calls such values inherent values, and he too distinguishes them from intrinsic values. See his, *An Analysis of Knowledge and Valuation* (La Salle, Ill.: Open Court, 1971), p. 391.

Six

THE POSTMODERN TURN: PLURALITY OF VOICE OR CACOPHONY?

James S. Kelly

Although our so-called postmodern culture, with its seeming rejection of the concept of truth, is often reflected in our educational institutions, I am sympathetic with Henry Giroux's claim that "[w]e need to combine the modern emphasis on the capacity of individuals to use critical reason in addressing public life with a critical postmodernist concern with how we might experience agency in a world constituted in differences unsupported by transcendent phenomena or metaphysical guarantees."[1]

Postmodernism, in the broadest sense, questions the logic of foundations. Postmodernists see all theories as historical and social constructions, and too often view the subject as constructed, but without responsibility for agency. But giving up on truth, including moral truth, is not the path to follow, despite the lack of transcendence and metaphysical certainty that the postmodern turn has reinforced. "[P]ostmodernists," claims Giroux, "are arguing for a plurality of voices and narratives—that is, for different narratives that present the unrepresentable, for stories that emerge from historically specific struggles."[2] But a difficulty emerges. Lacking firm footing, knowledge claims have given way to political maneuvering. With the new voices of those arguing that the texts and visions of dead white males no longer fully answer all the interests of all members of our diverse society, comes a politics of power brokerage where discussion centers on what degree various interest groups receive of their supposedly fair share as political consumers. As the critical evaluation of value issues dissolves into the wrangling of interest-group politics, plurality of voice turns into cacophony. I turn now to the metaphysical and epistemological roots of this difficulty, and suggest a grounding for normative claims.

The authors of *Habits of the Heart* tell us that:

> When science seemed to have dominated the explanatory schemes of the external world, morality and religion took refuge in human subjectivity, in feeling and sentiment. Morality and religion were related to aesthetics, the realm of feeling par excellence . . . . Nonetheless, theologians and moralists believed feeling had some cognitive content, some access to the external world . . . . But with the emergence of psychology as an academic field . . . the purely subjective grounding of expressive individualism became complete.[3]

There is more to this story, of course, but the bottom line is that the rise of scientific naturalism has pushed morality into a denigrated, purely subjective realm of emotion and feeling. Given the meta-physical and epistemological presuppositions of scientific naturalism, that result was inevitable. Scientific naturalists maintain that the methods of modern science are the only way to gain knowledge of the world, and that reality is delineated categorically in the way in which it is conceptualized in scientific thought. To bring out these presuppositions, and illustrate the ostensibly objective mode of knowing, consider the sentence: "The brick is red." In order to make sense of this sentence as a linguistic act, we must assume there are things in the world, in this case, bricks. We assume existence as a category in terms of which we delineate reality. In the history of philosophical thought there has been great debate on the exact nature of such things, whether they are physical objects, collections of sense data, or collections of ideas. But what is not subject to dispute is the category of existence; without such a presupposition our thoughts collapse. When we say of the brick that it is red, we are saying it exemplifies certain properties or features. Exemplified properties or features constitute the category of factuality. So there is, in the existence sense, a brick; and it is a fact that the brick is, in the exemplification sense, red. For the scientific naturalist, all explanation is to be carried out in terms of the categories of existence and factuality with all things and properties construed as physical. Since, on this view, the only data-gathering powers of the human mind are sensory observation and perhaps introspection, only these powers allow us to gain access to reality, which is construed in factual terms. Facts are acquired through our sensory observations.

Following the logic of these presuppositions, Bertrand Russell concludes: "while it is true that science cannot decide questions of value, that is because they cannot be intellectually decided at all, and lie outside the realm of truth and falsehood. Whatever knowledge is attainable, must be attained by scientific methods; and what science cannot discover, mankind cannot know."[4] On this supposedly objective view of knowing, there are no objective values. Our subjective choices cannot be evaluated as true or false, and thus the normative dimension of the world is an illusion. When we are confronted with an utterance such as: "Burning helpless cats for fun is wrong," the presuppositions of scientific naturalism do not allow such utterances to be true or false. For wrongness is not a property or feature of acts. We have no sensory access to wrongness; we do not hear it, see it, smell it, touch it, or taste it. To think otherwise invites us into the troubled den of G. E. Moore and the realm of mysterious, non-natural properties and what John Mackie calls "queer" facts.[5] Non-natural properties are not discoverable by empirical investigation, and it thus becomes a mystery how we can know about morality. Also, talk about moral facts typically involves strange properties or relations somehow acquired by a faculty of moral intuition. The scientific naturalist who claims that reductive strategies allow us to construe moral facts simply as natural facts, moreover, faces the daunting task of explaining the *justificatory* potency of such facts. Still, some philosophers think we nonetheless infer wrongness from our grasp of the facts. But that view brings us face to face with the Humean problem of deriving an "ought" from an "is." At that point intuitionists wave their hands in the direction of a solution to how we can know moral truths. Avoidance of these issues will be seen to be a plus for the view I endorse here.

Thomas Nagel states: "The connection between objectivity and truth is closer in ethics than it is in science. I do not believe that the truth about how we should live could extend radically beyond any capacity we might have to discover it . . . ."[6] What we need to make out, if Nagel's belief is accurate, is that people have epistemic powers enabling them to appropriate normative reality, thereby showing that people have the capacity for goodness, the capacity to know through a process of deliberation and critical assessment what is required in particular circumstances. But what epistemic powers enable us to access normative reality?

Interpreting Dorothy Smith, Sandra Harding maintains that feminism should distrust the particular form of objectivity and epistemology found in enlightenment science rather than disparage objectivity or epistemology's policing of thought *per se*. Harding writes: "Europeans and men are thought to conceptualize the self as autonomous, individualistic, self-interested, fundamentally isolated from other people and from nature, and threatened by these others unless the others are dominated by the self."[7] This fits with the view that what dominates in our culture is an objective mode of knowing where the paradigm of successful explanation includes manipulation and control. It includes the modern preoccupation with the kind of human needs that can be satisfied by manipulatory action and the kind of knowledge that will increase our power to satisfy them. It shifts the emphasis from humanistic to materialistic interests and values. Human needs beyond the realm of manipulatory power are thus ignored. Harding looks favorably upon the African world view in which the affective dimension of people is viewed as critical for gaining knowledge. She maintains that "women's subjugated position provides the possibility of more complete and less perverse understandings . . . [which] can transform the perspective of women into a 'standpoint'—a morally and scientifically preferable grounding for our interpretations and explanations of nature and social life."[8] But why this standpoint is an improvement is not clear. What is the new form of objectivity that is to be embraced, and is it epistemically superior?

Alison Jaggar argues that most cognitive accounts of the emotions follow the positivists in focusing on the distinction between the objective world of observations and facts and the personal world of feelings and sensations. She sees that cognitive accounts make it difficult to maintain a critical attitude toward feelings as appropriate or not to specific contexts. Jaggar argues:

> When intentionality is viewed as intellectual cognition and moved to the center of our picture of emotion the affective elements are pushed to the periphery and become shadowy conceptual danglers whose relevance to emotion is obscure or even negligible. An adequate cognitive account of emotion must overcome this problem.[9]

Jaggar recognizes the long-standing claim that values and emotions are inextricably intertwined and that without the capacity for emotional responses it would be a mystery how we would rank our values. She argues that in a hierarchical society there is emotional hegemony and emotional subversion, for the predominate norms and values are likely to serve the interests of the dominant groups. Consequently, the resulting emotional makeup of people will be inappropriate for feminism. Jaggar maintains that dominant values "limit our capacity for outrage" and "lend plausibility to the belief that greed and domination are inevitable human motivations; in sum, they blind us to the possibility of alternative ways of living."[10]

Jaggar goes on to identify conventionally unacceptable or inappropriate outlaw emotions as emotions of typically subordinated individuals. Outlaw emotions, she claims, are epistemologically subversive to dominant conceptions of the *status quo* and can have political importance by challenging conventional descriptions of the world. She tells us: "Only when we reflect on our initially puzzling irritability, revulsion, anger or fear may we bring to consciousness our 'gut-level' awareness that we are in a situation of coercion, cruelty, injustice or danger."[11] Jaggar's claim is that we must take the emotions seriously for they play an important role in the knowledge that is part of the epistemic privilege of the oppressed. Yet to avoid the difficulties surrounding the politics of power in a diverse culture, such outlaw emotions will be *epistemologically* subversive, in any interesting sense, only if they allow some access to reality that results in an alternative way of perceiving the world for the better. Jaggar's focus on the epistemic potential of emotion is headed in the right direction, but she fails to allow that affective, value experiences can be knowledge-yielding in their own right. She fails to investigate the *semantic* content of emotions.[12]

Before engaging directly the issue of the semantic content of emotions, consider Sidney Callahan's similar claim that our strong and persistent feeling that something is wrong often influences our actions.[13] Although we are often unable to articulate why we act on the basis of our feelings, the discomfort resulting from them keeps us from too quickly making important decisions on the basis of mere abstractions. But we need the details about how this understanding comes about. Are emotions causally required to jar our cognitive abilities, or do the emotions themselves have semantic content? Psychologist Martin Hoffman argues that empathy guides moral judgments and may provide informational input necessary for impartial observers to come to agreement on moral judgments.[14]

But, even combining the insights of Callahan and Hoffman, we must note that feeling strongly that something is wrong, say, apartheid, and reaching consensus on the judgment that racial segregation *ought* not be engaged in, is theoretically insufficient. For mere consensus on moral judgments, or shared sympathies is not enough. It leads to a sophisticated relativism unless it is plausible to believe that consensus can be reached on moral truth. We face our original difficulty. Our culture embraces the objective mode of knowing where our value experiences and emotional reactions are not taken to be knowledge-yielding, but denied epistemic weight. Without epistemic weight it is difficult to understand how our gut-level awareness can be interpreted as awareness that things are not as they *ought* to be. Jaggar tells us that emotions have epistemic potential. Someone who feels upset, within a patriarchal system, at the telling of a sexist joke may be evincing an outlaw emotion. Her claim that an outlaw emotion is epistemically subversive and points to a reliable appraisal that a sexist way of viewing the world ought to be changed has *epistemic* weight only if the appraisal is grounded in reality.

When we feel indignant, our feeling has semantic content, and is subject to critical assessment. Construing the feeling as merely a causal product of our apprehension of the facts leaves unanswered the question of how it is subject to rational appraisal. Rational appraisal language, for the naturalist, is left without any appropriate subject matter. Rational appraisal language presupposes a causal structure different from that allowed by the minimalist naturalistic categories of factuality and existence. Talk of human attempts to know, for instance, presupposes an effort to get things right, an intention or inherent structure of meaning, on the part of the person making the attempt. This is not so for the description and explanation of natural events. Nor can it be so, since the categorical presuppositions of the scientific naturalist are minimal and do not allow for inherent meaning. For the naturalist, behavior is explained solely in terms of the non-semantic causal nexus, as is any other natural event. But in the case of the rational appraisal of people, reasons are causes and often serve to justify as well as to explain.

The naturalist cannot plausibly deny this. Naturalistic theorists must appraise their own scientific activity in rational appraisal terms. Thus, naturalists must assume that their own activity is subject to rational appraisal, that it can be shaped and moved by reasons and that it is subject to mistakes. Naturalists, then, can hardly deny that rational appraisal is applicable to the persons about whom they theorize. Certainly it is appropriate to say one has justifying reasons for being angry, that such anger is, under certain conditions, rational. But given the limited categories of the naturalist, such rational appraisal seems inappropriate. Emotions, I argue, are not simply effects of the comprehension of facts, but are perceptions of supervening normative requirements and give rise to the ideas of value and normativity.

Consider the somatic sensation of pain, often theoretically portrayed as a raw feel involving no semantic content. When my tooth is in pain, the content of my experience is not simply the shooting, sharp, felt pain. I take it that something is not as it ought to be and this motivates me to go to the dentist. Suppose I am correct, and that there is damage to my body. Moreover, suppose that my reasons for thinking that something is wrong with my body provide adequate explanation for my claim that something is wrong. An adequate explanation for my claim is my sincerely saying under normal conditions: "I have a toothache." My taking it that something is wrong, moreover, is evidence for the correctness of my claim. The occurrence of my feeling that there is something wrong with my body invests my claim that something is wrong with some probability. My body's not being as it ought to be also provides justification for why I take it that something is not as it ought to be. The occurrence of the feeling depends on the actual presence of what is taken to be the case. I take it that something is wrong with my body because something is wrong. My *feeling* that something is wrong with my body is a knowledge-yielding epistemic encounter.[15] Of course I may be wrong, especially if I venture the factual claim that the damage is decay in my right bicuspid. It may be referred pain due to damage elsewhere. My somatic sensation, my *feeling*, has semantic content and is a *value experience* providing me with access to reality. I come to know that something is not as it ought to be. The feeling has meaning for me.

Now suppose the local school ruffian, to use a familiar example to extend the point and the level of semantic analysis, has found a healthy, unowned cat. The ruffian ties the cat to a stake, pours gasoline over it and ignites it. Nora, having witnessed this act, is asked how she felt about it. She responds that she felt terrible and that the cat should not have been tortured. What are we to say about what Nora takes to be the case? Is her claim that what was done to the cat is wrong, true or false? On my view, Nora's value claim is grounded in her emotive experiences resulting from her encounter with the facts. If her apprehension of the facts changes, so may the supervenient normative content of her experience. What ought to be done cannot be separated from the factual, contextual circumstances.

For instance, if Nora discovered that the cat harbored a virus that threatened the life of a community and could only be destroyed by burning, this new factual information could alter the normative content of her feeling. She might still feel a bit ill at ease and wish things had been other than they are, but she would feel good that a horrible disease has been avoided. Thus, although it at first appeared to Nora that the cat-burning ought not be condoned, the new circumstances would allow her to say, upon coming to know the facts, that her initial feeling was a *mistake*. She mistakenly took it that what was semantically present to her through her value experience was normatively required by the situation. Nora's feeling, then, is subject to critical assessment, as appropriate or not relative to the given circumstances. Thus, value experiences are subject to logical appraisal much as are sensory experiences. Value experiences are epistemic encounters. They are perceptions of the supervening normative requirements that certain facts normatively require other facts. Value experiences and sensory experiences are subject to error. Both are epistemic in nature.

Consider again the utterance, "burning helpless cats for fun is wrong." By recognizing that emotions have semantic content and allow for epistemic encounters, we can see that the utterance has a truth-value and that people have the categorical capability of accessing the normative dimension of reality. Wrongness is not a property or a queer fact. It is not inferred from facts, although it supervenes on facts. Taking the basic value concept to be ought rather than good, we can reduce "X is good" to "X is more or less the way it ought to be."

Following E. M. Adams, we can take "the basic value sentence to be of the 'ought'- form which under philosophical clarification becomes something like 'If X is F, then X (or Y) ought to be G' .... The 'ought' ... belongs to the conditional as a whole, not to the consequent. The connective 'If ... then ... ought ... ' expresses the value requiredness that is said to obtain in the objective situation."[16] Consider the statement: "If the cat is being burnt for fun, then the burning of the cat *ought* to stop." The fact that the cat is being burnt for fun normatively requires that the act be stopped. As I have argued, our perception-like value experiences enable us to access this value requiredness, to come to know that one fact requires another. It is not inferred from factual premises. Our epistemic renovation expands our vision of the ontological categories as well as our conception of humanity and human capacities. As our factual claims are linked to reality through our sensory experiences, our normative claims are linked to reality through our value experiences.

We must be careful not to mix metaphysical and epistemological issues, although they are, of course, linked. The metaphysical claim that morality is a category on a par with existence and factuality rides on the epistemic claim that people have the categorical capability of accessing moral truths through value experiences, much as people have the epistemic power to access facts through sensory experiences. Since the case for an ontological category can only be made plausible if there are reasons for believing that people have the categorical capability of epistemically experiencing the ontological category, the metaphysical claim must be the best account available of all the linguistic and phenomenological data. Thus the claim that there are moral truths is not an empirical claim justified by appeal to facts, but an *a priori* claim required to make sense of the phenomenological and linguistic data. Particular moral truths are, however, justified by critical assessment of our apprehension of factual and value structures in particular contexts.

Most of us have had spontaneous, affective emotional responses to a host of circumstances. A recent replay on television showed vividly, and in slow motion, the pain and agony of a football player as his leg was twisted and broken. When reflecting on how I felt about what I had seen, I focused on my spontaneous feeling, not in terms of its own properties, but in terms of its *semantic content* that I felt. I felt shocked and ill at ease, but I also felt that what had happened *ought* not to have happened. The semantic content of my value experience, what I felt, can be expressed in language much as the semantic content of a sense perception can be expressed. Expressing is distinct from describing in that what is semantically in the experience is put in language, to be grasped or understood. Likewise, when Huckleberry Finn struggles with his conscience over what to do about the escaped slave, Jim, he feels that he *ought* to help Jim, and does. I can report what Huck felt and the content of what I report is what Huck would say in expressing himself. As the semantic content of our perceptual experiences can be put into language, so too can we linguistically express the semantic content of our value experiences.

When I report that the football player's leg is broken, the semantic content of what I say resides in the semantic content of my *sensory* experience. Likewise, when I say that things are not as they ought to be, or that Huck felt that he ought to help Jim, the semantic content of my utterances resides in the semantic content of my *value* experiences. The cases are analogous, both kinds of experience have semantic content. Our utterances are linked to reality, in the one case through sensory experience, in the other through affective, value experience. We need to refrain from denigrating value experience as non-knowledge yielding, while allowing epistemic access through sensory experience. As Jaggar has noted, the affective aspect of experience becomes but a dangler which the steely-eyed naturalists, with their sometimes bizarre machinations, reduce to brain happenings or try to eliminate.

I have argued that emotions play an epistemic role in ethical decision-making very nearly on a par with the role of sensory observation in obtaining facts. Thus our value experiences provide us access to normative reality and our affective responses to the world of facts can, under critical assessment, amount to epistemic encounters. Our value experiences are expressible in language and embody a semantic dimension, as do sensory experiences. Value experiences and sensory experiences are meaningfully spoken of as subject to appraisal as correct or mistaken relative to the context. Thus, both sensory and value experiences have a semantic and logical character, both are epistemic in nature.

Few seriously deny that sensory experience has become highly reliable within scientific inquiry, but prior to a well developed theoretical structure and critical method for assessing the conflicts of the senses, rationalists thought of our sensory experiences as too fluctuating to serve as a basis for knowledge. Lacking a track record, a theoretical framework and a critical method for assessing value experiences, it is not surprising that there are doubts about their epistemic weight. Still, the considerable moral agreement that exists suggests that we do have epistemic powers backing the many moral platitudes and habits of judgment that we share. Explicit recognition of such powers and the development of a theoretical framework to give direction and intelligibility to our value experiences holds out considerable promise for further resolution of disagreement and for filling the void that is the focus of much postmodern thought.

Notes

1. Stanley Aronowitz and Henry Giroux, *Postmodern Education: Politics, Culture, and Social Criticism* (Minneapolis: The University of Minnesota Press, 1991), p. 117.

2. *Ibid.*, p. 69.

3. Robert Bellah, Richard Madsen, William Sullivan, Ann Swidler, and Steven Tipton, *Habits of the Heart* (New York: Perennial Library, Harper & Row, 1986), p. 46.

4. Bertrand Russell, *Religion and Science* (Oxford: Oxford University Press, 1935), p. 243.

5. See John Mackie, *Ethics: Inventing Right and Wrong* (New York: Penguin, 1977), pp. 38-42.

6. Thomas Nagel, *The View from Nowhere* (New York: Oxford University Press, 1986), p. 139.

7. Sandra Harding, *The Science Question in Feminism* (Ithaca, N.Y.: Cornell University Press, 1986), p. 171.

8. *Ibid.*, p. 26.

9. Alison Jaggar, "Love and Knowledge: Emotion in Feminist Epistemology," *Inquiry*, 3:2 (June 1989), p. 156.

10. *Ibid.*, pp. 165-166.

11. *Ibid.*, p. 167.

12. See James S. Kelly, "Semantic Presence," in Edmond Wright, ed., *New Representationalisms* (Brookfield, Vermont: Ashgate Publishing, 1993).

13. Sidney Callahan, "The Role of Emotion in Ethical Decisionmaking," *Hastings Center Report* (June/July 1988).

14. Martin Hoffman, "The Contribution of Empathy to Justice and Moral Judgment," in Nancy Eisenberg and Janet Strayer, eds., *Empathy and Its Development* (Cambridge, England: Cambridge University Press, 1987).

15. The above is an instantiation of Adams's analysis of an epistemic encounter; see E. M. Adams, *The Metaphysics of Self and World* (Philadelphia: Temple University Press, 1991), pp. 131-32.

16. E. M. Adams, *Philosophy and the Modern Mind* (Chapel Hill, N.C.: The University of North Carolina Press, 1975) reprinted (Lanham, Md.: University Press of America, 1985), p. 131.

Seven

THE BUSINESS OF THE ETHICAL PHILOSOPHER

Tom Regan

In the opening pages of *Principia Ethica*, the young G. E. Moore—for Moore was not yet thirty when he wrote this historically influential work—remarks that "it is not the business of the ethical philosopher to give personal advice or exhortation."[1] Moore clearly is not saying that ethical philosophers overstep the bounds of their discipline if they endorse some general rule or principle, or declare that certain traits of character are virtuous. In *Principia*, Moore himself does both. Rather, he is arguing against the propriety of ethical philosophers, in their capacity as ethical philosophers, of issuing advice or exhortation regarding facts that are, in his words, "unique, individual, absolutely particular."[2] "There are," Moore writes, "far too many persons, things and events in the world, past, present, or to come, for a discussion of their individual merits to be embraced by any science. Ethics, therefore," he goes on to say, "does not deal at all with facts of this nature, facts that are unique, individual, absolutely particular; facts with which such studies as history, geography, astronomy, are compelled, at least in part, to deal. And, for this reason," he concludes, in the words already quoted, "it is not the business of the ethical philosopher to give personal advice or exhortation."

I think Moore is partly right, and—maybe—partly wrong. He is right certainly when he implies that no ethical philosophy—no science of ethics—can possibly address *all* the facts of the sort he describes, of which, as he notes, there are "many million."[3] But he is mistaken, I believe, to the extent that he implies that ethical philosophers necessarily have wandered off the straight and narrow path of their profession if they choose to consider *some* such facts—the particular case of Baby Jane Doe, for example, the executions of Sacco and Vanzetti, or the construction of the Tellico Dam. To my mind, at least, it is entirely appropriate for moral philosophers to consider the "individual merits" of such matters and, depending on their findings, to register their judgment, for or against.

Possibly Moore would agree. I say possibly because, in evaluating the merits of the Baby Jane Doe case, for example, we are not evaluating just *one* "unique, individual, absolutely particular" fact. In the nature of the case, we are obliged to consider a *constellation* of many such facts, the child's present condition and the evidence for alternative predictions about her future, for example, not simply one fact standing alone, in isolation from everything else. Thus, if Moore means that ethical philosophers should not assess the merits of such constellations of facts, I believe he is mistaken, whereas if he believes that it is only atomic facts, as it were, that are beyond our reach, then perhaps he is correct.[4]

But there are, of course, many other things that ethical philosophers will be called upon to do, if, or as, they are tempted to swim in the turbulent waters of the everyday world. One needs the *relevant* facts, after all; and the more, the better, whether the question is the construction of a hydro-electric dam or the electrocution of convicted murderers. And one needs to think about these facts, and other relevant matters, with logical care. One needs, too, a good dose of conceptual clarity, a nose for logical nuance, a mind cleansed, so far as this is possible, of insupportable bias or prejudice. And one needs, besides, some well-considered moral principles about what is right and just, good and evil. A tall order, this, by any reckoning, an ideal which, perhaps, we are wont never fully to realize, try as we might.[5]

For many moral philosophers alive today what I am saying is more in the nature of orthodoxy than heresy. Applied ethics, or practical ethics, is part of the contemporary moral philosopher's bag of tools, and all that I am saying, I think, is that it is appropriate that we have and use these tools in a responsible manner in the conduct of our professional life. That this represents an important change in the conception of ethical philosophy compared to the dominant conception of, say, sixty or fifty or even thirty years ago, is evident to anyone familiar with twentieth century Anglo-American ethics. The meta-ethical questions that set the agenda for ethical philosophers back then, I think, have not been so much answered as they have been tabled, at least temporarily, and I have no doubt, the cyclical swing of thought being what it is, that we are in store for another heavy, healthy dose of meta-ethical philosophy in the coming years. But for now at least, to find a place for practical or applied ethics within the profession is mainstream: "to the max," one might say.

Still, there is a difference, or so I am willing to concede, between applied ethics and advocacy and values. In one sense, it is true that anyone who argues for any conclusion, moral or otherwise, can be said to advocate that conclusion. Suppose we call this the *logical* sense of "advocacy." In this sense, Kant advocated the categorical imperative, Moore, some form of utilitarianism, and

Russell—well, Russell advocated almost everything, at one time or another, from Bradleian idealism to the theory of descriptions. But in another sense, advocacy involves something more. Consider standard dictionary definitions of the nouns, "advocate" and "advocacy," and the verb, "to advocate." Thus the noun "advocate" is defined as "a person who defends, vindicates or espouses a cause by argument"; the noun "advocacy," as "an act of pleading for or giving verbal support to a cause"; and the verb "to advocate," as "to plead in favor of; support or urge by argument; recommend publicly."[6] What unifies these definitions is the idea of doing something in favor of—defending, vindicating, supporting, pleading—a cause. Suppose we refer to this sense of "advocacy" as the *normative* sense. In arguing for their respective philosophical views about the Absolute and the present King of France, neither Bradley nor Russell, I take it, fit the label of "advocacy" in *this* sense. For neither saw himself, in making the respective claims each did, to be arguing for, let alone "pleading for or giving verbal support to . . . a *cause*."

This concept of advocacy—the one that is bound up with advocating in favor of a cause, the one I have called the *normative* sense, differs from the logical sense. Philosophically considered, a work of advocacy, in the normative sense, is one that, while attempting to adhere to standards appropriate to the profession, articulates certain goals, the "cause" which the work itself advocates. These goals may find their original articulation in such a work, or they may pre-date the work. Works of advocacy by environmental philosophers, feminist philosophers, socialist or capitalist philosophers, animal liberation or animal rights philosophers, for example, may be of either kind; they may, that is, either constitute the original articulation of the relevant goals, or they may add their voice to pre-existing goals. These goals, in turn, may be, to create a new word, status-quoist, reformist, or abolitionist. The cause advocated may be (1) to retain the current state of affairs, including certain policies or practices, in particular; (2) to reform the current state of affairs by keeping certain policies or practices in general, while reforming them various ways; or (3) to abolish—to bring to an end—certain policies or practices. The history of philosophy is crowded with works of advocacy in the normative sense, works that fit one or another of these descriptions.

In addition to the logical and normative senses of "advocacy," which to my mind are beyond philosophical suspicion or controversy, there is a third sense which needs to be distinguished. Suppose we call this the *political* sense. In this sense, advocacy involves more than affirming a position, as in the logical sense, and more than writing an essay or book that advocates a cause, as in the normative sense. The political sense involves *active public participation in efforts to forward the cause,* efforts that go beyond advocacy in the logical or normative sense, such modes of advocacy as attempting to exert pressure on those who hold political office; helping to organize boycotts; speaking at conferences, rallies or demonstrations, with the intention of informing or empowering other activists; or participating in marches, or in sit-ins and other forms of civil disobedience, for example, all in the name of furthering the cause. The question now to be asked, is whether *this* kind of advocacy of a cause—what I have called *political advocacy*—is "the business of the ethical philosopher."

My own answer to this question is, no. In saying this, I do not mean that philosophers should not actively engage in such political means of advocacy as demonstrations and civil disobedience. On the contrary, I not only believe that such political advocacy is entirely appropriate, I have myself been a political advocate, both in the anti-war and the animal rights movements in each of the ways I have indicated.

What I mean in answering the question as I do is this: when philosophers engage in such activities as these, they do so in their capacity as *concerned citizen, not in their capacity as ethical philosopher*. The *grounds* for their political advocacy of the cause they advocate, their reasons for believing the cause is just or right, are likely to be distinctively *philosophical*—the very grounds they may have articulated in the essays or books that advocate the cause, in the normative sense. My point is only that once philosophers enter the political arena, the arena of political pressure and public protest, they do so, not as philosophers who happen to be citizens, but as citizens who happen to be philosophers. So, in my view, it is not the business of the ethical philosopher, *qua* ethical philosopher, to be an advocate in the political sense. Philosophers who engage in such extra-philosophical activities, I believe, do so, not in the name of philosophy, but in the name of political or social change. Which is fine, I hasten to add. It is just not philosophy. I return to this matter below.

But while political activism is not the business of the moral philosopher *qua* moral philosopher, being a moral philosopher should not paralyze the philosopher's political will. More than being logically consistent, it makes moral sense to take our moral convictions out of the study and into the street, if one thinks that one's sense of personal integrity demands it. Moral philosophers are not immune to bouts of bad faith, moments when we explain away our failure to assume the role of political activists in the cause we defend philosophically because, we say, assembling at the barricades is not the business of the moral philosopher. Our ivory towers should not a prison make, and while I do not wish to argue here that an unwillingness to enter the political struggle necessarily casts doubt on the sincerity of someone's moral convictions, a fuller, more complete life arguably demands political activism, not simply normative theory.

Whatever we might think on this matter—and I assume we may not all be of one mind—moral philosophers, in their capacity as moral philosophers, clearly can do more than write learned articles or books. For it *is* philosophy, and thus part of the business of the moral philosopher, when, as increasingly happens, philosophical advocates of a cause offer a *summary* of their philosophical advocacy—their *normative* position. Suppose the philosophical advocate is invited to some campus or to some other public venue, to give a forty-five minute talk for the non-philosophical public. Is it reasonable to assume that the finer details, the nuances of, say, a four-hundred page book can be condensed into forty-five minutes? Only the authors of *Cliffs' Notes* will be tempted to suppose so. Nevertheless, it is not unreasonable to expect and demand something by way of philosophy, a sketch, in the nature of the case, by way of philosophical advocacy in the normative sense, from the ethical philosopher. Granted, it is damnably difficult to say in a comparatively few words what it has taken one many more words to say to one's own best satisfaction. Still, even within these time constraints, and even in the face of an audience of the philosophically unwashed, ethical philosophers can do ethical philosophy. We can allude to some of the relevant facts, exhibit the logical form of some of the most important arguments, and diagnose some of the possible prejudices. It is, let us agree, not philosophy at its best and fullest. But this is no reason to say that it is not, or that it cannot be, philosophy at all.

Because more and more ethical philosophers are turning their attention to advocacy in the normative sense, an ever increasing number are finding themselves in the position I have just described. Philosophers working in health care ethics, business ethics, and professional ethics, for example, regularly participate in conferences where the majority of those in attendance are not professional philosophers. I believe this is a salutary development, both for the profession and for society at large. It is, however, a mixed blessing. The very increase in participation by philosophers in society's grappling with the major moral issues of the day can create a family of unwelcome problems, some personal, some of more general interest to the profession. As ethical philosophers, I believe we are well advised to be aware of what some of these problems are. At least my experience in response to my advocacy suggests as much.

That experience has been largely, but not exclusively, gained from my involvement in the animal rights movement. A number of my philosophical writings advocate animal rights in both the logical and the normative sense. The same is true of many of my public lectures, including those presented on various campuses. Moreover, as I have already indicated, I have also been an advocate of animal rights in the political sense, having participated in sit-ins, protests, rallies and the like. Philosophically, the position I advocate is abolitionist in nature. I argue that the nonhuman animals who are raised for food, killed for reasons of fashion, and "sacrificed" in the name of science, for example, are treated unjustly; further, that the injustice of these practices cannot be eliminated by reforming them in various ways, for example, by increasing the size of cages; and that, therefore, the right thing to do is to abolish these practices altogether.

Whether true or not, my position certainly can be perceived as a threat to the interests of others—for example, those whose career and livelihood are tied to business-as-usual in commercial animal agriculture, the fur industry, and the bio-medical industrial complex. As I have discovered, some of those who are threatened, including high-ranking academics, voice their disfavor with my ideas about animal rights in the vocabulary of slander.

In what follows I relate some of my experiences.[7] In doing so, I hope I will not be misunderstood. I have not chosen to highlight some more or less recent occurrences in my life for reasons of self-aggrandizement. My interests, rather, are to determine what, if anything, might be learned from the treatment I have received as an advocate of a cause; to consider how this might possibly benefit others who are contemplating or who already are engaged in such activity; and, generalizing on my experience, to speculate about some of the threats and challenges we face, not individually and alone, but collectively, as a profession. As my experience illustrates, philosophical advocates of some causes may need to be prepared to encounter vicious, personal, and demeaning professional attacks. I have been called a dangerous zealot, a firebrand, a rabble rousing demagogue. I have been likened to Hermann Goering, to monomaniacal mental patients who think they are Jesus Christ or Napoleon, and, on one occasion, I was described as the Jim Jones of the animal rights movement. Concerning my campus lectures, I have been accused in them of advocating violence, which is false; of spreading lies, which is false; of being anti-science, anti-rational, and anti-intellectual, which is false; of asserting that I have the right to impose by violent means my notion of ethics on others, which is false; of inflaming my audience to commit unlawful acts, which also is false. On another occasion someone suggested that I am the point man, so to speak, for laboratory break-ins, which is false; and on still another someone implied that I was under investigation for the crime of murder, an absolutely groundless allegation. Finally, my *The Case for Animal Rights* has been dismissed as entirely lacking in scholarly merit, of being a lengthy tendentious non-sequitur in which I substitute zealotry for reasoned argument—a work in which my appeals are entirely emotional.

Now philosophers cannot relish the opportunity to be the target of *ad hominem* attacks, or to be on the receiving end of remarks that slander their character or degrade their professional standing. All this is bad enough. What is worse—and here I believe my experience does not differ qualitatively from that of many other philosophers who advocate other causes—is the realization that the attacks aimed at me are part of a larger, national strategy, involving powerful political figures and professional organizations. By way of example, consider first the following statement contained in the American Medical Association's 1988, "Animal Research Action Plan." "The animal activist movement must be shown to be not only anti-science but also . . . responsible for violent and illegal acts that endanger life and property."[8]

Next consider these remarks by Frederick K. Goodwin, M.D., former Administrator, Alcohol, Drug Abuse, and Mental Health Association: "The animal rights movement is, in large part, a young persons' movement, and it is made up of young people who tend to substitute sentiment for reason. In effect, they are saying, 'Because I feel strongly about not using animals in research, it's true for me.'"⁹ Goodwin goes on to dismiss, in a tone of righteous indignation, what he calls the "facile, pathetically misinformed, and/or dishonest arguments" animal rights advocates urge against animal research.[10]

Lastly, for present purposes, we have the declamations of former United States Representative Vin Weber (R-MN), founder of the Animal Welfare Caucus, contained in an invitation to a fundraising event featuring Health and Human Services Secretary, Dr. Louis Sullivan: "It is my pleasure to invite you to meet a national leader in the fight to counteract the mindless emotionalism and violent tactics of the animal rights movement."[11] Later on in his invitation Congressman Weber declares that "the tactics employed by the animal rights movement are nothing short of terrorism. . . . Calling animal rights activists' destructive methods arguments is giving them too much credit."

The list goes on. Certainly there is no difficulty in multiplying examples of this rhetoric of derision as practiced by people in high places, and, as my earlier remarks confirm, in lower places, too. What some research scientists have said about me in particular, in other words, had already been said by their national leaders about the animal rights movement in general. And this, as I have said, is important to understand. For the more an ethical philosopher's advocacy threatens powerful political and economic forces with a vested interest in the status quo, the greater the risk that the philosopher will be called upon to endure the slanderous attacks of those who are threatened. Individual ethical philosophers who choose to run this risk normally stand alone, without much by way of organized interest in or support from the larger philosophical community. Perhaps this is as it should be. After all, those philosophers who align themselves with a cause *voluntarily* choose to do so, and, so, arguably must be prepared to reap the sometimes bitter fruits of their advocacy. Nevertheless, the attack on advocates, if my experience is any guide, can cross the boundaries of the personal and encroach upon the profession, so that the attacks upon the individual and attacks upon the profession can become all but inseparable. The following two examples illustrate this point.

The first involves a scientist who registered his displeasure with my having been invited to his campus. He noted, fairly, that I lacked "an adequate scientific background." But then he argued that, *for this reason*, my presentation would *not* be "an open and objective, but [instead would be] a sophisticated rationalization of an emotionally [sic] and biased point of view." This is a familiar theme, at least as familiar as C. P. Snow's *Two Cultures*.[12] Viewed from the perspective of the scientific component of Snow's two cultures, *either* one reasons from "an adequate scientific background," in which case one is able to conduct an "open and objective" discussion, *or* one speaks without the benefit of "an adequate scientific background," in which case one can at best muster something by way of "a sophisticated rationalization of an emotional and biased point of view." Given this perspective, to the extent that moral philosophers lack "an adequate scientific background," or are perceived to lack one, they will be seen as lacking the ability to offer an "open and objective" presentation, and will instead be seen as quasi or pseudo professionals who are able only to evince their emotions behind the smoke and mirrors of intellectual sophistry. In this way, individual ethical philosophers, who advocate a cause in the normative sense, can trigger slumbering dogmas about ethical philosophy in general. In a very real sense, then, part of the attempt to discredit the individual practitioner of ethical philosophy can consist in attempts to discredit the practice.

A second variation on this main theme was made clear to me by the comments of an influential psychology professor, who happened to be among the most vicious in his personal attacks upon me. Along with these attacks, the professor commented on what he saw as the *arrogance* of ethical philosophers who, in his view, assume that, because they "study ethics," they are "the guardians of other people's ethics."[13] "In this country," this particular professor continues, "personal ethics is a matter for the individual conscience, and neither priest nor philosopher have an inherent right, or a widely acknowledged special expertise, that allows them to dictate to others, certainly not by violent means, the ethical judgments they should make."

These comments are perfectly general; they are not aimed at me in particular but at ethical philosophers in general. Even if we ignore the reference to "violent means," these comments, in my view, are confused. I myself do not know a single ethical philosopher who views herself or himself as the guardian of other people's ethics, or who believes that she or he is in a position to dictate what ethical judgments others should make. That ethical philosophers often advocate controversial ethical positions, in both the logical and normative senses of "advocate," is unquestionably true. And that, in doing so, they often argue in favor of, defend, attempt to vindicate or support a cause that is at odds with the ethical judgments of others, also is true. But neither of these truths entails anything about the philosophical advocate's assuming guardianship of other people's ethics or dictating to others what ethical judgments they should make. How widespread these misunderstandings are, I am unable to confirm in any detailed fashion. My own experience, both on my campus and beyond, however, suggests that they are very widespread indeed. The advocacy of individual ethical philosophers can occasion vigorous if misinformed indictments of ethical philosophy in general. Once again, therefore, part of the attempt to discredit the individual practitioners of normative advocacy can consist in attempts to discredit the practice.

Perhaps we might learn something useful from the family portrait of ethical philosophers that emerges from the preceding. To begin with, there appears to be something of a time-lag between the pace at which philosophy changes, on the one hand, and the pace of change observable in the non-philosophical community of scholars, on the other. For even while it is true, as I observed earlier, that the meta-ethical questions that dominated Anglo-American moral philosophy for a large part of the twentieth century have not been so much answered as they have been shelved, it seems very unlikely that when we return to them with greater collective concentration, we will do so only in order to exhume the ghost of logical positivism, which seems to be the epistemological ideology that underlies the unflattering family portrait of ethical philosophers summarized in the above—the disreputable image of what it is to be an ethical philosopher.

Second, and relatedly, the sheer staying-power of the assumption that science is objective while arguments about value are emotional attests to the not-too-blissful ignorance, on the part of some academic scientists, of much of the recent work in the philosophy of science. Recognition of this fact might serve the salutary function of reminding us of the importance of familiarizing the next generation of scientists with this literature, lest this harmful assumption continue to hold sway. So that, third, there is in my view a real need for philosophers, both ethical philosophers and philosophers of science, to make greater contributions to the real education of scientists, in our classrooms and beyond. But, finally, doing this likely will not be an easy task. If, unlike science, which is valorized because it is *objective and rational,* ethics is denigrated because it is *subjective and emotional*; and if, unlike scientists, who *discover* the truth, ethical philosophers are perceived to be people who want to *dictate* other people's values, then the sometimes cool, the sometimes hostile reception scientists shower upon the suggestion that their students need a course in ethics is hardly remarkable. Clearly, the challenge ethical philosophers must face, in discussions about curricular change in the sciences, is likely to be formidable.

However these matters are to be resolved—and I claim no special wisdom regarding the solutions—my central points are these: that philosophical advocates of a cause, while they speak for themselves, often are perceived as representatives of ethical philosophy in general; that when, as sometimes happens, efforts are made to discredit the individual philosopher, the efforts sometimes will include attempts to discredit the profession; and that in choosing to assume the role of philosophical advocate of a cause, individual ethical philosophers should realize that, like it or not, they may be called upon not only to defend their views and endure slanderous attacks upon their person, but also to explain and defend the discipline of ethical philosophy itself. None of this, in my view, constitutes a sufficient reason for not electing to advocate a cause, in the normative sense, if the force of argument leads one to such a conclusion; but it does, I think, go some way toward suggesting the variety and magnitude of the challenges one might face, if one decides to do so.

I turn now to my final point. It concerns academic freedom. Those who have most vehemently attacked me, both personally and as a scholar, frequently have insisted that they were not denying my right to free speech. As one of my principal detractors wrote: "Anyone, from Farakkhan to Regan, has a right to speak on a university campus no matter how abhorrent his views are to any segment of the community." This *sounds* eminently fair, and it would be fair if philosophical advocates, including those with "abhorrent views," could be assured that the traditions of academic freedom will prevail in their case. Not surprisingly, such a guarantee requires sustained vigilance.

On my own campus, for example, certain individuals who strongly disagree with my views on animal rights once objected to my participation in a campus program because "North Carolina State University should not be perceived as supporting Tom Regan's position on animal rights because it might offend research funding organizations and cause the loss of grants." In this case, fortunately, the sponsors refused to be intimidated and the program went on as scheduled. However, it was only by accident that I discovered the existence of this attempt to silence my voice. And this, as I say, was *on my own campus,* where I have taught for twenty-five years.

On *other* campuses, the main story line differs. Sometimes objections are voiced because I am said to be a violent terrorist who will incite my audience to riot. In fact uniformed police and other law enforcement officers have attended my campus lectures, "just in case . . . ." At other times it is because "the issue is not one of intellectual debate consecrated by our commitment to academic freedom, but rather one of *anti-intellectual actions* that have been specifically condemned by our Academic Senate."[14] Whether one who practices anti-intellectual actions should be permitted the academic freedom to perform them is less than clear.

Nevertheless, despite efforts to the contrary, to the best of my knowledge my freedom to speak, both on my own campus and elsewhere, has never been denied. In this, I have been fortunate indeed. Clearly, if those people who had invited me to speak had failed to insist upon my right to do so, I would have been denied the exercise of this fundamental right.

This, then, is a final dimension of philosophical advocacy that is worth considering. Precisely because such advocacy can threaten powerful, entrenched special interests, one can anticipate various efforts aimed at silencing the advocate. Moreover, because the advocate is an ethical philosopher, and in view of the fact that attempts to discredit the advocate sometimes include allegations that discredit ethical philosophy in general, those of us who are ethical philosophers, in my view, have, if anything, an even greater obligation to insure that the traditions of academic freedom prevail.

Perhaps all that we should do, as professionals, can be done effectively by using the resources of already existing committees within, say, the American Association of University Professors and the American Philosophical Association. If this is true, then by all means let us honor Occam's sage advice, and not multiply committees beyond necessity. But it is worth asking ourselves, both those of us who are advocates in the normative sense and those who are not, whether something more is needed, even if we conclude, after informed reflection, that nothing is. On this matter, even Moore, who had well-considered views about the business of the ethical philosopher, would agree.

Notes

1. George Edward Moore, *Principia Ethica* (Cambridge, England: Cambridge University Press, 1903), p. 3.

2. *Ibid.*

3. *Ibid.*

4. There is, perhaps, a certain tension in Moore's views, given his famous method of isolation as an approach for judging which things are good in themselves. For those things which are judged best by him, are certain facts, certain states of consciousness, which perhaps can lay some claim to being "unique, individual, absolutely particular."

5. For somewhat lengthier comments on this ideal, see, for example, my "Introduction" to *Matters of Life and Death*, 3rd ed. (New York: McGraw-Hill, 1993).

6. *The Random House College Dictionary*, revised ed. (New York: Random House, 1981).

7. A number of academic research scientists, whose views about animal rights differ fundamentally from mine but who had observed first-hand the style and substance of my campus lectures, kindly wrote letters in my defense—letters in which they indicated their sense of outrage over how I was being treated by some of their peers. Unless otherwise indicated, the accusations I list and the material I quote are contained in letters and other communications written in response to my having been invited to offer a campus lecture. Because no good purpose would be achieved by identifying either the authors or their respective institutions by name, I have chosen not to do so. I should also add that some members of the biomedical and animal agriculture community have raised their voices in my defense.

8. "Use of Animals in Biomedical Research: The Challenge and Response," An American Medical Association White Paper (Chicago: American Medical Association, 1988).

9. Frederick K. Goodwin, "In Animal Rights Debate, the Only Valid Moderates Are Researchers," *The Scientist*, 67 (September 1993), p. 6.

10. *Ibid.*

11. The material quoted is from Weber's invitation, on Congress of the United States

House of Representatives stationery, dated September 1990.

12. C. P. Snow, *The Two Cultures and the Scientific Revolution* (Cambridge, England: Cambridge University Press, 1959).

13. See note 7.

14. See note 7.

Eight

THE RISKS OF ADVOCACY

William Aiken

Should moral philosophers be advocates? Should we venture forth from our ivory towers to advocate a cause in the public forum? It depends upon the type of advocacy in question. In his essay, "The Business of the Ethical Philosopher," Tom Regan classifies advocacy into three types: logical, normative, and political.[1] Logical advocacy is simply supporting a conclusion with arguments. Normative advocacy involves arguing for a cause which advances certain goals dealing with social policies and practices. Political advocacy involves active public participation in efforts to forward a cause.

I see no reason why a moral philosopher must remain only a logical advocate in the public arena, a sort of neutral expert witness who is adept at constructing arguments and at drawing out implications of various arguments and at spotting weaknesses in the arguments of others. Certainly these functions are important and public debates are frequently in need of such logical precision and clarity. But there are three reasons why moral philosophers should go beyond this and become normative advocates who advance definite goals dealing with social policies and practices.

First, when I advocate in the normative sense, I am not merely promoting my conception of the good, I am also affirming my belief in the importance of rational argument. To value rational argument is to believe that it can lead a person to abandon faulty positions and to adopt better ones. So in a sense, I must be willing to normatively advocate what I believe to be the best position in the public marketplace of ideas if I am going to practice the very philosophy which I preach. If I refuse to put forth my views for criticism then I am rightly judged hypocritical.

Second, it must be frankly acknowledged that there really is no purely neutral stance from which to approach controversial normative matters. We are always somewhat of a partisan not only of a particular theory of the good and the right, but also of a distinctive method of inquiry and argumentation. It is important that I recognize this and that I make the case that the approach which I adopt is a fruitful and helpful one for the issue at hand. Merely constructing arguments or plotting out the logical consequences of arguments sounds more theory-neutral than it really is. It is not enough for me to merely perform a risk assessment, I must advocate that quantified risk assessment is indeed relevant to rational decision making in this instance. Exclusive adherence to logical advocacy may lead to a mistaken assessment of its degree of impartiality.

Third, because we do not live isolated from the emotionally charged overtones which accompany many controversial social normative issues, and because we often do have our own beliefs and strong feelings about these matters, there is a great danger of self-deception here. Though I may insist that I am merely doing logical advocacy and so mask, even to myself, my unwarranted partiality and unexamined biases under the guise of logical neutrality, my analysis will nonetheless be influenced by these unexamined assumptions.

It is not clear that there even could be a pure logical advocacy which is not laced with some normative judgments and preferences. So I see no advantage in attempting to adhere exclusively to this type of public advocacy. And, given the problems involved, I do not see how moral philosophers in good faith can avoid embracing normative advocacy. Retreat to the pretense of merely constructing arguments and drawing logical inferences is insufficient.

So when involved in public normative debates, moral philosophers should go beyond mere logical advocacy and be willing to advocate in the normative sense. Advocating in this sense requires, however, that I attempt to adopt professional standards of reasoning. So I must construct and defend reasoned arguments in support of the cause I advocate. And my belief in the desirability of the cause itself must be revisable. If the desirability of the cause is not itself subject to criticism and scrutiny, then my advocacy degenerates into a case of "faith seeking understanding" wherein my adherence to the cause precedes my development of arguments to support it. This would hardly be desirable; it would render me more a dogmatist or an ideologue than a philosopher who advocates a cause. Though the potential social effects of such advocacy may be great, normative advocacy is primarily concerned with theory even when it is in the guise of justification for adopting a practice or radically altering social institutions. It is ultimately a form of rational argumentation and not a form of political activism.

As long as moral philosophers engage in normative advocacy, within our circle of professional colleagues we expect our antagonists to abide by the same set of professional standards and rules for argumentation. But as we venture further and further into the public arena, normative advocacy appears more and more impotent as a means of achieving our ends. This can happen even within the confines of the university. It is shocking to find that academics sometimes use what we all know to be fallacious arguments and mere rhetoric in our politically significant in-house disputes. This willingness to abandon high standards of reasoning and normative argumentation in favor of politically significant and normative argumentation in favor of political expediency within the halls of academia is particularly disturbing. But such expediency should be expected beyond those halls. As moral philosophers turn to the real public forum where social causes are further or hindered, we are faced with a dilemma. Do we continue to play by strict rules imposed by normative advocacy in the furtherance of our cause, or do we join everyone else who is fighting in the public arena and adopt political advocacy? So the significant question surrounding advocacy is whether philosophers should practice *political* advocacy, and abandon the constraints imposed upon them by the standards for argumentation required by the profession. Should we be satisfied with being a Hegel-type or should we rather strive to be an Angela Davis-type, or somewhere in between?

Of course it is not hard to argue that such political advocacy is permissible for citizens living within a democracy. A variety of arguments can be cited. It could be argued that political advocacy is a responsibility of citizenship in a pluralistic democratic state whose effective functioning presumes conflicting adversarial voices pleading divergent causes. Or it could be argued that the political community functions under a set of rules governing discourse and decision-making which presuppose political advocacy. Or, we could just appeal to the pragmatic argument that political advocacy is the most effective way to further our cause. However it is justified, let us grant that political advocacy is certainly permissible. However, even if it is, I think it is important to ask whether moral philosophers *should* turn to partisan advocacy to further their cause.

Of course, only philosophers would ask such a question in the first place. Every marketing, public relations, or political science major knows that in the public forum, where success is measured by the ability to control and manipulate public opinion, rational argument is not necessarily the preferred tool of persuasion. Public opinion and ultimately public policy are in the hands of the political handlers for whom image is everything, and the agents of political action committees for whom the power of money constitutes the most effective argument. And then there are the advertising moguls who adeptly play the emotions of the public like a harp, harmonizing fear, hatred, and patriotism with envy, pity, and insecurity. If the point, as Marx said, is to change the world then philosophers have been missing the point for quite a while. Should they eschew their ivory tower, and book an interview on Geraldo, Sally Jessie, or Oprah to plead their case with every unprofessional rhetorical trick they can muster? This should do far more for their cause than the mere writing of professional articles or the public presentation of carefully structured arguments. Walking the walk may entail a substantial deviation from the standard political naivete of the academy. It might even be argued that too much preoccupation with professional standards suggests a lack of commitment to the cause. Perhaps I only want to talk the talk, or perhaps

I am more concerned for my precious professionalism and my reputation as a model arguer than I am for the cause I say I care about. It is not difficult to stereotype the mere normative advocate as an effete intellectual snob who is politically impotent.

It would take a very persuasive argument to defend the claim that moral philosophers should never engage in political advocacy. Since any of a variety of counter examples could defeat this claim, it would take some type of principled argument to defend it. I do not think there are any such arguments. Maybe such an argument could be constructed by appeal to consistency in willing, wherein a special responsibility to consistently use reasoned argument is derived from the moral philosopher's commitment to reasoned argument as the appropriate tool to investigate moral problems. So any act of political advocacy by a moral philosopher would entail a violation of that special responsibility and so would be unjustified. But, of course, we can always question the worth and consequent necessity of such consistency. Even if there may be no principled arguments against moral philosophers engaging in political advocacy, I believe there are some persuasive practical considerations which would suggest that such activity is unwise and should generally be avoided by moral philosophers. First, there is no reason to suppose that moral philosophers are particularly good at political advocacy, since nothing in their practice or training prepares them for this activity. It is probably the case that their training in argumentation puts them at a disadvantage. Suppose however, that somehow I acquire the knack of such advocacy and become skilled at it. I am not likely to survive as a normative advocate in the public forum, because if I am really good at political advocacy, I am likely to become seduced by the awesome power which less than rigorous arguments and rhetorical tricks can have over audiences. Advertisers and public relations folks are not dumb and there is a seductive magic in their craft as the overwhelming impact of negative campaigning in the 1994 election demonstrated. I can become easily corrupted by the power of partisan reasoning especially when preaching to the uncritical among the believers, or bashing my opponents or rousing deep and powerful emotions. Though this may serve to motivate others to enact my social agenda it can also, I fear, creep into and undermine my ability to do professional level normative advocacy, or at least my inclination to continue to engage in it. It is difficult to return to the rather dry world of academic argument after being exposed to the exciting world of public advocacy. So the ability and willingness of moral philosophers to do normative advocacy can be undermined by the practice of political advocacy.

Their effectiveness in doing normative advocacy can also be jeopardized. My credibility as a normative advocate is undermined when I leave the private world of professional argument and enter the public world of partisan debate where only winning matters. My opponents will automatically categorize me as a partisan or a lobbyist regardless my intention or the brilliance of my argument. These matters are beyond my control. So my effectiveness to advocate with *rational* argument may be hampered by my involvement in political activism or partisan advocacy. This is particularly unfortunate, since what moral philosophers are trained to do, and thus should be best at doing, is providing rational argument and critique. So as philosophers we may well be hurting our cause by jeopardizing our believability among opponents when we engage in partisan scholarship, less-than-fully-professional argument forms, and political activities for the sake of political advocacy.

So for the sake of the causes we hold most dear and which we advocate in our professional writing, we should stick to what we do best, rational argument and criticism within the standards of our profession. We should restrict our advocacy to normative advocacy. This is not a trivial pursuit. It can have a powerful impact upon the world as is illustrated by the influence of an Augustine, a Machiavelli, a Hobbes, a Rousseau, or even Marx himself who was a better thinker than doer. So even though it may be permissible for moral philosophers to engage in political advocacy, we would most effectively utilize our resources and preserve our intensity and our potency by avoiding political or partisan advocacy especially of the causes which we defend and normatively advocate in our professional writing and speaking. Ironically, this seems to imply that the less we know about the arguments which support a particular cause, the more prudent it would be to use political advocacy, and the more we know about the arguments, the less prudent it would be to use it. I doubt if this result would be embraced by those who argue that moral philosophers are equally warranted in engaging in both types of advocacy.

Note

1. Tom Regan, "The Business of the Ethical Philosopher," ch. 7 in this volume.

Nine

PHILOSOPHERS AND ADVOCATES

Robert K. Fullinwider

There are two questions embedded in Tom Regan's "The Business of the Ethical Philosopher."[1] One is: what is the relation between philosophy and advocacy? The other is: when and how is advocacy appropriate for us?

I start with the proposition that philosophy and advocacy are antagonistic. How could the matter be otherwise? Advocacy is about action in the here-and-now. It takes place in the Cave of shadows and illusions. It aims to shift our allegiance from one shadow to another, to prompt our embrace of a better illusion. Philosophy is about what lies outside the Cave—about that permanent reality only dimly reflected in the flickering shadows of our daily lives.

Inside the Cave we attach ourselves to the transient, the ephemeral, the confused, the corruptible. Today's certitude is tomorrow's heresy, tomorrow's panacea today's failure. Since we live life in the Cave there is every reason to be serious about its circumstances, every reason to try to make it a better place even if the changes we effect are unavoidably flawed, confused, misdirected, and short-lived. Still, living in the Cave is one thing and understanding our condition as en-Caved is another. That understanding, if we can achieve it, reveals the enduring, permanent limits of what we can know, what we can be, what we can hope for. That understanding is the object of philosophy. Philosophy aims for a vision of completeness and wholeness. It seeks the sunlight—the ground, the inescapable, the transcendental, the quiddity, the Archimedean point.

Good advocacy, because it is shadow-play, deflects the philosophical vision, and good philosophy, because it looks at the sun, is blinded for effective advocacy. Thus, advocacy and philosophy are antagonistic.

Even if my simple picture here is true, it does not answer the question whether, and how, *we* might be advocates. For *we* are complex individuals, not pure philosophers. We are scholars, educators, intellectuals, public servants, citizens—and possibly philosophers—all at the same time. Answering the question of advocacy means teasing out the aims, obligations, and privileges that attach to our several roles.

First, what is an advocate? An advocate is "one who defends, maintains, publicly recommends, or raises his voice in behalf of a proposal or tenet" or "who pleads, intercedes, or speaks for . . . another."[2] We expect advocates to defend their causes and plead their cases vigorously and forcefully. In the adversarial contexts of the law court and the electoral contest, in particular, we expect advocates to give the very best coloration to their own sides and to cast opposing views in their worst light. We do not expect advocates to tell us the weaknesses in their own positions or point out the strengths in their opponents' beliefs.

An advocate may be motivated by more than the truthfulness of the proposals or tenets she advocates. She may or may not believe in the cause of the person she pleads for. In court, for example, the lawyer-advocate's role is to make the best case she can; it is the judge's or jury's role then to pass judgment. The judge and the juror, not the advocate, are expected to exercise the virtues of judiciousness by seeking balance and fairness, comprehensiveness, and logical coherence; they, not the advocate, are expected to come to judgment without pre-commitment to one side or the other.

Similarly, in political competitions, partisans, advocates, and contestants sometimes offer claims they may privately consider dubious and make promises they suspect they cannot keep. They may advocate a view not because they believe in it but because it is instrumental to their achieving success at something else, such as acquiring political office. Like judges and jurors, we voters ideally are expected to weigh and sift the claims and counter-claims of political contenders in order to reach balanced or measured choices in the voting booth.

Though advocates may promote views or causes impersonally or instrumentally, they may also advocate what they personally think good or important and do so precisely because of their judgment of goodness or importance. They may raise their voices because they think that valid tenets and desirable proposals are not getting an adequate hearing; they may speak out to counter false and harmful doctrines.

One-sidedness is built into the advocate's role. The advocate speaks for a policy, cause, or person, not for-and-against it. When the representative from the local police department visits a school to speak against drugs, she does not give the case for drug use alongside the case against. The advocate of safe sex dwells on the dangers, not the pleasures, of risky sex. The advocate of free speech does not emphasize the value of domestic tranquility, and the advocate of animal liberation does not limn the glories of porterhouse, medium rare.

So, is the kind of one-sidedness characteristic of advocacy appropriate to academicians in late twentieth-century United States? What are we academicians, anyway?

Academics are *scholars*. This means we are members of communities trained to make open and good-faith use of certain techniques of inquiry and argument. As scholars, we have a legitimate interest in the way the communities organize themselves and in the conditions for their support. Our advocacy on behalf of academic community standards, institutional improvements, or public support for scholarship arises from, and need not compromise, our role as scholars, although advocacy that is dishonest and in bad-faith is inconsistent with our role. Our advocating, say, structural changes in the American Philosophical Association to make it more inclusive of unorthodox philosophical styles is organic to our role as scholars, while our advocating that the Association endorse abortion rights is not.

Academics are *educators*. Almost all of us are attached to universities and colleges where our main job is instructing students. Our ultimate concern as educators is the full development of students' intellectual and moral capacities. Educational success is measured by the growth of a student's powers of thought and action, not by her adoption of a particular doctrine, tenet, or cause. Educators are not advocates; but they may use advocacy as a tool to strengthen the intellectual habits and critical powers of students. A teacher as teacher has no side but may become one-sided to counter-balance already existing student prejudices and tendencies. Advocacy is not inconsistent with education, but its place is subservient to the educator's ultimate concern. For example, a teacher may advocate a particular public policy on abortion with the purpose of stimulating students to engage the abortion question more effectively or fruitfully, but not with the purpose of getting the students to subscribe to that policy.

Academics are *intellectuals*. I mean that we possess in high degree not just the particular techniques of our scholarly field but general, all-purpose powers of analysis, investigation, and argument. These powers are socially valuable, and simply in virtue of possessing them, intellectuals may owe some duty to use them in response to public needs—just as a person with medical knowledge may be thereby bound to respond to another's medical need. But more: modern intellectuals do not happen spontaneously. We have the powers we do because of deliberate social investment in universities and other institutions of training and research. Thus, we may owe in return a duty to use our special powers for socially good purposes. In virtue of being intellectuals, we may have duties sometimes to speak about public affairs and even to become advocates.

Relatedly, academics are a kind of public servant, or at least many of us. Large numbers of us work in public universities dedicated to serving the public good and improving the common weal. Indeed, we might think of the entire system of public and private universities and colleges in this country as a single public institution meant to improve the economic, political, and cultural opportunities of all citizens. As public servants of a sort, we academics may have some responsibility to use our training for public purposes, even to become advocates for socially important causes.

We are at best public servants *of a sort*, and we may best discharge our responsibilities as public servants, and as intellectuals too, by doing what we do best: teaching our students and doing our scholarship. Still, our role as special kinds of people in special kinds of institutions may give us reasons to lend our voices to public debate. We can assist public debate by offering concepts, categories, and classifications that help sort out arguments, unearth assumptions, and clarify goals: conceptualizing, classifying, and clarifying are, after all, what we do best. But we may also adopt a cause or promote a policy, either as a way to enrich the public debate, or for the sake of the cause or policy itself.

Finally, as Regan notes, we academicians are also *citizens*. Our private commitments give us motives to use our training and talents on behalf of various public ends and political goals. Our role in the academy does not debar our acting as advocates in a private capacity, but our private advocacy can conflict with our academic responsibilities if it undermines our ability to teach or discredits our scholarly communities.

Thus, as philosopher-scholar-educators in universities in late twentieth century industrial or post-industrial society, we possess several reasons for and against being advocates of various sorts. Whether we do well or ill in choosing to be advocates will depend very much upon the particularities of our advocacy: particularities about the cause we advocate, the manner, and the circumstances.

We should not forget, however, the basic antagonism between philosophy and advocacy, and between scholarship and politics. The academy, ideally, is a place where discourse is characterized by open and good faith argument and all of its members hold themselves to high standards of reason, although Regan's essay reminds us how we frequently fall away from this ideal. Politics and public action generally are governed by a different norm: success. The political arena, even at its best, is a constrained struggle to control the instruments for imposing the will of some on the will of others. In the academy resolution need never occur, agreement need never be reached; discussion can go on forever. In politics talk must end at some point and action be taken. Decisions must be made, policies instituted.[3] The successful political campaign is not the one that makes the public smarter, or even kinder and gentler, but the one that wins public opinion to your side. It is no surprise, then, that political advocacy features hyperbole, distortion, disguise, dissimulation, personal attacks, inflammatory rhetoric, reckless charges, and outright lies. Persuasion, not truth, is the object, and the stakes are high.

The problem for academics as public advocates, however, is not just that they should not stoop to hyperbole and distortion. Even when it is thought of in its best forms, public persuasion is an art that scholarly training does not supply. We philosopher-scholars are not especially accomplished in what Aristotle called rhetoric, the methods of persuading a popular audience, an audience untrained in the speaker's particular science or discipline. To be effective before such an audience, according to Aristotle, the advocate must "be able to reason logically, to understand human characters and excellences, and to understand the emotions."[4] Taking a Ph.D. at Princeton, Chicago, or Stanford will train our powers of reasoning logically, certainly, but will not make us astute judges of character and emotion.

An advocate must possess these abilities and understandings because her own character and her audience's emotional dispositions are as implicated in her persuasion as are her reasonings. Indeed, a substantial part of the last leans on the other two. As Regan notes, it is difficult to condense a complex argument into a forty-five minute speech, but this difficulty is inherent in advocacy, not just a mere nuisance. Arguments in advocacy must be simple and must draw their strength as much from what is unsaid as from what is said. They must draw their strength from what the hearer adds or does not add to the advocate's few words, and what the hearer adds or does not add is partly a function of the advocate's own character as conveyed in her words.[5] In guiding her audience through what she *says*, she must establish confidence that she would be a safe guide through the *unsaid* as well.

As Regan observes, among the things a hearer may add to an advocate's words are confused views about philosophers and ethics due to confused perceptions about academics arrogantly putting themselves forward as guardians of people's values. Regan suggests that we need to educate the public out of such confusions. That is not a bad idea, but the point I am pressing is that, if we are to be advocates, we must educate *ourselves* at using the materials at hand for persuasive argument. Those materials include the common confusions an audience brings with it—confusions no less liable to engender agreement as disagreement with the advocate's views. The rhetorical challenge for the responsible advocate is to find in an audience the common ground for by-passing both the confusions that lead to rejection and the confusions that lead to embrace of her views. To the extent that we academic philosophers measure up to such a challenge, it is in virtue of our role as teachers, where we have to learn to communicate with untrained minds full of popular confusions.

My argument here thus takes issue with a theme implicit in William Aiken's comments in "The Risks of Advocacy."[6] Aiken notes that philosopher-scholars are committed to rational argument according to the standards of the profession. He further notes that in the public forum, rational argument is not always the preferred tool of persuasion, thus limiting an effective role for philosophers. The unstated assumption here is that providing a rational argument in the public forum is the same as providing a rational argument by the standards of philosophical scholarship. But I take it to be the force of Aristotle's discussion of rhetoric to call this assumption into question. I am arguing that it is a mistake to think we philosophers are already educated to make rational arguments in the public forum, in virtue of our professional standards, if only the public would listen to us.

Rather, we have to educate ourselves to the distinctive forms of rational argument appropriate to public debate.[7]

Political advocacy certainly holds out dangers to philosopher-scholar-educators. Regan warns the philosopher-advocate who enters the public forum to expect calumnies and slanders, threats and intimidation, cheap shots and hardball. But we should not need *that* warning; it is already prefigured in Plato's own career at the beginnings of our profession. Plato is the one, after all, who announced the basic antagonism between philosophy and advocacy, between seeking the sunlight and playing at shadows. Yet even he could not resist the lure of advocacy and the prospect of subjecting power to the discipline of truth. Off he went to Syracuse to make kings philosophers. His subsequent letters to Dion, Dionysus, and others tell the story. In them we have Plato defending himself against various intrigues and power plays;[8] lamenting the "malicious reports" and "slanders" against his name;[9] puffing his reputation as a smart guy;[10] advising on the importance of appearing "conspicuous" and "renowned" for one's truth, justice, and generosity;[11] recommending "veiling" the real meaning of his doctrines and promoting them instead as paths to prosperity;[12] and complaining about not getting paid.[13] Plato the philosopher, meet Plato the spin-doctor. But a Roger Ailes he was not.

Philosopher-scholar-educators should not shy away from responsible advocacy, but we need to have a keen sense of our capabilities and liabilities as advocates. In public affairs, midwifery may be more our strong suit. We might better ease the resolution of a pregnancy, helping what is potential not be stillborn or miscarry. But as for arranging the impregnation itself well, in that ambition we may overreach.

Notes

1. Tom Regan, "The Business of the Ethical Philosopher," ch. 7 in this volume.

2. *Oxford English Dictionary*.

3. Of course, in the university, decisions have to be made as well, insofar as faculty must be hired, curriculum instituted, and the like. So the university is not without its own politics, but the politics are on behalf of the purpose of the university, which is to be a forum for pursuing scholarly questions that never have to be resolved, never have to be decided if evidence and argument remain divided.

4. Aristotle, *The Complete Works*, ed. Jonathan Barnes (Princeton: Princeton University Press, 1984), p. 2156.

5. *Ibid.*, p. 2155.

6. William Aiken, "The Risks of Advocacy," ch. 8 in this volume.

7. For a similar argument, see Leonard J. Waks, "Philosophers and Social Responsibility in Technological Society," in Joseph C. Itt and Elena Lugo, eds., *The Technology of Discovery and the Discovery of Technology* (Blacksburg, Va.: The Society for Philosophy and Technology, 1991), pp. 391-405.

8. Plato, *The Collected Dialogues*, eds. Edith Hamilton and Huntington Cairns (Princeton: Princeton University Press, 1961), pp. 1572-73.

9. *Ibid.*, pp. 1570-71.

10. *Ibid.*, pp. 1564-65.

11. *Ibid.*, p. 1569.

12. *Ibid.*, p. 1581.

13. *Ibid.*, pp. 1561-62, & pp. 1595-96.

Ten

THE LOST CHILDHOOD OF *HOMO ECONOMICUS*

Roger Paden

Perhaps the two most striking features of *Homo economicus* or "He," that now-familiar rational utility maximizer who first appeared in the theories of the English political economists of the seventeenth and eighteenth centuries and who today has come to dominate much of the industrial world, is that He is male and middle-aged. Not only is *Homo economicus* now middle-aged, but He seems always to have been middle-aged, as if, like Adam from God, He sprang full-grown from the minds of Smith and Bentham. Currently, He plays a central role in many moral and political theories. I will investigate the role He plays in some of them, in particular utilitarianism, in light of His seemingly miraculous conception and eternal maturity, leaving it to others to explore the ramifications of His gender. I will attempt to establish three points. First, I will argue that the modern theories are necessarily committed to the thesis that He never had a childhood. Second, I will argue that this thesis is false, that He must have had a childhood. Third, I will argue that because modern moral and political theories are committed to this thesis, they are seriously flawed, both theoretically and practically.

It is no mere theoretical oversight that *Homo economicus* is portrayed as lacking a childhood. His lack follows from the essential nature of modern moral and political philosophy. In *After Virtue*, Alasdair MacIntyre draws a distinction between modern moral theories and the pre-modern moral theories of the predecessor culture that illustrates this point. According to MacIntyre, pre-modern moral theories consisted of three parts: "human-nature-as-it-happens-to-be (human nature in its untutored state), . . . human-nature-as-it-could-be-if-it-realized-its-*telos*," and the "precepts of ethics" which, if followed, would "enable [people] to understand how they [can] make the transition from the former to the latter."[1] On the other hand, according to MacIntyre, modern moral theories consist of only two parts: a characterization of some essential "feature or features of human nature; and the rules of morality, . . . [which are to be] explained and justified as being those rules which a being possessing just such a human nature could be expected to accept."[2] On MacIntyre's view, pre-modern moral theories are teleological in the sense that their authors were interested primarily in the development of human beings toward their *telos*.

Modern moral theories, on the other hand, even consequentialist theories such as utilitarianism, are not teleological in this sense. Instead, they could be said to be individualistic. Typically, what is meant by this claim is that in these theories such phrases as "the good of society" are to be understood as referring to nothing more than the sum of the goods of the individuals that make up society. Individualism, in this sense, can be contrasted with social holism. Modern moral theories adopt this kind of individualism both through their assumption that no intrinsic goods exist above or outside the individual and in their practice of analyzing all social goods into individual goods. However, modern moral theories are also individualistic in another, more literal, sense. They are based on the idea that there are no intrinsic values inside the individual. Just as the good of society does not stand independently over and against the good of individuals, neither does any independent good lie beneath the individual's conscious desires and choices. An individual has no moral interior because the individual's desires act as the moral given. Because desires serve as the logical foundations of the theories, they are, in-themselves, necessarily beyond moral criticism. If an individual desires it, then, as Bentham put it, "Prejudice apart, the game of push-pin is of equal value with the arts and sciences of music and poetry."[3] The only morally significant properties of a desire are its objective properties; its strength, duration, and direction. Its subjective properties, its moral quality or worthiness, are irrelevant. Desires must be judged by their objective properties, not by some independent moral standard, such as that which was provided in pre-modern theories by a conception of the human *telos*. On the modern view, the good of a person is regarded as a superficial phenomenon. It can be read off the surface by assessing all of a person's desires. Modern moral theories tend to be individualistic in this way, treating people as indivisible social atoms.

The acceptance of this form of individualism most clearly differentiates modern from pre-modern moral theories. Modern moral theories, because they lack any conception of the moral depth of persons that could be provided by a conception of a human *telos* must be based on superficial factors, on human-nature-as-it-happens-to-be. This commitment to a conception of the interior-less individual defines modern moral theory, and *Homo economicus* is just such an individual.

Charles Taylor has made a similar point in his criticism of utilitarianism. He compares a utilitarian "simple weigher" of desires with a "strong evaluator."[4] On

Taylor's view, in strong evaluation, unlike simple weighing, the value of a desire is thought to be a function, not just of its strength, but of its place in the overall structure of a person's character. As Taylor points out in a discussion of a person addicted to overeating, a strong evaluator may reject even a strong desire, such as the addict's desire for a chocolate sundae, not just because it conflicts with another desire, say a desire to be healthy or thin, but because it is despicable to be controlled by an addictive desire. A strong evaluator, therefore, has a kind of moral depth that a simple weigher such as *Homo economicus* lacks, a kind of depth that MacIntyre attempts to articulate through his concept of *telos*.

However, while Taylor's concept of strong evaluation allows people the same internal moral complexity as MacIntyre's concept of *telos* without being burdened by the excess metaphysical freight of Aristotle's teleological biology, it is silent on the issues of character development that played such a large role in pre-modern moral theories. The virtue of the appeal to *telos* made, on MacIntyre's view, by all pre-modern theories, is that it implies that human beings are necessarily involved in what MacIntyre calls a "quest," an essential process of moral self-development.

One consequence of this is that, on MacIntyre's view, pre-modern moral theories, unlike most modern theories, must necessarily be theories of moral development. This comes out in two ways. First, pre-modern theories are not only based on the assumption that desires can be morally evaluated, but they also suggest a moral ideal of a person whose desires are both moral and harmonious toward which people should develop. A moral person, on this view, will, over time, cultivate harmonious moral desires. How this is done and what it requires occupied Aristotle throughout most of the *Nicomachean Ethics*. It is not, however, a subject that seems to interest many modern moral theorists. On Taylor's view, the reason for this is that modern morality does not permit the strong evaluation of desires. As a result, there is no conceptual space for this type of moral development. Of course, *Homo economicus* may undertake to change His desires so that He or His society achieves a greater net satisfaction. But this would only make Him more efficient, not more morally developed.

Pre-modern theories also typically include discussions concerning the development of the virtues. This is especially true of the virtue of *phronesis* or moral judgment, the development of which, according to Aristotle, requires long practice, stretching back into childhood, in a supportive moral community. Modern moral theorists, on the other hand, rarely discuss moral virtues at all, let alone, their development. In part, this is because modern theorists have focused on the articulation of universal moral rules that can be fairly applied to diverse groups in modern cosmopolitan societies. But the focus on rules also can be explained by the fact that modern theories are committed to the idea that the most basic modern virtue, prudence—now understood to be the ability to maximize preference satisfaction over time—is not something that needs to be developed.

For modern theories, prudence is an essential human trait lying at the heart of *Homo economicus*'s identity: He is by nature a rational utility maximizer. While He may become more efficient as He learns more about the world or develops simple, easily used rules-of-thumb, such changes do not constitute a qualitative development. Prudence is His unchanging essence. There is simply no need for him to be concerned with its development.

Like the physical atoms of the early Greek philosophers, *Homo economicus* is essentially unchanging. This explains His eternal maturity. Because He does not need to develop morally, as He is, from the beginning, already fully mature and fully virtuous, He needs no childhood. His lack of childhood is also consistent with the fact that He does not need to develop His desires. His eternal maturity is, therefore, over-determined, a consequence of the complex transformation of pre-modern moral theory into a technical, calculative science in the modern world.

It is a mistake, however, to base a moral theory on a being who lacks a childhood. A moral theory addressed to such a creature is empty and misleading, because a being such as *Homo economicus* is inconceivable. This may be true for many reasons, but I shall focus on the claim that a being without a childhood could not be prudent: no creature can be a rational utility maximizer without first becoming a strong evaluator, and to be a strong evaluator, a creature must have a childhood. As my argument will be similar to an argument advanced by Derek Parfit, I will begin with a discussion of his argument.

In *Reasons and Persons*, Parfit argues against what he terms the "self-interest theory" of rationality.[5] According to this theory, each person should always do what is in his or her long-term self-interest. Parfit contrasts this theory with what he terms the "present-aim theory," according to which we ought to do what would best fulfill our present desires. The two theories differ only in that the self-interest theory is based on a "requirement of equal concern . . . [according to which a person] should be equally concerned for all parts of his future."[6] A person who is so concerned with all parts of his future, in contrast to a person who adopts the present-aim theory, would be, in our language, prudent.

Parfit argues that this type of prudence is irrational. His best argument for this claim turns on the question of personal identity.[7] The self-interest theory, he argues, presupposes a notion of self-identity according to which a person is identical with himself at all stages of his life and not identical with other persons. Based on what he takes to be the best philosophical articulation of this concept, Locke's view that personal identity is simply a matter psychological continuity, Parfit argues against both these presuppositions. If, as Parfit argues, relations of personal identity over time and personal differences across individuals at the same time are matters of degree, then a wedge can be driven between the two aspects of the basic ontological presupposition of the self-interest theory. If, in the words of one commentator, "it is rational to be more concerned for oneself than for others, and if what distinguishes oneself from others also distinguishes temporal stages within one's life, so that one is more closely related to nearer stages, then it cannot be irrational to be biased toward the nearer future."[8] It would be rational to adopt the present-aim theory, to be imprudent.

If successful, this part of Parfit's argument would show only that prudence is irrational. However, as Parfit points out, many philosophers have argued that, given Locke's criterion of psychological continuity, prudence should not just be irrational; it should be impossible.[9] Given that some people succeed in acting in a self-consciously prudent way, therefore, this argument seems less an argument for the impossibility of prudence than an argument against Locke's reductionistic criterion of personal identity. However, Parfit, who accepts Locke's reductionistic criterion, rejects the argument that Lockean individuals could not be prudent by arguing that, although it would not be rational for them to be prudent, they may be compelled to be prudent by some kind of hard-wired instinct. He argues that, although such an instinct would seem irrational to a Lockean individual, it would make evolutionary sense, as a prudent person would be more likely to successfully reproduce.[10] I find this argument to be unconvincing. First, instinctual prudence would seem an extravagant and inefficient way to promote reproductive success. Second, the self whose good prudence seeks to insure is not the self of evolutionary theory. Not only do we desire many things other than reproductive success, but we desire some things that conflict with reproductive success. Prudence is not the servant of a narrowly conceived libido, as required by this argument, but rather serves many masters. Finally, it would seem that prudence is an uncharacteristically weak instinct as it is so often overwhelmed by immediate desires. In any case, however, the Lockean criterion cannot be the basis on which people identify with their "future selves." Nevertheless, although actual people are not Lockean individuals, I will argue that *Homo economicus* must be. As such, He could not identify with His future selves, and, therefore, He could not act prudently.

Note, however, that I have changed the terms of the argument. I speak not of "*identity*," but of "*identifying*," and I claim not that it would be *irrational* for *Homo economicus* to be prudent, just that He could not *act* prudently. By doing this, I intend to set aside the question of the correct philosophical theory of personal identity in order to discuss the necessary psychological presuppositions of prudent actions.

Clearly, the concept of prudence presupposes some notion of stable personal identity through time. It is also clear that prudent actions can be self-consciously undertaken only by someone who psychologically identifies with his or her future selves. These two points need to be kept distinct, for the psychological identification cannot be accomplished merely through the adoption of the philosophical thesis that future selves are ontologically identical with a present self; nor can it be based solely on the Lockean belief that the future selves will be connected to a present self through a continuity of memory and consciousness. Instead, such an identification requires the adoption of a favorable evaluative attitude toward the future selves.

To illustrate this point, let me adopt Parfit's practice of using examples from science fiction. In "We Can Remember It for You Wholesale," Philip Dick describes a society that has developed a technology that can modify memories.[11] Not only can memories be electronically erased, but new memories, even the memories of complete lives, can be implanted. In *Total Recall*, the novelization of the movie version of this short story, the central character, Doug Quaid, discovers that the memories that he has of his life have been implanted in him by agents and for purposes unknown.[12] Setting out to recall fully his true identity, he uncovers evidence indicating that he was an agent employed by the current administrator of Mars to help suppress a rebellion staged by weakly telepathic mutant workers. While working on this task, Quaid, or "Hauser," as he was then known, became sickened by the sadistic tactics of the administrator and defected to the rebels' side. After this defection his old memories were erased, his present memories implanted, and he was setup in a new, safe life on Earth. In hopes of uncovering the details of his past, Quaid decides to journey to Mars to find the leader of the rebellion. Unfortunately, it turns out that the memories of his supposed defection were themselves implanted to fool the telepathic rebels as part of a larger plan devised by the administrator and his agent, Hauser, to discover the hiding place of the rebel leader. The plot succeeds as the unintended results of Quaid's search for his identity: the rebel leader is discovered and killed; Quaid is captured; and the rebellion apparently suppressed. Acting on Hauser's original desires, the administrator then places Quaid in a machine that will reimplant all of Hauser's memories and stronger desires in Quaid's brain. Quaid, however, resists this forcible recall, as, in effect, an unwanted conversion to an evil cause.

Quaid's resistance to his reintegration with Hauser is understandable; but not from the perspective of a Lockean or utilitarian theory of personal identity. For, after Hauser is recalled, Quaid will be connected to Hauser-Quaid though a continuity of memory and consciousness. Of course, Hauser-Quaid will be different from Quaid, but perhaps not as different, for example, as Paul was from Saul. But just as, on Locke's theory, Paul was the same person as Saul, Hauser-Quaid will be the "same person" as Quaid. Thus, on this view, Quaid will not cease to exist upon Hauser's recall because his memories and consciousness will be incorporated into Hauser-Quaid. From either a Lockean and utilitarian perspective, therefore, Quaid would have no reason to reject Hauser's recall: he would not die as a result of it, and he could look forward to a life which promises great satisfactions. After all, Hauser-Quaid would be the hero of the counter-revolution, the favorite of the very powerful and wealthy administrator, while Quaid would be nothing more than a failed and imprisoned revolutionary. It would seem that a prudent person in Quaid's position would *demand* Hauser's recall. To do otherwise would be to act with a childish petulance at having one's present desires frustrated; it would be to demonstrate an inability to consider the long-run; it would be the height of imprudence. But Quaid is not a Lockean. From his perspective, and from our's, Hauser-Quaid is simply not Quaid. He is not Quaid because he holds values that are completely at odds with Quaid's. Quaid rejects the recall of Hauser, because, believing Hauser to be evil, he does not identify with Hauser or with Hauser's future desire-satisfactions.

Quaid's attitude toward Hauser is strikingly similar to Taylor's description of the attitude of the food addict toward his addiction. Although both Hauser and the addiction might well be thought by Quaid and the addict respectively to be part of their present or future selves, they are judged to be foreign and despicable parts with which neither can identify. Clearly, this kind of identification with parts of the self requires a positive act. As these examples show, we do not identify with our future selves, or with parts of our present selves, merely because of some simple psychological continuity. We can identify with them only if we judge them morally worthy. Our identity is in part morally constructed. As Kuato, the mutant leader of the rebellion pointed out, *pace* Locke: "A man is defined by his actions, [by his moral character,] . . . not by his memories."[13] Taylor seconds this idea when he writes: "Our identity is defined by our fundamental [or strong] evaluations."[14]

If this is the case, then because *Homo economicus* is constitutionally incapable of strong evaluation, He cannot identify with His future selves. Although sharing memories and consciousness with those selves, He would lack a stable identity. He would be, in short, a purely Lockean individual. As a Lockean individual, however, He would not be able to act prudently, for such a person would have no reason to value future satisfactions on par with equally strong present satisfactions. *Homo economicus*, therefore, could not adopt the self-interest theory. Instead, given the narrowing of His horizons caused by His inability to identify with His future selves, He could only adopt Parfit's present-aim theory. He must be imprudent.

Prudence or self-interest, therefore, cannot serve as the foundation of any moral or political theory. Actions undertaken to promote long-term self-interest presuppose both the continued existence of a self and the ability to identify with that future self. This last, however, presupposes the ability to make strong evaluations. Prudence, therefore, cannot be a basic virtue. It requires the presence of other virtues, which as Aristotle argued requires a moral environment and a history of moral development. It requires a childhood.

Something is seriously wrong with many modern moral and political theories: they are committed to the theoretical existence of an impossible creature, a pure rational utility maximizer. However, if *Homo economicus* were to exist, He could not be such a creature. He also would have to be a strong evaluator and, therefore, He would have to have had a childhood in which He learned more fundamental values. But if prudence presupposes more fundamental values, then any moral theory that portrays morality as nothing more than a kind of universalized prudence and moral reasoning as nothing more than a kind of simple weighing must be wrong. A neutral, purely calculative, quasi-scientific approach to practical reasoning is impossible.

I have argued that *Homo economicus* must have undergone some kind moral development in His theoretically suppressed childhood. I would be the first to admit that I do not fully understand the process of childhood moral development, although, given my original argument, I must assume that the self and moral values must be equally primordial. However, let me disguise my ignorance with some jargon. Let us say that the self and its fundamental values are developed through a pedagogy of the self, which probably begins shortly after birth and continues at least through early childhood. Clearly, this pedagogy, like all pedagogues, can go well or badly, and obviously some parents and some societies are better teachers than others. Moreover, one might suspect that a society that is based on the denial of the possibility of moral development might be, in both senses of the word, constitutionally incapable of offering moral instruction.

As Plato pointed out in his discussion of the inevitable degeneration of corrupt cities, a society can be judged in part on how successfully it transmits its central values to its children.[15] The central theme of Plato's ideal histories of the various kinds of corrupt cities is that societies based on incomplete or inadequate ideals cannot maintain themselves over several generations. It might be possible to construct a similar ideal history of modern society, completely and self-consciously based on the ideals of modern moral and political theories, a society whose citizens accepted *Homo economicus* as an accurate characterization of human nature and the ideal of virtue. The history would illustrate the problems encountered by a society based solely on these values.[16] Such a history, I believe, would closely resemble the histories Plato sketched of oligarchic and democratic societies.

An ideal modern society fully grounded on modern moral theory would be designed to be the home for *Homo economicus*. It would not be designed to be a home for children. As a result, it would have great difficulty raising children according to its ideal. It probably would find it difficult to address child care and development issues.[17] Because it would be blind to the issue of moral development, thinking that prudence is an essential property of all people, it would not undertake to teach virtue. As a result, it would tend to raise only Lockean children who could identify only with the current contents of their minds. Such individuals, as we have seen, would lack stable identities and would tend to act imprudently. Adults might notice a growing tendency in their children to be more interested in today than in tomorrow, to be unwilling to make long-term investments and long-term commitments, and to act irrationally or imprudently on sudden fits of anger or waves of compassion. Like Plato's description of democratic people, they would be a peculiarly unstable and unpredictable generation, composed of shallow and unintegrated people, who would be, as Taylor points out, increasingly subject to identity crises.[18] In Plato's metaphor, their lives would resemble a fabric embroidered with every kind of ornament, brightly colored, and entertaining, but insubstantial and disorganized.[19] Lacking depth, their lives would be, to borrow Marcuse's term, "one-dimensional."[20]

The society would be unable to pass its ideal on to its children. Its failure will present itself as a decline in prudence. However, the imprudent behavior of necessarily prudent beings can only be explained by a failure to perceive outcomes accurately, and the obvious way to overcome such a perceptual failure is to make outcomes more obvious, for example, by imposing sanctions on imprudent behavior to make its imprudence more clear. However, because this strategy does not address the necessary moral foundations of prudence, its probable result would not be to make people into long-term utility maximizers, but instead, to make them into more clever short-term utility maximizers. Therefore, attempts to teach prudence would, in the end, only reinforce imprudence. Unfortunately, the failure would very likely give rise to calls to increase sanctions still further, creating a downward spiral into authoritarianism. It seems, therefore, that an ideal modern society could not sustain itself, but would, as Plato might have argued, tend to transform itself into a society of imprudent short-term utility maximizers living under an increasingly authoritarian government.[21]

The practical and theoretical problems that beset modern moral and political theory can be related to its attempt to suppress *Homo economicus*'s childhood. We might be wise, therefore, to abandon our ageless wonder, our modern individual. In rejecting modern individualism, however, we would have to return to a more realistic conception of people, one which places them in a society and gives them a childhood. Such a move would place at the forefront of philosophical and social concern questions concerning the nature of moral development and the nature of the morally deep self. These questions, however, cannot be adequately addressed until we give up our belief in the eternal maturity of *Homo economicus*. The road away from the moral and political problems of modernism leads away from *Homo economicus*, through childhood, to the morally deep self.

Notes

1. Alasdair MacIntyre, *After Virtue* (Notre Dame, Ind.: Notre Dame University Press, 1981), pp. 50-51.

2. *Ibid.*, pp. 49-50.

3. Jeremy Bentham, *The Works of Jeremy Bentham*, ed. John Bowring, vol. 2 (New York: Russell and Russell, 1962), p. 253.

4. Charles Taylor, "What Is Human Agency?" in *Human Agency and Language* (Cambridge, England: Cambridge University Press, 1985), pp. 15-44.

5. Derek Parfit, *Reasons and Persons* (Oxford: Oxford University Press, 1984).

6. *Ibid.*, p. 313.

7. *Ibid.*, pp. 199-320.

8. Alan Goldman, "Reasons and Personal Identity," *Inquiry*, 28 (1985), p. 379.

9. See Parfit, *Reasons and Persons*, pp. 307-311.

10. *Ibid.*

11. Philip K. Dick, "We Can Remember It for You Wholesale," in Edward L. Ferman and Robert P. Mills, *Twenty Years of the Magazine of Fantasy and Science Fiction* (New York: G. P. Putnam's Sons, 1970), pp. 196-215.

12. Piers Antony, *Total Recall* (New York: Avon Books, 1989). The Hollywood entertainment industry grinds on.

13. *Ibid.*, p. 199.

14. Taylor, "What Is Human Agency?", p. 34.

15. Plato, *Republic*, Books 8 & 9.

16. Clearly, our society is not yet completely modern in this sense.

17. For an interesting discussion of one aspect of this problem see, Garry Wills, "H. R. Clinton's Case," *New York Review*, 39 (5 March 1992), pp. 3-5.

18. Taylor, "What Is Human Agency?", p. 34; and Charles Taylor, *Sources of the Self* (Cambridge, Mass.: Harvard University Press, 1989), p. 19.

19. Plato, *Republic*, section 557(c).

20. Herbert Marcuse, *One-Dimensional Man: Studies in the Ideology of Advanced Industrial Society* (Boston: Beacon Press, 1964).

21. Both Hobbes and Plato argued that authoritarianism is the proper form of government for imprudent people.

Eleven

ELEMENTS OF A NATURALISTIC REALISM IN ETHICS

Jonathan Jacobs

1.

One of the most striking developments in philosophical theorizing about ethics in recent years is the resurgence of interest in formulating ethical theories that are naturalistic and realistic.[1] The sorts of non-cognitivism that dominated the subject for many years no longer have the general appeal that they once had. In part this is because the bias of the subject was to meta-ethics to the neglect of normative issues. Now there is a growing interest in closing the gap between the two. Naturalistic and realist approaches have merit in this regard, since by their nature they tend to take empirical issues about motivation, action, need, interest, and human welfare more seriously. A naturalism or realism that is not closely attentive to facts about people as natural and social beings would not have much promise of success.

I will present some considerations in favor of a version of naturalistic realism, and use them to formulate some general objections to non-cognitivist and relativist approaches to ethics. The view I will endorse can be called *practical realism*. According to practical realism, natural and social facts about people have normative significance because people are practical reasoners. We may say that there are moral facts, as long as it is understood that this is not because there are additional value entities or properties in the world, but because facts have normative significance *for* practical reason.

The point of setting up the issue this way is that it identifies the basic problems of ethics as problems for practical reason. The central issue is not a theoretical one of how to derive values from facts, or motivational efficacy from belief. Ethics, as Aristotle long ago argued is primarily the business of practical reason, in that it has to do with what is included in an understanding of what it is good to do. The intelligibility of human action and practical reason is to a large extent ethical intelligibility. Practical reason has as its object what is good in action. We understand action when we know what it aims at and why. There are deep and difficult problems about how to live, what to do and why, but they just are not best formulated as grounded in semantic or logical problems about *deriving* ethical facts or motives from non-ethical facts. Whether we take the relation between the non-moral and the moral to concern moving from fact to value or moving from belief to motive the relation is not deductive or semantic one.

Theorists such as Gilbert Harman argue that even if there were moral facts they "do not seem to play a role in explaining why anyone makes the particular observations he makes."[2] He argues that whatever moral facts could be correctly said to exist must be relative" to one or another set of conventions."[3] Thus, moral considerations are convention-based, but even if they had a convention-independent status they would be idle, cognitively and motivationally. I reject both claims, and hold that there are convention-independent, factual moral considerations and that knowledge of them can be motivational. Conventions do not constitute moral considerations but may register and reflect them.

This sort of naturalistic realism does not deny that the metaphysical and epistemological issues of value are genuine or significant. But they are mainly issues for the practical employment of reason. Well-ordered practical reason can achieve a comprehension of the ethical significance of facts and can be motivating. Moreover, the account of what it is for practical reason to be well ordered involves reference to its objects. Practical reason is not just a capacity to generate consistent prescriptions, or to link causal beliefs with ends of action supplied by desire or the passions.

According to some theories, there are ethical facts in the sense that certain distinctive objects or qualities exist and are intuited or perceived. So, whether or not there are ethical facts depends on how many objects exist in the world and what kinds of objects they are. But I do not mean that ethical facts are a special kind of value-thing, detected by a special faculty. They are the plain-old facts understood by practical reason. Practical reason does not stipulate or project values. It recognizes the normative significance of facts for action. That just is the activity of reason in its practical employment. This kind of naturalism enables us to avoid being pulled in the direction of Intuitionism, on the one hand, and skepticism on the other.

Here is an example of what I mean by facts being ethically significant, and how an account is realist without commitment to additional entities. Suppose a pile of logs falls off the back of a truck and lands on someone. It is a fact that there are logs on that person; it is a fact that the person is in distress; and it is a fact that it would be a morally good thing to help that person. That it is a good thing to help the person is not another fact "on the pile," so to speak. It is explained in terms of the significance of the facts of the situation for practical reason. It is not a further entity or a property of oughtness. The significance of the situation is understood, but not by detection of an additional distinctive fact, especially not a non-natural one.

Naturalism might be taken to involve defining moral terms in non-moral terms. It might be taken to involve identifying a criterion of right or good action in terms of an end we aim at by nature. It might be taken as an account of moral properties as properties that supervene on natural properties. Or, it can center on the explanation of moral judgment in terms of human sensibility. In that sense, even emotivism could be regarded as a species of naturalism.

G. E. Moore thought naturalism amounted to something like the definitional version, and thought it hopelessly mistaken. That view depends on certain semantic principles and commitments which are not part of practical realism. Naturalism does not turn on the prospect of producing definitions of ethical terms in non-ethical terms.

J. S. Mill's project in *Utilitarianism* was close to the version based on human desire and sensibility. He says:

> actions are right in proportion as they tend to promote happiness; wrong as they tend to produce the reverse of happiness. By happiness is intended pleasure and the absence of pain,[4]

And

> The utilitarian doctrine is that happiness is desirable, and the only thing desirable, as an end.[5]

The idea here seems to be that there is a basic, common motivational structure in people; we are pleasure-seekers. There is something people desire as an end, by their nature. And so, it is good that that should be maximized. Mill's view does not seem to turn on definitions, nor does it turn on a more Aristotelian idea of there being an intrinsic end for human nature, though there is something that action aims at as an end. Happiness, for Mill, is not the realization of the constitutive capacities of human nature. It is a state, the desirability of which is explained by an empirical account of what in fact people aim at. And what people aim at is pleasure. His theory is naturalistic in being based upon facts about psychology, action, and motivation, and in his attempt to fashion an empirically supported endorsement of the qualitative superiority of some pleasures. In attempting to avoid valuations that are not fact-based, he uses as a criterion, the preferences of people with the widest range of experience. It turns out that one of the things they desire is the general happiness. People are naturally endowed with social feelings, and the cultivation and education of their sensibility can yield a lasting, generalized concern for human welfare. With respect to moral value and moral motivation, Mill seeks to keep the account naturalistic. My account differs considerably from Mill's. Much of the difference has to do with claims about practical reason being a capacity for knowledge and motivation.

A third version of naturalism involves the claim of supervenience, and has figured prominently in contemporary discussion. Much of the revival of moral realism involves endorsing variants of realism that are naturalistic rather than intuitionistic. The point is to show how ethics can be realistic, cognitive and objective without appeal to any facts but those discoverable by the natural and social sciences and common sense. In David Brink's version of naturalism, for example, there are moral facts, dependent on natural and social facts, and supervening on them. So there is an object of moral knowledge. Its object does not transcend the natural order, or require a special faculty of cognition or perception in order to be known. Brink says:

> According to the naturalist, moral facts and properties both weakly and strongly supervene on natural facts and properties. Moral facts and properties strongly supervene on natural facts and properties because some sets of natural properties necessitate certain sets of moral properties. Because he rejects a semantic test of properties, the ethical naturalist denies that this necessary relation represents either logical or conceptual necessity; instead, it represents metaphysical necessity or necessity *a posteriori*.[6]

My view will differ from supervenience theories in an important way. Supervenience theorists still see the basic problem of ethics as a theoretical problem. They take the main concern to be to locate values in a world of facts. If we are to hold on to realism and cognitivism, then it seems that values either constitute an additional set of facts, or they emerge from or supervene on natural and social facts. On the view I endorse, practical reason can achieve a substantive understanding of moral considerations and be motivationally efficacious. It is not a matter of recognizing relations between properties, but of recognizing the normative significance of facts. The claim that there are moral facts can be taken in different ways. One is that the goodness, badness, justice, cruelty and other ethical properties of situations, actions, and characters are matters of fact in the sense of there being a distinct value entity or property or a supervenient property. The other way is that these ethical properties are not ontologically supervening but that given what the facts are, something is morally good or bad for practical reasoners.

Practical reasoners fit factual considerations into conceptions of worth. They can understand them in terms of how they figure in the significance of action. Reasoning is not practical only in guiding action. It is also practical in formulating conceptions of what is good to do and why. In order to formulate them, we must have an understanding of facts about human abilities, propensities, and circumstances. Facts have objective ethical significance for practical reasoners, though there are not value entities.

This is different from Brink's view of the constitution of moral facts. He says:

> Ethical naturalism, on this construal, claims that moral properties are constituted, composed, or realized by different combinations of natural and social scientific properties. Moral properties are nothing over and above organized configurations of natural properties.[7]

Brink claims that the supervenience of values on natural and social facts is necessary but *a posteriori*. On my view there are truths for practical reason that are not first discovered by theoretical reason. Factual moral considerations are the object of reason in its practical employment. Given what is required for human well-being, facts have objective ethical significance. If it would be unfair, callous, and dishonest to do something, it is not because four things exist, an act, and three properties of it. An act or situation has real or objective moral significance *for* practical reason that we do not project onto it, but neither would it be right to say we detect it first by theoretical reason. What is morally good to do is an objective matter ascertained by practical reasoning. We can explain in factual terms what is really wrong with cruelty or slavery for example, or why justice is a virtue. This is a matter of practical cognition. Ethical judgment is not the result of a cognition of facts being joined to a non-rational, independent desire. Nor is it a matter of attributing value to facts by projection, or theoretically detecting supervening values. People are moved to act because they are beings to whom desire is essential, but their desires can be informed by reason. Practical reasoning includes articulating desire in conformity with understanding. It is a capacity both to form cognitive conceptions of what is good, and to be moved by them. The conceptions are world-guided in the sense that they can register an objective understanding of the ethical significance of facts.

2.

When we consider what is ethically important, whatever meta-ethic we go in for, it is likely that a plausible, shareable sense of what is important will be supported by factual considerations about human nature, social life, emotions, needs, and purposes. It is almost incredible that anyone should think that ethics should be centered on an examination of how we use the word "good," or on what sorts of feelings are typically associated with the use of certain ethical terms. Similarly, it is almost incredible that anyone should think that ethical values are utterly free creations, unguided and unconstrained by facts about how the world is. Whether or not it is ethically good to care for an abandoned infant has nothing to do with how we use words or unguided radical choice, and it would be shocking if anyone *really* believed that they were decisive.[8] The same goes for the badness of slave trade and the ethical goodness of people dealing honestly with each other. Any conception of what is right and wrong that did not centrally involve reference to facts about human nature and social life could not be taken seriously in a lived, practical sense.

It is often argued that because ethics concerns norms of evaluation it cannot have the objectivity that natural or social sciences aspire to, or that ethics is essentially a cultural product for which there are no completely general standards or criteria of appraisal. The objections take many forms and often involve the additional claim that attempts at objectivity are specious and dangerous projects of extending one cultural construct beyond its boundaries.

One fundamental flaw in this sort of view is basic enough to strategically undermine it. Of course we live by convention, and we must fashion concepts and norms. This is one of the distinctive marks of human *nature*.[9] We do not live by instinct alone and our lives are structured and oriented by our concepts, understandings, reasonings, and commitments. It is natural for us to live by convention. But the conventional dimensions of human life are not simply detachable from human nature, and are not altogether constitutive of it. Conventions are not programmed developments of a primary human nature. But neither are their attendant conceptions of what is conducive to well-being ungrounded in a primary human nature. They are grounded in the possibilities and limits of human convention, and these supply the considerations for an objective normative appraisal of conventions.[10]

The power of Aristotle's analysis is particularly evident. His account of human nature is a kind of normative naturalism. He is unbothered by some more modern concerns about the distinction between facts and values. As Sarah Broadie remarks:

> Indeed, what many have considered the most fundamental of all distinctions in ethics, that between judgments of fact and judgments of value, seems to have passed over Aristotle's head.[11]

This is not altogether a loss. There is perhaps taxonomic clarity to a psychology of action that sharply divides belief and desire, and reason and non-reason. It simplifies the account of the character of deliberation and evaluation. At the same time, though, it implausibly restricts the function of reason to instrumental calculation, and it reserves the ground of prescription for desire or sentiment in a way that excludes the role of rationality in valuation. Good and bad are notions of practical reason which are not decomposable into rational and non-rational parts, occurring in pure samples. Because the practical employment of reason often is valuational, and sometimes ethical, we are interested in the normative significance of facts. The normative significance in ethical contexts has to do with a contentful understanding of what is needed for people to live well, and with what are reasonable requirements of people with respect to action. People typically do not have a systematic understanding of human needs, emotions, and motivation and do not need one. But they do make choices and judgments on the basis of an empirical appreciation developed in experience which involves reason and understanding.

We are animals with a certain constitution, fitting us for only certain kinds of environments and activities. We have dispositions, powers, and susceptibilities that we may not understand very well, but are nonetheless elements of our constitution. The plasticity of human life is very extensive, and given the variety of exercises of valuing, it might seem that moral values arise essentially from subjective bases in sensibility and convention. Human second natures, forms of life and practices, and modes of self-understanding are where ethical theorizing might well be thought to find its subject matter. Normative theories are human constructions, and they are for the evaluation and direction of human life. Our ideals, emotions, and needs are not somehow utterly free creations of the mind or will. Our freedom of thought and action is the exercise of capacities that we did not make. Many human desires, interests and purposes do not answer directly to natural needs or inclinations. Yet, what we can do is constrained by our natural constitution and how the world is. Nor does the fact that we are *rational* animals liberate us from our animality. We each live one unified life, the life of an animal capable of rational activity. Our rationality enables us to guide our action by understanding of our nature.

For ethical theory to succeed, we must take seriously the fact that there is a common human nature. This does not mean that ethical theory should uniquely determine a best set of social conventions down to the level of all ethically relevant details. What is ethically good has so much to do with the conditions and possibilities of our lives that it is implausible that some single set of conventions could yield the one best way to live. There almost certainly is no such thing. Nor does basing ethical theory on objective considerations entail that ethical principles will be absolute or exceptionless. What it *does* involve is that ethical thought should be guided by factual considerations some of which have to do with a common human nature. This nature is something for us to discover through action, experience, and reflection and inquiry.

The project for ethical theorizing is to explain what is normatively significant about human nature. Human second natures may be in some ways incommensurable. This is not evidence for ethical relativism or the lack of a common, human nature. The diversity we find is interesting and problematic because it is diversity of development of a common human nature. In large part, this enables us to recognize the varieties and possibilities of human life.

Some human purposes must be responsive to non-optional needs even if there are many ways to meet them. Much of what is central to human good at the most basic level is not a cultural product. But there are successful and unsuccessful ways of meeting the challenges of nature, and traditions are amenable to rational criticism. Ideals and aspirations also can be ethically appraised. There is an object for practical reason that is common across space and time and that cannot be reductively decomposed into relative conceptions dissociated from each other and from a common human world.

Ethical knowledge is not a special body of knowledge concerning a special class of facts. Ethical facts are natural and social facts considered from the point of view of practical reason. They are not distinct metaphysical laminates layered into the plain old facts. It *is* a fact, for example, that deliberately causing the suffering or humiliation of others for the sake of sport is wrong. But the wrongness is not a non-natural property nor is it discerned by a special sense. Nor do normatively significant facts have any peculiar prescriptive force or properties. The facts do not make us do anything. We are moved to act by taking facts to be considerations with a certain weight and significance for practical reason. What makes a fact an ethical consideration is what it has to do with an objective understanding of human goods, needs, and interests.

The kind of fact-based ethical theory I endorse allows for pluralism in the respect that not only are human needs and interests diverse but what is ethically sound depends on the facts of our settings and circumstances. Ethical theory need not rationally require only one set of economic, social and political arrangements. Yet it is profoundly implausible to claim that because there are so many possibilities for the organization of personal and social life, there are no objectively rational conditions for what count as ethically good lives. There may not be a best way to live, but there are many bad ways. What is good or bad is not altogether a matter of convention. The fact that our ethical beliefs and practices are often bound up with political, religious, and scientific beliefs and customs does not exempt them from rational assessment. Ethical views are sometimes based on conceptions of people that we know to be false, crazy, or supported by lies.

Members of a group with a murderous obsession for the persecution of another group are either in error about some morally relevant considerations, or ignorant of them, or have a disordered moral sensibility. If they are stubbornly indifferent to the suffering of others we must not simply insist that they just have different desires or attitudes, or that certain moral reasons are not reasons for them. We *know* they have different desires and attitudes. We need an explanation of this in terms why they count certain kinds of things as ethically relevant in the ways that they do.

Non-cognitivists and anti-naturalists are right that intellect alone or facts alone cannot make reason practical. But to note that motivation and action involve elements other than factual knowledge need not lead to a clean break between them. Reason is practical. What makes it practical is not that it is connected to desires or motives independent of it, but that one exercise of reason is to comprehend facts in terms of conceptions of good. These conceptions do not have non-rational sources. They are cognitive recognitions of the significance of facts for practical reasoners with a certain constitution. It is in this sense that facts are prescriptive; namely, they are objects of *practical* cognition. This kind of naturalism is the most plausible explanation of the content of moral beliefs, the generality of moral considerations, the possibility of improvements or worsenings in moral understanding, and the variety of considerations relevant to ethically significant practical reasoning.

Some philosophers argue from ethical disagreement to ethical non-cognitivism or to the denial of ethical objectivity. If there are ethical facts, would we not find more agreement on what they are and how they should count as reasons for action? I do not see why cognitivism would ensure agreement. What it would do is enable rational agreement. Anyway, I suspect that we find more agreement in ethical belief than philosophers often acknowledge. What partially masks agreement is the fact that people do not act well and often produce specious rationales for acting badly. The problem is not that we lack a common human nature, facts about which constitute ethical considerations, but that we lie, hate, misunderstand, and fail to know or care. The problem is not the relativity of ethical values but the greed, resentment, falsification and distortions that disfigure moral belief and practice.

Honest disagreements among informed, reasonable, decent people are bound to occur. I am not suggesting that there is a unique, right course of action in all cases. I claim that the kinds of considerations that go into formulating and addressing ethical matters are factual. Whether people in distress should be aided, or young children cared for, or scarce goods allocated on terms other than force are ethical matters which arise out of facts and are to be resolved in terms of facts. People can recognize that there is a common human nature that is ethically significant. In any case, neither difference in belief nor difference in practice support relativism unless there is no better explanation for them. Naturalistic realism supplies plausible explanations for both agreement and non-agreement, by taking seriously naturalistic considerations that justify ethical positions and judgments.

Practical realism also takes into account the changes in natural and social conditions without unraveling into relativism. Not only do conditions and problems change, but our personal and social ideals and ambitions change, and ethical thought must be responsive to those changes. Some ideals and ambitions it simply excludes: genocide, tyranny, deliberately causing suffering for one's own enjoyment, deliberately impeding development of cognitive and emotional capacities are examples. Different understandings of basic needs are ethically possible. What someone needs to lead a decent life has some general requirements, but a great deal of what counts as need depends upon circumstances. Security against starvation or constant threat is more certain than what someone needs to live decently in their own social setting. Our needs also encompass protection against cruel or arbitrary treatment, brainwashing, and an indeterminate range of other abuses or deprivations. When we get to questions such as whether people should choose their own mates, or whether minimum levels of health care should be publicly funded, the significance of custom, convention, economic conditions and other highly variable factors become centrally important. That people should not sell their children into slavery is clear; that primogeniture is unethical is not so clear. Practical wisdom about these matters must incorporate both highly general considerations and details of local contingencies. Moreover, both justice and utility take time. Ethical thought might yield a conception of what changes in practices and institutions are to be made, but it also must take into account what sorts of dislocations, resentments, and uncertainties the changes are likely to cause. The manner of change is no less ethically significant than the end aimed at.

People who already share a good deal of fact-based ethical understanding have the luxury to deny that ethical understanding *is* fact-based. Ethical views can appear to be largely a matter of approval and disapproval, or the product of choices unguided by knowledge, if there is substantial agreement in them. Thinking that morality is non-cognitive or not fact-based is socially tolerable when there is wide agreement on fundamental beliefs and practices. The differences among people do not strain the community to destruction. The widespread convergence may really be supportable by factual considerations, even if they are not actually accepted as the basis for it. Whatever soundness there is in a moral belief or practice is in large part to be judged with reference to naturalistic considerations, even where the appreciation of them as such is inarticulate.

Ethical attention, ethical imagination, subtlety in judgment, and other virtues of practical reason have to do with appreciating the normative significance of facts. That is one respect in which practical wisdom is naturalistic. A second respect in which it is naturalistic is in how it is developed. As Aristotle pointed out, its starting point is habituation through which we can become disposed to find pleasure in the right things and to choose to do what is best. Habit is not an alternative to practical reason. It is the matter which it informs, but for practical reason to be well ordered it must inform matter receptive to it. Coming to have a certain character and a particular set of ethical commitments, perspectives, and dispositions of action is itself a naturalistic process. Practical wisdom is thus naturalistic in a two-fold way, in terms of its object and its development.

If we are inattentive to the naturalistic character of ethical phenomena and take them to be wholly stipulative, or cultural constructs, we are almost certain to deceive ourselves about their sense and significance. Nor is it good enough to remark that we take their naturalistic basis for granted, while claiming the interesting problems lie elsewhere. Facts about human nature are always relevant to what counts as an ethical issue and cannot merely be taken for granted. Fashioning sound norms and ideals is made possible by a practical understanding of a natural, factual order of which we are part.

One conclusion that can be drawn from this characterization of naturalistic realism is that well-ordered practical reason that underlies sound ethical thought and action involves an important kind of self-knowledge. In involving an understanding of the ethical significance of facts, it is an understanding of human needs, goods, and interests that have extensive, contentful generality. Action in accordance with our understanding of them involves exercising knowledge of our nature as the ground of values to be realized.

Notes

1. For a survey of some important recent positions in defense of naturalism and realism, see Geoffrey Sayre-McCord, ed., *Essays on Moral Realism* (Ithaca, N.Y.: Cornell University Press, 1988). See also David Brink, *Moral Realism and the Foundations of Ethics* (New York: Cambridge University Press, 1989).

2. Gilbert Harman, *The Nature of Morality* (New York: Oxford University Press, 1977), p. 130.

3. *Ibid.*, p. 132.

4. J. S. Mill, *Utilitarianism*, ed. G. Sher (Indianapolis, Ind.: Hackett Publishing Company, 1979), p. 7.

5. *Ibid.*, p. 34.

6. Brink, *Essays on Moral Realism*, p. 175.

7. *Ibid.*, p. 177.

8. For a critique of the existentialist's notion of radical choice, see C. Taylor; "Responsibility for Self" in *The Identities of Persons,* ed. A. Rorty (Berkeley: University of California Press, 1976).

9. For a treatment of the character and importance of convention in human life and human good, see James Wallace, *Virtues & Vices* (Ithaca, N.Y.: Cornell University Press, 1978), ch. 1.

10. For an extended discussion of convention and its relation to practical wisdom, see my *Being True to the World: Moral Realism and Practical Wisdom* (New York: Peter Lang Publishing, Inc., 1990).

11. S. Broadie, *Ethics with Aristotle* (New York: Oxford University Press, 1991).

Twelve

THE VALUE OF HUMAN LIFE: AN ABSOLUTIST STRATEGY FOR ATTACKING CONSEQUENTIALISM

Joram Graf Haber

When will the world realize that a million men are of no importance compared with one man?
—*Thoreau*

Moral Absolutism is a theory ordinarily regarded to be opposed to consequentialism.[1] By "consequentialism," I mean a principle of the form: "An act is right if and only if the act produces the highest ranked state of affairs that is open to the agent to produce." By "moral absolutism," I mean a principle of the form: "For some values of O, where 'O' represents an action type, in no situation could it be right to O." So construed, consequentialism and absolutism are contradictories of each other.

Many consequentialists have offered what is thought to be a foolproof strategy for attacking absolutism. They have charged that for any value of O resulting in a state of affairs S, it is always possible for there to be an alternative to O-ing such that a state of affairs S* obtains where S* is worse than S. The strategy here is to make S* a state of affairs that includes everything bad that S includes and more of the same.

There are two versions of this strategy. In its strong form, the strategy is to make S* include all that is included in S so that S is a subset of S*. In its weak form, the strategy is to make S* and S separate sets, with S* including all that is *bad* about S and then some. I propose to show that in either form the strategy fails, by arguing that for some values of O, there is a state of affairs that is so bad that nothing could be worse. Though most of what I say applies to the strategy's strong form, I shall focus on the weak form, since this is where much of the discussion lies. To keep things simple, I will consider "killing the materially innocent" as a value of O, with S serving as the avoidable death of an innocent person and S* serving as the avoidable deaths of n number of persons, where n >1. The principle in question is "It could never be right to kill an innocent person," and the view to be discussed is that the avoidable deaths of n number of persons is not a worse outcome than the avoidable death of one person.

1.

An explicit defense of this strategy is found in Samuel Scheffler's critique of Robert Nozick's thesis that rights function as side-constraints.[2] Of this thesis, Nozick asks whether it is not irrational to violate a side-constraint C if the refusal to do so results in other more extensive violations of C?[3] His answer is that it is not irrational, since side-constraints reflect the Kantian principle that individuals are ends that must never be used for ulterior purposes.[4]

Scheffler, to be sure, is unconvinced. He writes: "It is natural to interpret Nozick's defense of side-constraints as an appeal to the disvalue of certain features of violations of the constraints. But if that is the proper interpretation of his defense, then clearly . . . [it] . . . is inadequate."[5] And the reason for this is that acts that violate C have some feature that has high disvalue. But if that is the case, then, however high the disvalue of a violation of C might be, a greater number of equally weighty violations will obtain if C is not violated. Thus, "appeals to the disvalue of violations of [C] are powerless to explain why it is wrong to violate [C] when doing so will prevent [other] identical violations of [C]."[6]

Other philosophers have wielded this strategy. Kai Nielsen, for one, uses it to solve the case of the "fat man in the cave." A fat man leading a group of potholers out of a cave is stuck in the mouth of a cave in which water is rapidly rising. Unless he is promptly unstuck, the group will all be drowned. He can be unstuck, but only if the others blast the rocks with the explosives they have, causing the death of the man caught in the rocks.

Of this case, Nielsen writes:

> If there really is no other way of unsticking our fat man, and if plainly, without blasting him out, everyone in the cave will drown, then, innocent or not, he should be blasted out. This . . . does not reveal a callousness toward life, for the people involved are caught in a desperate situation in which, if

such extreme action is not taken, many lives will be lost and far greater misery will obtain . . . . Surely we must choose between evils here, but is there anything more reasonable, more morally appropriate, than choosing the lesser evil when doing or allowing some evil cannot be avoided?[7]

Philippa Foot provides us with other examples. There is the driver of a runaway tram who can turn either to one track on which five men are working or another track on which one man is working. Which way should he turn? There is the patient who needs a massive dose of a lifesaving drug in short supply while at the same time there are five other patients each of whom can be saved by one-fifth of that dose. To whom should we give the drug? And there is the pilot whose aeroplane is about to crash and who is deciding whether to steer from a more to a less inhabited area. Which way should he steer?[8] As Foot puts it about each of these cases: "we feel bound to let one man die rather than many if that is our only choice."[9] The thinking here is that between two states of affairs, S* and S, S* is worse than S if S* includes everything bad that S includes and then some. For the faithful: "the good of the many outweighs the good of the few."

It will be noticed that in none of these cases does the causal chain run through the will of anyone but the agent. I have deliberately excluded cases like Bernard Williams's "Jim and the Indians,"[10] in which one agent will kill others if some other agent does not kill one. Though cases like these are informative and occupy much of the literature, they have been intentionally omitted in order to avoid the complications that arise from such thorny problems as the act-omission distinction and the doctrine of double effect.

2.

There are a number of philosophers who do not think that the right course of action in cases like these is the one that will minimize premature deaths. And the reason for this is that they do not share the view that S* is worse than S. Wittgenstein intimates as much when he writes: "*No* torment can be greater than what a single human being may suffer," and "the whole planet can suffer no greater torment than a *single* soul."[11] But it is one thing to have a strong moral vision and another to have a theory about it. Wittgenstein has the vision but not the moral theory.

There are, however, two bases for the "not worse" thesis. The first is that S* is not worse than S because there is no value-comparative truth about S* and S. The second is that there *is* a value-comparative truth about S* and S, and S* is not worse than S because it is exactly as bad as S. Following Jonathan Bennett, I shall refer to the former as the "incomparability thesis" and the latter as the "equality" thesis.[12]

John Taurek is the clearest champion of the incomparability thesis.[13] If faced with the choice of giving a lifesaving drug to five people who could all be saved by it, or one who could be saved by it but only if he got it all, Taurek says he would flip a coin. He rejects the view that from an impartial standpoint, S* is worse than S. There are, for Taurek, only the standpoints of the parties involved. And since, from each party's standpoint, it is a worse thing that that party should die rather than the other, it follows that no one party's loss is greater than another from some alleged but chimerical impartial point of view.[14] In a word, what Taurek is denying is that separate losses can be meaningfully tallied in a value-comparative way.

Grisez and Shaw also seem to champion incomparability. They write:

> Human life [should be] regarded not as a concrete, specific, essentially quantifiable object but as a good in which each person participates but which none exhausts or sums up in himself. In such a view of reality it is simply not possible to make the sort of calculation which weighs lives against each other ... and thus determines whose life shall be respected and whose sacrificed. The value of life, each human life, is incalculable, not in any merely poetic sense but simply because it is something not susceptible to calculation, measurement, weighing, and balancing.[15]

The word "balancing" in this passage suggests that Grisez and Shaw are advancing a thesis of incomparability. Oddly, they seem also to champion equality. They suggest that since the value of life is infinite, the disvalue of S* is, like the disvalue of S, exactly equal since they both are infinite. Thus, Grisez and Shaw write:

> If it were true that any action ... is permitted in certain circumstances, then no good intrinsic to the person would be safe from invasion .... It would always be possible to conceive of circumstances in which the person could be sacrificed to the attainment of ulterior ends .... It would then make no sense to speak of the "infinite" value of the human person. Far from being infinite, the value of a person would be quite specific and quantifiable, something to be weighed calculatingly in the balance against other values.[16]

But it is by no means clear how one can defend the incomparability thesis together with the equality thesis. The truth of one commits one to the falsity of the other. But neither is it clear that Grisez and Shaw defend equality. They seem *not* to defend it, if the following passage is characteristic of their thinking:

Consequentialism would work if choices were between possibilities which differed from one another *only* in the quantity of good they promised. If, for instance, one had a pure case of bringing about the deaths of more people or fewer people, and nothing else of human importance were involved, one would surely prefer to kill fewer. The greater good/lesser evil would be so clear that no choice would be required or even possible.[17]

Note the counterfactual comparability of S* and S. Grisez and Shaw imply that while, *as a practical matter*, one could not be placed in a position of having to choose between S* or S, all things being equal, such a position is *logically* possible. But if that is what they think, then they are not committed to the equality thesis.

3.

It is questionable whether anybody could defend either of these theses, or whether anyone would want to do so. After all, it seems hard to deny that S* is worse than S, if S* includes everything bad that S includes and more of the same. Nevertheless, I want to defend the equality thesis. I want to argue that S* is *not* worse than S, and my reason for doing so has to do with the value I place on an individual's life. The argument is forthright and simple. I start with the premiss that life is infinitely valuable and argue from here that if that is so, then a state of affairs S in which a life is terminated is a state of affairs that is infinitely bad. If S, however, is infinitely bad, then so is S*, since once you have infinity you cannot add to it. Consequently, S* is not worse than S but has identical moral disvalue.[18]

The argument derives its strength from an analogy with mathematics. Intuitively, if a set contains an infinite number of members, then a second set, containing all of the members of the first plus one not contained in the first, contains exactly the same number of members as the first set contains. Thus, if S is infinitely bad, it follows that S* is as well.[19]

Previously, we saw Scheffler take Nozick to task for tacitly appealing to the disvalue of certain features of violations of side-constraints in order to account for their absolutist force. Scheffler argued against this tactic by reasoning that however high the disvalue a violation of C is, at least as much disvalue will obtain if C is *not* violated. In criticizing Nozick, Scheffler's goal was to show the irrationality of the view that in "no situation could it be right to O." As Scheffler puts it: "Appeals [to the disvalues of violations] . . . make all violations of the constraints look *equally objectionable*." (emphasis added)[20] Scheffler is right, of course, if the disvalue that obtains is high though less than infinity. But if the disvalue that obtains reaches infinity, then Scheffler has assumed what remains to be proved.

Consider more closely Scheffler's train of thought. He says it cannot be wrong to O solely because O-ing results in S. For if that were true, then it would be wrong to O even if the only alternative to O-ing were an act resulting in S*. But since S* *is* worse than S, it follows that in some situations it is permissible to O.

If, however, S is infinitely bad, then S* is equal to S and Scheffler has produced no argument to the contrary. Indeed, Scheffler has unwittingly assumed that the disvalue of S is less than infinity, and argued from there that S* is worse. And while the belief that S* is worse than S is compelling, just as compelling is the belief that the value of life is infinite. Thus, Scheffler's argument succeeds if, but only if, we accept an axiology which places the value of life at less than infinity. Consequently, one can agree with Scheffler that tactics such as Nozick's make all violations look "equally objectionable," yet wonder why this should count as a strike against Nozick. Without his axiology, Scheffler's argument counts as much *for* Nozick as it does *against* him.

4.

It would be helpful, of course, if it were possible to prove the equality thesis. Is such a proof possible? If by "proof" is meant "demonstrate," then the answer is no. But the equality theorist, who assumes that life has infinite value, is in no worse a position than the consequentialist, who places the value of life below infinity and who also cannot prove the truth of her position. Of absolutism at least, Bennett has freely admitted that there is no way to disprove it, and he would ostensibly say the same of equality. Referring to absolutism, he says: "The principle is consistent and reasonably clear."[21]

Why then think that the equality thesis is no less plausible than its consequentialist rival? The main reason is our fundamental conviction that persons are beings with infinite value. Now I am more sure that we have this conviction than I am of its theoretical grounding. For some absolutists, the conviction is laid down by a moral authority whose edicts are accepted without question. For others, the conviction has its source in the Kantian view that persons are beings for whom states of affairs have value in virtue of a person's beliefs and desires.[22] For my own part, I am inclined to accept the Kantian view believing, as I do, that persons are beings who, as Kant put it, are "above all price." A virtue of this view is that it explains why things have value relative to each other while the value of persons is incommensurable.

Of course, in putting forward this view, I must give up the view that S* is worse than S. That is the cost of defending equality. What is gained, however, is the well-entrenched view that an individual's life has infinite value and cannot be quantified in any meaningful sense. The question we must ask is whether the benefit of the thesis is worth the cost, for the cost of the thesis is the compelling belief that S* is worse than S especially when S is a subset of S*. The dilemma is this: Either it is true that life has infinite value and false that S* is worse than S, or it is true that S* is worse than S and false that life has infinite value.

Bennett has doubted whether anyone could really stick by the equality thesis and follow through with its implications. One of these, he says, is that the first time something as bad as S occurred, the universe would become infinitely bad so that nothing that happened later could serve to make it worse. Such a view would, in addition, generate a permission to evil-doers to the tune of: "Go ahead and do what you like; it can't make things any worse than they are."[23]

As to the first objection, I admit that the equality thesis entails the view that the universe has become infinitely bad and I unhappily accept this conclusion. As to the second objection, it may be that there is nothing about the badness of the states of affairs that makes it more wrong to kill n rather than one person, but that if you have killed one person it is a further wrong action to kill another. But even if the equality thesis does generate a permission to evil-doers to repeat their misdeed, the consequentialist is not in any better position. The equality theorist has a *tu quoque* to this effect: Even if S* is worse than S, as the absolute badness of each becomes greater, with the difference between them being, say, only a single life, the relative difference shrinks without limit. Thus, the relative difference between a million lives and a million and one lives is negligible. Think here of Bernard William's facetious remark that consequentialism "will have something to say even on the difference between massacring seven million, and massacring seven million and one."[24] So for plenty of cases though admittedly not all the consequentialist has nothing more powerful to say to persistent evil-doers than does the equality theorist.

Bennett, to be sure, is unpersuaded. He says:

> The relevant notion is not relative difference but absolute difference. Between one life and two, as between a million lives and one, there is an enormous difference, namely the difference of one precious life. It is because of the absolute size of that difference i.e., because a human life is so valuable, however many lives have been lost that I judge that the serial murderer who kills his ninetieth victim is doing a really terrible thing, adding a great deal of badness to the world. Thinking in terms of relative value, I contend, is a seductive moral infirmity that one should fight to avoid.[25]

But calling such thinking a "seductive infirmity" is not to deny that the consequentialist is committed to that line of thought. Indeed, if the equality theorist offers up a *tu quoque*, Bennett offers up an *ad hominem* of his own: The "infirmity" he speaks of, he is committed to, whether or not he finds it is to his liking.

5.

It may be urged that the differences between consequentialists and equality theorists are largely illusory, since many consequentialists place the value of life just short of infinity. That makes the differences between them more apparent than real. Because many consequentialists place the value of life at infinity minus one, they are, in effect, practical absolutists. Furthermore, it may be urged that they are in an even better position, since this allows them to hold that S* is worse than S.

I do not begrudge consequentialists this view. I add only that, as a moral philosopher, I am interested in knowing if there is a possible world in which O-ing would be permissible even though in the actual world it would never come about that that would be so. I want to know, that is, whether the belief I have that it could never be right to O is one that is based on the contingencies of the world or one that is based on *a priori* principles.

If consequentialists are right, there *is* a possible world in which O-ing is permissible, since they would sooner deny that persons have infinite value than they would that S* is worse than S. I trust consequentialists can live with this result given the putative allure of their overall theory. They might reason that if they must reject the conviction that people are infinitely valuable so as to preserve the view that S* is worse than S, then so much the worse for that conviction. After all, consequentialists often suppose that where theory and intuition clash, it is natural to suspect the intuition in question.

Equality theorists are not so accommodating. They would sooner deny that S* is worse than S than acknowledge that persons have less than infinite value. They are so repulsed at a possible world in which O-ing is permissible which implies that we could quantify value over persons, that they would rather accommodate their counter-intuitions than accept the consequentialist alternative.

Furthermore, equality theorists may suspect that the reason their conclusions are counter-intuitive is itself attributable to consequentialist values. Consider, for instance, what G. E. M. Anscombe, an absolutist if not exactly an equality theorist, has to say about procuring the judicial execution of the innocent: "If someone really thinks, *in advance*, that it is open to question whether such an action . . . should be quite excluded from consideration—I do not want to argue with him; he shows a corrupt mind."[26]

In the light of this comment, consider what Bennett has said he finds "intolerably strange" about the equality thesis:

> The equality theorist has to say that as the serial murderer works through his successive victims it is not the case that things are becoming worse. When the police, having found two bodies of victims who have been raped and strangled, then find a third victim's body hidden in the undergrowth, the policeman who says, sickened, "Things are even worse than we thought" is not speaking the literal truth—according to the equality thesis.[27]

I do not accuse Bennett of having a "corrupt mind." He is not like Mary Anne Warren who, in a well-known paper, favorably compares the premature death of a newborn infant to the loss of a great work of art because of their deleterious outcomes.[28] But I do think that *qua* consequentialist, Bennett does undervalue the life of a person in finding such reasoning "intolerably strange." From the perspective of the equality theorist, "things are not worse than we thought" since they have already become infinitely bad. To think otherwise, he insists, is to devalue life in theory, if not in fact. Thus, far from depreciating the disvalue of the activities of the serial murderer, the equality theorist appreciates the disvalue of the activities of the common murderer.

6.

To be sure, more must be said of the suggestion that consequentialism's devaluation of persons is itself responsible for the counter-intuitiveness of the examples used against absolutism. Support is needed for the view that equality theorists are appreciating the disvalue that attaches to a state of affairs S rather than depreciating the disvalue that attaches to S*. Insisting that consequentialists are logically committed to the idea of relative disvalue, and that that idea is morally repugnant, equality theorists must strengthen their claim that human life has infinite value.

One way of arguing that people have infinite value involves a certain appeal to the sympathetic judgment of an impartial observer.[29] The claim can be made that if an impartial observer were told the story of the premature death of a single person, he could not help but conclude that such a story would be as catastrophic as a story about the premature deaths of n number of persons. There is, however, an important caveat. The story of the one must be told in sufficient detail to bring out in full the sympathetic judgment.[30] And what this means is that the story must be told in a way that exhibits the full particularity of the person as a distinct individual with a rich biography. Novelists are particularly good at this, and we could expect to find through a study of literature many poignant tales that would exhibit this perception. If, however, the story is told in a way that conceals the particularity of the person, then the absolutist's position will fail to convince. Thus, the absolutist cautions against telling the stories in such a way that their only relevant difference lies in the number of deaths obtaining. This is how consequentialists tell their stories and why it has the effect of clouding the absolutist's position.

To exemplify this tactic, suppose we are told that n persons will be killed unless we kill one person. That is our choice, and we are to suppose that there is no escaping it. What ought we to do? *Prima facie*, it is natural to suppose that we ought to kill the one person. Suppose, however, we are informed that the one to be killed is a significant other perhaps our beloved child. Given the full particularity of our relationship with our child, it is natural to conclude that a state of affairs S in which the person is killed is a state of affairs that is as bad as its alternative.[31] And this would be true even if the choice were between S* and S, where S is a subset of S*.

But, it will be asked, what is impartial about this judgment and why accord it *moral* status? To the contrary, it seems eminently partial and anything but moral. The answer to this question lies in the fact that, while for me the death of my child is every bit as bad as the deaths of many other people, I know that every individual is the child of some parent who places as high a value on that child as I do on mine. Knowing this, I generalize to the view that my judgment on this particular case is characteristically moral, since there are nonmoral facts that are the reason for my judgment. Otherwise put, I judge that for any individual, that individual is infinitely valuable. In this way, the attitude I have about the value of persons is one I can prescribe to all moral agents.

Notes

1. An earlier draft of this chapter was presented at Syracuse University, July 1990, as part of a National Endowment for the Humanities seminar on Consequentialism. I am grateful to Jonathan Bennett for the many helpful comments received on that occasion as well as to members of the seminar.

2. See Samuel Scheffler, *The Rejection of Consequentialism* (New York: Oxford University Press, 1988), pp. 87-90.

3. Robert Nozick, *Anarchy, State, and Utopia* (New York: Basic Books, 1974), p. 30.

4. *Ibid.*, pp. 30-31.

5. Scheffler, *The Reflection of Consequentialism*, p. 88.

6. *Ibid.*, p. 87.

7. Kai Nielsen, "Against Moral Conservatism," *Ethics*, 82 (1972), p. 228. For a competing analysis of this case, see Alan Donagan, *The Theory of Morality* (Chicago: University of Chicago Press, 1977), pp. 177-180.

8. See Philippa Foot, "The Problem of Abortion and the Doctrine of the Double Effect," *Oxford Review*, 5 (1967). Reprinted in Philippa Foot, *Virtues and Vices and Other Essays in Moral Philosophy* (Berkeley: University of California Press, 1978), pp. 19-32. For a list of cases of this sort, see Kai Nielsen, *Ethics Without God* (London: Pemberton Books, 1973), ch. 4. See also my *Absolutism and Its Consequentialist Critics* (Savage, Md.: Rowman & Littlefield, 1994) for a collection of essays that discuss these cases.

9. *Ibid.*, p. 24.

10. See Bernard Williams, "A Critique of Utilitarianism" in J. J. C. Smart and Bernard Williams, *Utilitarianism: For and Against* (New York: Cambridge University Press), pp. 98-99.

11. Ludwig Wittgenstein, *Culture and Value*, ed. G. H. von Wright in collaboration with Heikki Nyman. Trans. Peter Winch (Chicago: University of Chicago Press, 1980). P. 46e. Compare this with: "Man was created as a single individual to teach us that anyone who destroys a single life is as though he destroyed an entire world." (*Mishnah*, tractate Sanhedrin 4/5).

12. Correspondence, July 1990.

13. See John Taurek, "Should the Numbers Count?", *Philosophy and Public Affairs*, 6:4 (Summer 1977), pp. 293-316.

14. For a critique of Taurek, see Derek Parfit, "Innumerate Ethics," *Philosophy and Public Affairs*, 7 (1978) pp. 285-301, and William Shaw, "Elementary Lifesaving," *Southern Journal of Philosophy*, 18:1 (Spring 1980), pp. 87-97. For a defense of the view that numbers do not count but only at the level of supererogation, see Charles Fried, "Correspondence," *Philosophy and Public Affairs*, 8 (1979), pp. 393-397.

15. Germain Grisez and Russell Shaw, *Beyond the New Morality: The Responsibilities of Freedom*, 3rd ed. (Notre Dame, Ind.: University of Notre Dame Press, 1988), p. 136.

16. *Ibid.*, p. 134.

17. *Ibid.*, p. 132.

18. With the exception of Grisez and Shaw, it is doubtful that any absolutists are also

equality theorists.

19. Admittedly, the argument rests on a raw, unarticulated conception of "infinite value." On the one hand, the term is used in the mathematical sense of immeasurability accounting for the claim that once you have infinity, you cannot add to it. On the other hand, the term is used in the metaphysical sense of wholeness, something, with apologies to Anselm, akin to "value greater than which it is impossible to conceive." And while it needs to be determined just how the two conceptions are logically related, it is hard to deny that life is, in some sense, infinitely valuable. For an excellent discussion of "infinity" in both its mathematical and metaphysical sense, see A.W. Moore, *The Infinite* (New York: Rutledge, Chapman and Hall, 1990).

20. Samuel Scheffler, "Introduction," *Consequentialism and Its Critics* (Oxford: Oxford University Press, 1982), p. 10.

21. Jonathan Bennett, "Whatever the Consequences," *Analysis,* 26 (1965-1966), p. 84.

22. For a Kantian defense of absolutism generally, see Alan Donagan, *The Theory of Morality* (Chicago: University of Chicago Press, 1977).

23. Correspondence, July 1990.

24. Williams, "A Critique of Utilitarianism," p. 93.

25. Correspondence, July 1990.

26. G. E. M. Anscombe, "Modern Moral Philosophy," *Philosophy,* 23 (January 1957), pp. 16-17.

27. Correspondence, July 1990.

28. Mary Anne Warren, "Postscript on Infanticide" in Richard Wasserstrom, ed., *Today's Moral Problems* (New York: Macmillan, 1975). The "postscript" is to Mary Anne Warren, "On the Moral and Legal Status of Abortion," *The Monist,* 57:1 (January 1973).

29. Josef Popper-Lynkeus has employed such an approach in his book, *Das Individuum und die Bewertung menschlicher Existenzen* (1910), translated by Andrew Kelley and me as *The Individual and the Value of Human Life* (Savage, Md.: Rowman and Littlefield, 1995).

30. It may also have to be told prior to the story about the deaths of the many.

31. There may be an algorithm here to the effect that we are desensitized to the suffering of others in direct proportion to the number of persons whose suffering we learn of. Also operative here may be a concept of diminishing marginal disvalue analogous to the economic one of diminishing marginal utility. Just as the consumer of a good

tends to devalue that good after the consumption of the nth good, so too, as moral consumers, we tend to devalue a state of affairs after we have appreciated the death of the nth victim where here, n is equal to one. Another way of putting this is to say that our moral imagination is stretched to its limits immediately after we sympathetically appreciate the death of the one.

Thirteen

ON BENEFITING PEOPLE BY CREATING THEM

Julian Lamont

Does bringing people into existence benefit them? People may ask this question in two ways. They may be asking whether future people would have pleasurable lives. Alternatively, they can assume that the lives would be pleasurable and still ask themselves if *causing someone to exist* is itself a benefit to that person. Derek Parfit devotes himself to this more subtle question in Appendix G of *Reasons and Persons*. Parfit says "I shall argue that the answer Yes is not, as some claim, obviously mistaken."[1]

As Parfit correctly notes, the answer has implications for arguments about population policy. Parfit comments:

> This question has been strangely neglected. Thus, in a Report of a U.S. Senate Commission on Population Growth and the American Economy, it is claimed that "there would be no substantial benefits from the continued growth of the U.S. population." The Report never considers whether, if extra Americans are born, this might benefit these Americans.[2]

But the answer to Parfit's question has implications for arguments about population policy only if some *moral* sense of the term "benefit" is used in the question. This is important as it affects the focus of my analysis. If causing people to exist benefits them only in some non-moral sense of "benefit," then the result is uninteresting, at least from the point of view of arguments about population.

By "moral sense of benefit" I mean that if an action would benefit someone, then this provides us with some *prima facie* reason for performing the action. So, if bringing more people into existence benefits them in a moral sense, this gives us some *prima facie* reason for bringing them into existence. Such benefit would have implications for policy and for personal choices about procreation including the procreation of severely handicapped infants. In what follows, I shall consider whether causing a person to exist benefits that person in a way which has moral implications.[3]

I shall show that we can consistently explain certain normal moral obligations without affirming a *prima facie* obligation to benefit future people by creating them. I will use Parfit's arguments as a testing ground for this claim. In addition, I shall argue that, while an affirmative answer to Parfit's question may not be *obviously* mistaken, it probably is.

1.

When does an action benefit someone? Here is a suggestion for determining whether an action c benefits a person X:

> *Suggestion 1*: Call the world which would be actual were c to occur, world P, and the world which would be actual were c not to occur, world Q. Then c benefits person X if X is better off in world P than in world Q.

Before considering the implications of this suggestion, it is important to note a simplifying assumption which will make the discussion less cumbersome. The simplification is to assume that there is *one* world which would be actual were c to occur, and that there is *one* world which would be actual were c not to occur.

So, using this criterion, does an action c, which causes person X to exist, benefit X? The criterion above suggests comparing P and Q and asking whether X is better off in P than in Q. But X does not exist in Q. There is no entity whose position can be compared across the worlds. If one takes benefiting someone to involve making a comparison of the life of that person between the cases where c occurs, and where c fails to occur, then X is not benefited by c. To be sure, X exists because c occurs in world P. But there is no relevant entity for comparison across the worlds. There is no relevant entity we can identify and say of it that it is better off than it is in the other world.

Another possible suggestion for a criterion for determining whether an action c benefits a person X is as follows:

> *Suggestion 2*: c benefits person X if, relative to X's self-interested preferences, the world P ranks higher than the world Q, where P and Q are as described in suggestion 1.

If we make the plausible assumption that, *ceteris paribus*, people will normally rank a world in which they exist higher than a world in which they do not, then, under this criterion, *c* benefits X. It does not matter here that X does not exist in one of the worlds. We simply use X's preferences to rank the worlds. People certainly can rank a world in which they do not exist. I shall assess Parfit's arguments under the assumption that Suggestion 1 is correct and then examine the considerations in favor of Suggestion 1 over Suggestion 2.

2.

Parfit distils three points from his argument in Appendix G. First, the claim that causing people to exist benefits them need not imply the implausible view "that it is bad for possible people if they never become actual."[4] This is a purely defensive point and will not concern us much here as it is not in contention. Parfit puts his second point in two ways:

> Must I claim that, while it benefited me to have had my life saved *just after* it started, it did not benefit me to have had it started? I can defensibly deny this claim . . . .
>
> if it benefited me to have had my life saved just after it started, I am not forced to deny that it benefited me to have had it started.[5]

Parfit's claim is that the belief that someone whose life is saved is benefited, even if the life is saved just after it started, supports the position that someone whose life is started is also benefited. This claim of support is open to an objection if we adopt Suggestion 1.

Once we have a person whose life we can save, we have a person who we can make better off because of our actions; our actions can improve the life. Being better off, having our life improved, and being benefited, all involve a comparison between what our life is like in a world where the act occurs and what our life is like in a world where it does not. Parfit considers a similar type of comparative criterion which he calls "The Two-State Requirement."[6] As we will see in a moment, this requirement is flawed. Nevertheless, in so far as it has a comparative structure, Parfit's arguments against it are useful tests for Suggestion 1.

Parfit puts forward for consideration the proposal that we should treat similarly the cases of someone who ceases to exist and someone who never exists. He then suggests a possible reply to the proposal on behalf of a supporter of the Two-State Requirement.

> It might be replied that, when someone dies, there is a particular person who has ceased to exist. We can refer to this person. In contrast, there are no particular people who never exist. We cannot refer to any such person.[7]

Parfit then makes the following rejoinder:

> This might be a good reply if we were claiming that, in causing people never to exist, we could be harming these people. But we are making a different claim. This is that, in causing someone to exist, we can be benefiting this person. Since this person *does* exist, we can refer to this person when describing the alternative. We know who it is who, in this possible alternative, would never have existed. In the cases that we are considering, there is not the alleged difference between having ceased to exist and never existing. Just as we refer to the person who might now have ceased to exist, we can refer to the person who might never have existed. We have not been shown why, in applying the Two-State Requirement, we should not treat these two states in the same way.[8]

Parfit is claiming that in causing someone to exist, we can be benefiting the person. Parfit's claim does not lack a referent. Anyone denying that it does would be mistaken. But someone who claims that there is *no entity which is benefited* does not have to make this mistake. The *existing* person did not benefit by the procreative act *and* there is *no* entity which did so. The person who exists is not an entity which benefited from the procreative act: the person *is not better off in the actual than in the alternative world which does not contain the act*. There is no relevant entity which can be used for counterfactual comparison. A *general* lack of reference then does not cause the trouble for Parfit's position if we adopt Suggestion 1. The trouble is due to *the lack of any moral entity that benefited from the act.*

I am making two claims here. The first is that the person who exists is not an entity which benefited from the procreative act because there is no world with that person and without *c* which can be used for the critical purpose of comparison. The second claim is not directly related to the question which Parfit is addressing. It is helpful in establishing the more general point that not only does the person who is caused to exist not benefit, but there is *no* entity which is benefited by the causal action except perhaps incidentally. For suppose we could turn some entity into a person—say we could inject a plant with a drug to make it turn into a person. Even in this case the plant does not benefit, in the moral sense, from our action even though we have a clearly identifiable pre-existing entity and even though we may be able to do something to the plant to benefit the future person.[9] It may even be the case that we can counterfactually refer to people who never existed, as we might with "the person who would have resulted if the couple had

had intercourse at time t." But this entity would not be one which would have benefited from intercourse. A general lack of reference then is not the problem, but the lack of an entity *which actually benefited from the action*. Persons, dogs, cats and other animals are the type of entities that can benefit, morally speaking, from actions. Non-existent people are not. They are not persons we can do good or ill by. In procreating we do not begin with someone who first of all does not exist, and then have sexual intercourse so that the person is better off because now that person exists.

3.

Let us look more closely at the claim that the person who exists is not an entity which benefited from the procreative act and examine Parfit's objections to the Two-State Requirement to see if they are applicable to Suggestion 1. According to the Two-State Requirement: "We benefit someone only if we cause him to be better off than he would otherwise at that time have been."[10] Parfit argues:

> If someone now exists, and has a life worth living, is he better off than he would now be if he had died, and ceased to exist? Suppose that we answer Yes. In applying the Two-State Requirement, we count having ceased to exist as a state in which someone can be worse off. Why can we not claim the same about never existing? Why can we not claim that, if someone now exists, with a life worth living, he is better off than he would be if he never existed? It is true that *never existing* is not an ordinary state. But nor is *having ceased to exist*.[11]

Parfit then goes on to ask what happens if we answer No to his first question.

> The defender of the Two-State Requirement might next change his view about the state of being dead, or having ceased to exist. He might claim that this is not a state in which someone can be worse off. He can then claim the same about never existing.
>
> With this revision, the Two-State Requirement becomes too strong. It implies that saving someone's life cannot benefit this person, since the person saved is not better off than he would have been if he had ceased to exist.[12]

Parfit's questions are confused and this infects his statement and treatment of the Two-State Requirement. His first question begins the confusion when he asks whether the saved person, let us call him Peter, is better off than he *now* would be if he had died. But there is no sense in asking how a person *now* would be if he had died. The person, if he had died, would now no longer exist. Parfit carries this confusion into the statement of what might be said by someone who answers Yes to his question. He says "In applying the Two-State Requirement we count having ceased to exist as a state in which someone can be worse off."[13] But why would we want to count *having ceased to exist* as a *state*? We do not want to say "Peter is in a bad way. He is in the state of not existing." Peter, if he no longer exists, is in no state *at all* now.

This view catches us on the other horn of Parfit's dilemma because it is tantamount to the view that having ceased to exist is not a state in which someone can be worse off. But this is a quite reasonable position to hold. Having ceased to exist is not a state in which someone can be worse off. It is not a state which someone can be *in* at all. However, in holding this view we do not get into the trouble that Parfit describes. Parfit believes that such a view implies that saving someone's life cannot benefit that person. It is not clear how this follows. If Mary swims out and rescues John, then she has done something which has benefited him. By Suggestion 1 we can determine whether she has benefited him by comparing the world in which she rescued him with the one in which she did not, and asking which world he is better off in. Although there may be many competing views about what makes a person better off, it is not controversial to say, in this case, that John is better off in the world in which Mary rescues him than he is in the world in which Mary does not.

Having ceased to exist is *not* a *state* that anybody is in. When we say that Peter is dead this should be understood in the way it is intended in ordinary discourse, not as a predication of a state to a still existing subject, but as a way of saying that the individual, who was Peter, no longer exists. This is where Parfit goes wrong in his characterization of what someone defending something like the Two-State Requirement would say is bad about death. He suggests that "we count having ceased to exist as a state in which someone can be worse off."[14] But this is a mistaken way of characterizing the situation.

It would be easy to become sidetracked into a discussion of what makes people better or worse off. But there is no reason to believe that the only way we will be able to explain why someone is worse off for not being saved is by saying that after the person has died that person is in a worse off state. Even using simple measures of welfare like preference fulfillment, we can avoid this type of claim. For instance, we can compare the world in which John is saved with the world in which he is not, and say that he is worse off in the world in which he is not saved, because fewer of his preferences are fulfilled in that world. This is how we should understand what is bad about death, since death is not a *state* that some unfortunate person is in.[15] Parfit's mistake in characterizing objections to his position can be traced back to his statement of the Two-State Requirement. He says: "We benefit someone only if we cause him to be better off than he would otherwise at that time have been."[16] Parfit takes the expression "at that time" to require that we compare the state of having ceased to exist with the concomitant present state of the person. This is why he calls the requirement, the Two-*State* Requirement. In his characterization of a person objecting to his position he construes the grammar of the expression "Peter is dead" as a comment on the *present state* of Peter. But it is not. We are predicating something of a person who lived in the past. We understand from the statement that some event occurred which caused Peter to die.

Understanding this allows us to generate the moral injunctions against premature death that we want. A person who is killed, or not saved, will normally fail to have preferences for a longer life fulfilled. We can compare the life under the scenario in which the person is saved against the one in which the person is not saved and say that the life is worse when it is not saved because fewer preferences are fulfilled. In effect, we can do everything we want to do without having to apply certain current predicates to non-existent people. When death is involved we need to remember to be careful in ascribing some predicates. Death has the distinctive quality of annihilating subjects.

4.

Parfit gives an alternative analysis of what it is to benefit someone. He says:

> The objectors might now turn to *The Full Comparative Requirement*: We benefit someone only if we do what will be better for him . . . .
>
> Because it covers saving life, the Full Comparative Requirement is more plausible than the stronger form of the Two-State Requirement. But if we can relax the latter, in both of our special cases, it may be defensible to relax the former, in the case of giving life.[17]

Unfortunately, The Full Comparative Requirement leaves unclear the status of the claim that causing people to exist benefits them because the requirement is ambiguous between readings like Suggestion 1 and Suggestion 2. However, it appears, because of his suggestion about relaxing it, that Parfit believes The Full Comparative Requirement does not support the claim. But his strategy here will be unacceptable to anyone who adopts Suggestion 1. If Suggestion 1 is correct, then it is only because the Two-State Requirement is stated and interpreted in an implausible way that anyone might find a need to relax it. Supporters of Suggestion 1 can claim that a similar but more plausible requirement will not need relaxation, and does not support the conclusion that causing people to exist benefits them. So Parfit cannot support the claim against supporters of Suggestion 1 in this fashion.

Let us consider Parfit's third point. Parfit's summarizes it as follows:

> Third, causing someone to exist is clearly a special case. It cannot be proved that this cannot be a benefit because it lacks some feature shared by all other benefits. This argument begs the question. Since this is a special case, it may be an exception to some general rule. Appealing to some general rule simply assumes that there cannot be an exception.[18]

Parfit's third point does not help his position. Parfit supports his claim of exception by drawing an analogy with relaxing the Two-State Requirement. But the relaxing is not necessary when a more plausible requirement is used. Hence this does not support Parfit's position. Furthermore, while some types of exception to the rule are acceptable, others are not. If Suggestion 1 is the correct criterion for determining benefit, it should not admit of exceptions. If it is not, it should be withdrawn and replaced by something better. To say that this suggestion is correct but that we are going to add on an extra meaning to the term "benefit" while still retaining its force in moral discourse would be less acceptable. This is reminiscent of discussions which occasionally crop up about predicates applying to God. God is said to be a special case. That, in itself, is reasonable enough. But it is not reasonable when it is used to justify uses of a term such as "good" which do not retain the crucial features that we associate with the term. In such cases, writers are not using the term to refer to behavior that the rest of us call good. In the case at hand I am suggesting that Parfit is at liberty to give an additional meaning to the term "benefit" but that he will then have to give an additional *argument* for why the new use of the term has any moral force.

5.

I have tried to show that we can adopt Suggestion 1 and support a conclusion contrary to Parfit's without getting into the troubles he describes. I have not argued that Suggestion 1 is right or that it is better than Suggestion 2. Which is the more plausible suggestion for determining whether an act is a benefit for someone, Suggestion 1 or 2? Our concept of benefit may not be well-formed and robust enough to decide between them, though I have some preference for Suggestion 1. When we talk about benefiting a person, I think we do believe it is important to compare the person's life between the two different situations. We can see this tendency even in Parfit. For instance, he asks rhetorically at one point: "Why can we not claim that, if someone now exists, with a life worth living, he is better off than he would be if he never existed?"[19] We can see in the expression "than *he would be* if he never existed" the tendency actually to compare how a person *would be* under the alternative scenario of never existing. But asserting things about how people *would be* if they had never existed is a misguided activity. We can see in Parfit's use of this expression, how natural it is to do this when considering the question of benefit. Suggestion 1 captures the intuition. Because we cannot meaningfully make the comparison in the case of causing to exist, we have a good reason to say that no benefit is present.

I have not provided a knock-down argument. The argument captures an intuition, avoids certain awkward claims, generates the normal moral claims we want, and avoids the moral claims we do not want. But at this point it may be wise to admit that conceptual analysis may not give us a definitive answer. My treatment of Parfit's third point may have been too unsympathetic. His suggestion may not have been to add an extra meaning to the term "benefit" but that the term itself is vague. Most moral categories have a degree of vagueness inherent in them. One of the things I have tried to show is that Parfit is mistaken in believing that we need to have an extended notion of benefit to explain adequately other areas like killing and saving. But these points do not directly address the question of benefit by creating. Apart from reasons of parsimony, can other reasons be given for resisting this extended use? I think so.

Because the conceptual analysis may not give us a definitive answer on the question of benefit in the case of causing to exist, we could try exploring the consequences of adopting the extended notion of benefit and hence the analysis of Suggestion 2. If we adopt the extended notion of benefit then we will be committed to the view that contingent future preferences of future persons for existence provide us with a *prima facie* reason to create them. Parfit seems to entertain this as a possibility, given his comment on the possible implications of his view for population policy. This is, on the face of it, an implausible moral view requiring strong independent reasons, or reasons of consistency, for its adoption. None of the commonly held beliefs about our obligation to continue the human race require this moral premise. Even total utilitarians, who hold that we ought to increase the total number of people in order to increase the total level of utility in the world, do not depend on this moral premise for their argument.[20] We have yet to find any plausible moral views which require us to extend our notion of benefit in a way that implies a *prima* facie obligation to benefit people by creating them.[21]

Of course, this implication could be resisted if we remove any moral force from Parfit's extended use of "benefit." Normally we suppose that if an action benefits someone then that gives us some *prima facie,* often easily defeasible reason for performing the action. To block the moral implication, we would have to sever all moral force from certain claims of benefit with respect to persons. This is a significant departure from normal usage, and hence another reason to resist the extension of the term "benefit" to this type of case.

Finally, by denying Parfit's extended use of the term "benefit," we do not rule out the use of other positive ways of describing creation acts. I can certainly be *glad* that my parents created me. And all the love and care they have given me is correctly described as a benefit. So it is not as if we are left dumb in these important areas by giving up the option of extending the use of the term "benefit."

6.

It may be objected that Suggestion 1 cannot support obligations which we now have to people who will only exist in the future and hence, that it will be necessary to adopt something like Suggestion 2 to explain these obligations we have towards future generations. But note that under Suggestion 1, a person can certainly act to benefit people who will only exist in the future. If Jones opens up a trust account for his granddaughter, then if and when she comes into existence, it can be truly said of Jones that he acted to benefit her. We can say of his granddaughter that she is better off in a world where Jones opened up the trust account than she would have been in a world in which he did not. On more substantial issues like the environment, we not only *can* act to benefit future people, we have *an obligation* to do so.

But there is an interesting variation on this example, which does cause problems for Suggestion 1.[22] Suppose a person, call him Arthur, had some money to spare and decided to put that money into a trust account for his future granddaughter. Suppose also that as a result of opening this account, Arthur gained a greatly increased interest in sex and that it is only because of this that he actually comes to have a granddaughter. Did the opening of the account benefit the granddaughter? I think the intuitive answer is that it did. Suggestion 1, however, implies that it did not. In the world in which Arthur does not open the account, the granddaughter does not exist and so there is no relevant entity for comparison. Suggestion 2 gives the answer that there is a benefit. So it looks as though Suggestion 2 gives the answer which is more in line with our intuitions. However, I think there is a reply which can be made here in support of Suggestion 1.

Why do we intuitively believe that Arthur benefited his granddaughter? We make the comparison in our minds between the situation in which the granddaughter does not have a trust account compared with the situation in which she does have one. This has important implications for the relevant possible worlds to use for comparison. The relevant world is a world where the causal chain is different. It is a world where the trust account is not opened but where the granddaughter nevertheless exists, rather than a world where the trust account is not opened and this causes the granddaughter not to exist. The same point about determining the relevant possible worlds can also be seen for cases of harm. Suppose Arthur does not use the extra money to open a trust account but instead uses it to purchase a forty-year time delay bomb which he plants in his backyard. Planting it has the strange effect of increasing Arthur's sex drive, and the ensuing causal change leads to the birth of his granddaughter who is then maimed by the backyard bomb. The suggestion is that the relevant world to look at when considering the question of harm is the one where the granddaughter exists but the bomb does not.[23]

If this intuition is correct, then it does not support Suggestion 2. In fact, it appears to be against the whole motivation of that suggestion, since Suggestion 2 does not require a comparison to be made between the alternative situations of the person. Instead, the intuition seems to be in the spirit of Suggestion 1, which requires comparisons, though the exact wording of Suggestion 1 will require some specification of which worlds are relevant for comparison.

7.

I have tried throughout to show that, *pace* Parfit, we can consistently explain certain normal moral obligations without at the same time affirming a *prima facie* obligation to benefit future people by creating them. My point has not been to show that no such obligation exists, though hopefully the discussion has made the task of showing that a little easier.[24]

Notes

1. Derek Parfit, *Reasons and Persons* (Oxford: Oxford University Press, 1984), p. 487.

2. *Ibid.*

3. For a discussion of this moral sense of benefit and of what type of entities can be benefited see Paul Bassen, "Present Stakes and Future Prospects: The Status of Early Abortion," *Philosophy and Public Affairs*, 11 (1982), pp. 314-337.

4. Parfit, *Reasons and Persons*, p. 490.

5. *Ibid.*, pp. 489-490.

6. *Ibid.*, p. 487.

7. *Ibid.*, p. 488.

8. Ibid.

9. For interesting related discussions of potentiality see Michael Tooley, *Abortion and Infanticide* (Oxford: Oxford University Press, 1983), chs. 6 and 7; and Bassen, "Present Stakes and Future Prospects."

10. Parfit, *Reasons and Persons*, p. 487.

11. *Ibid.*, pp. 487-488.

12. *Ibid.*, p. 488.

13. *Ibid.*, p. 487.

14. *Ibid.*

15. Many proposals for explaining the harm of death can be found in the collection *The Metaphysics of Death*, John Martin Fischer, ed. (Stanford, Cal.: Stanford University Press, 1993). In particular, see Fred Feldman, "Some Puzzles About the Evil of Death," which uses a comparative view to explain the harm of death.

16. Parfit, *Reasons and Persons*, p. 487.

17. *Ibid.*, pp. 488-489.

18. *Ibid.*, p. 490.

19. *Ibid.*, p. 487.

20. For an argument along these lines see William Anglin, "The Repugnant Conclusion," *Canadian Journal of Philosophy*, 7 (1977), pp. 745-755. For a critical reply to Anglin's argument see Peter Singer, "Anglin on the Obligation to Create Extra People," *Canadian Journal of Philosophy*, 8 (1978), pp. 583-585.

21. James Sterba, "Abortion, Distant Peoples, and Future Generations," *Journal of Philosophy*, 77 (1980), pp. 424-440, appears to be an exception to this claim. My argument here also applies to Sterba's claims about benefiting future people and hence to his discussion of the right to be born.

22. This variation on my example was suggested to me by André Gallois.

23. On the topic of the intransitivity of certain counterfactuals and the need to go farther than the closest possible world to find the most relevant possible worlds see David

Lewis, *Counterfactuals* (Cambridge, Mass.: Harvard University Press, 1973), pp. 33-36.

24. I am grateful to Chin Liew Ten, André Gallois, Frank Jackson, David Lewis, Tom Magnell, and Derek Parfit for their comments on an earlier version of this chapter. I would also like to thank the Fulbright Foundation and the Philosophy Departments at Princeton University, City University of New York Graduate Center, and University of Queensland for providing funding and facilities for me to undertake research for this chapter.

Fourteen

FORGIVENESS, MORAL REASSESSMENT, AND RECONCILIATION

Uma Narayan

1. Varieties of Moral Reassessment of Emotions

I wish to start with the suggestion that it is illuminating to understand forgiveness as *one* important facet of our abilities to morally re-evaluate the way we feel about other persons, and to attempt to change our feelings in the light of such re-evaluation. It would seem that all our conscious feelings are possible objects of such reassessment and change. Although I shall focus on forgiving another, I do believe one can forgive oneself, and suspect that much of what I say about forgiving another applies to self-forgiveness. Moral re-evaluations of our feelings can proceed along at least three different paths. First, we reassess *whether what we thought we felt toward X was in fact what we felt toward X*. Our re-assessment might lead us to conclude that we were mistaken in our understanding of the nature of our feelings. My dislike of X, which I attributed to her unappealing character, might on reflection turn out to be rooted in my envy of her success. This sort of reassessment is important if we acknowledge that we are often mistaken or self-deceived about our complex feelings toward others, and if we are concerned that our errors do not lead us to an incorrect picture of ourselves, and to unfair, unwise and uncritical ties to others. Second, we may re-evaluate *whether the way we felt towards X was warranted in the first place*. We might thus reassess our respect and admiration for X, when we discover that X is a hypocrite and coward. Our reassessments will strike us as important if we acknowledge that we are often mistaken in our reading of others, deceived by the faces they present to us, or by our desires that they be the sort of persons they are not. Third, we may reassess *whether it is appropriate to continue to feel toward X what was once appropriate to feel toward X*. We may discover that our feelings, though once warranted, are no longer so. For instance, though we might once have had good reason to love X, the sort of person X has since become may no longer warrant our continuing to love X. Such reassessments are important if we wish to react to changes in ourselves and others with discernment and sensitivity, and do not wish to be frozen in responses that no longer ethically make the sense they may once have made. I am not unaware that it is possible to love someone passionately without much that counts as a reason, and that love might be a response both to ethical qualities of a person, and qualities that make them engaging persons. The loss of either sorts of qualities might lead to a reassessment of one's continuing to feel love toward the person. Only reassessments based on changes in the *ethical* qualities of the person loved would constitute a moral re-evaluation of this third sort. Forgiving another is *one* particular form of this third sort of moral reassessment of our feelings. It consists of coming to feel differently toward X, because a reassessment of our feelings leads us to see that it is no longer appropriate to feel negatively towards X in a way that was formerly appropriate. I see forgiveness as a process, and the agent as "having forgiven" only at the successful culmination of this process. Until then, I would prefer to describe the agent as "attempting to forgive." What are the feelings whose reassessment and change constitutes forgiveness?

2. What Emotions Are Reassessed in Forgiveness?

The feelings that are reassessed and overcome in forgiveness are negative feelings that one felt justified in having towards another, due to a sense of having been *personally affected* by her wrongdoing. So arbitrary anger, unconnected to being wronged, and moral anger at wrongs to unconnected third parties are not the sorts of feelings reassessed in forgiveness. What Jeffrie Murphy terms "resentment"—a sense of justified anger—is probably one of the commonest negative feelings toward another who we believe to have wronged us.[1] Forms of moral anger at such individuals might include scorn, contempt, hatred, malice, and wrath.[2]

I shall focus on cases of forgiveness where someone has in fact been wronged, and where negative feelings are in fact justified. Of course, I might be mistaken in my belief that X wronged me, and resent X without justification. If, on discovering my mistake, I cease to resent X, I have not *forgiven* X. I may also engage in forgiving X while mistakenly believing her to be a wrongdoer. If I discover my mistake later, I would be inclined to say "I did forgive X, but now realize I had nothing to forgive her for." I do not think the negative feelings we overcome in forgiveness need necessarily be forms of moral *anger*. We may, for instance, react to being wronged with a sense of hurt. Though our emotional focus is on what we have suffered, there often remains a sense of the suffering being *due* to a wrong. We feel hurt *by* the wrongdoer's conduct, and have a sense of *grievance* about being hurt. In *some* such hurt responses to being wronged, anger may not phenomenologically *feel* like a component of our feelings. I am inclined to think that when we reassess such non-angry but hurt feelings that involve a sense of grievance, and overcomes them, and where this is tied to a change in our feelings towards a wrongdoer, we have instances of forgiveness. I do not wish to suggest that one could not feel both hurt and angry. I merely wish to focus on cases where one may feel hurt without *feeling* angry, and to suggest that some cases of overcoming such feelings constitute forgiveness. I do not think forgiveness requires overcoming *all* negative feelings toward a wrongdoer, but only those negative feelings that constitute *a sense of grievance* against the wrongdoer.[3] Thus, negative feelings that were not rooted in being wronged, say, prior dislike or mild contempt for the person, may well remain in the aftermath of forgiveness. A reduction in previous esteem, trust or affection for someone is also compatible with having forgiven that person. We may surely forgive a lover for a betrayal while no longer being able to love him. I think we set too high a standard for what can count as forgiveness, if we require that our feelings toward the wrongdoer be completely unaffected by the misdeed. What forgiveness requires is the ability to set aside our vivid sense of grievance toward the wrongdoer, which is not the same thing as feeling as if the wrong had never in fact happened.

3. What Sorts of Wrong Might We Forgive?

Conduct that culpably violates one's own rights seems to be the paradigmatic type of wrong one might forgive. I have argued that the wrongs one forgives must have a personal edge or stake, and wrongs other than the violations of our rights have this character. For instance, we are personally affected by wrongs to those close to us. While I lack the standing to forgive X for the wrong he did to my daughter, I might well forgive him for the indirect wrong he did to me in wronging her. We might also feel a personal stake in wrongs to third parties we are not emotionally close to, in institutional contexts where we feel a strong link to the institution. I might react with personal moral anger to one colleague's mistreatment of another, because I feel a personal stake in how our department functions as an institution, and might later forgive the colleague. We may react with personal anger to wrongs to others that are predicated on shared identities. A racist or sexist remark, pertaining to an identity I share, may be something I have a personal negative reaction to even if it is addressed to another person, and I may later forgive the wrongdoer for it. We can also feel justifiably personally wronged by breaches of "reasonable expectations" that do not constitute rights violations. We may have expectations of family members, friends and lovers, that are mutually recognized as reasonable, but which the parties would not characterize in terms of rights. Whether any particular expectation is reasonable may depend on the nature of the relationship and the understanding of the parties. Thus, I might expect friends to remember my birthday, keep my confidences, and assist me when I really need help, and feel wronged when these expectations are unmet. People do ask forgiveness for breaching such expectations, and receive forgiveness for them.

4. What Are Some Reasons for Reassessment in Forgiving?

My analysis of forgiveness thus far is deeply influenced by and sympathetic to Jeffrie Murphy's analysis of forgiveness as the overcoming of justified resentment. Negative feelings towards the wrongdoer *are* often morally appropriate *in the first place*. I share Murphy's analysis that such feelings of justified resentment are often tied to "certain values of the self," most importantly to our having self-respect.[4] I am also sympathetic to Murphy's insistence that reasons for forgiveness be "moral reasons."[5] Overcoming negative feelings towards a wrongdoer for purely selfish reasons, such as a desire to bask in a sense of moral superiority, arguably do not constitute cases of forgiveness. However, I have some differences with Murphy in that I do not think that *all* broadly moral reasons for overcoming negative feelings toward a wrongdoer constitute cases of forgiveness. There are cases where we might strive to feel differently because we perceive our feelings to be a nuisance, as something that impedes our functioning comfortably in ways that are valuable to us. My resentment at X might cause me to be inattentive to my students, or unkind to my pets. I might strive to overcome my resentment for these reasons, where my concerns seem arguably moral concerns. However, I am inclined to argue that the change in my negative feelings toward X, when motivated by these sorts of moral concerns, do not constitute a case of forgiveness. We do not have an instance of forgiveness in such cases because the reasons for overcoming resentment, albeit moral, are too far removed from the wrongdoer or the wrong. Reasons for forgiveness must, it seems, not only be moral reasons that reflect a reassessment of *continuing* with negative feelings, but reasons that bear directly on the wrongdoer or the wrong. Forgiveness must be based on the recognition that our negative feelings toward the wrongdoer are *no longer appropriate responses to having been wronged*. It must not merely be based on the recognition that the negative feelings are *inconvenient*, or impediments to completely *ulterior normative ends*. On my analysis, if Jane overcame her resentment at X merely on the grounds that it would help her avoid eternal damnation, she would have overcome her resentment, but not really *forgiven* X. I would like to suggest that reasons for forgiveness can be classified into four types. They can involve (1) a reassessment of the wrongdoer, (2) a reassessment of our relationship to the wrongdoer, (3) a reassessment of the wrong, and (4) a reassessment of our reactions to the wrong. I do not wish this classification to suggest that these reasons are neatly separable, since they often make reference to each other. I see the classification as helping to locate various foci of moral reassessment, where the re-evaluation might be primarily situated in different cases of forgiveness. I will explore cases of forgiveness based on these four different types of reasons.

Let me start with cases where forgiveness is primarily based on a *reassessment of the wrongdoer*. After the heat of moral anger has passed, we might recognize that the wrongdoer, though she did wrong us, is *genuinely not a bad person overall*. Her misconduct might come to seem only a minor diminution of her overall moral stature, and forgiveness may seem appropriate when faced with this recognition. To continue to feel negatively may seem to reflect an inability to respond with discernment to the whole person. Reassessment of the wrongdoer might also proceed from her asking for forgiveness, or because we know that she has sincerely repented. Apology and repentance confirm that the wrongdoer's moral machinery is working, and reveal her to be capable of moral reflection and change. It shows her to be a person who wishes to repudiate her immoral conduct. These features provide reasons to change our negative feelings in return. Forgiving a wrongdoer may sometimes involve not a moral reassessment of her *character*, but a reassessment of her current state of being. If we attend to the fact that a person who wronged us when she was powerful is now frail, powerless, defeated by life, and isolated by her incapacity to treat others well, it would be genuinely inappropriate to continue resenting her. She is, in some sense, no longer the person who wronged us, and no longer seems an appropriate target of our grievance. Perhaps it is something like compassion that moves us to forgive in such cases. Reasons for forgiveness may involve a reassessment of our relationship to the wrongdoer. On reflection, we may be moved by our history of past connection to the wrongdoer—previous kindness, mutual affection, shared good times. We are morally responsive when we are moved by a sense of the richness of our *past* ties to the wrongdoer, and led to overcome our sense of grievance on this account. Forgiveness may also be based on the *current* nature and ongoing value of the relationship we have with the wrongdoer. We might recognize that we are best at hurting those close to us, that rich and complex relationships create their own tensions, and provide ample scope for wronging each other. We may recognize the value and joy of the wrongdoer's presence in our life despite the wrong, and that the significance of our ties overflow the wrong done. I think we are often moved to forgiveness on these grounds. While forgiveness may help us to sustain our love for others who wrong us, our love for them might also assist our abilities to forgive them. Reasons for forgiveness might be provided by a *reassessment of the wrong* done to us. We might continue to perceive the conduct as wrong, but come to see it as a different kind of wrong, one more deserving of forgiveness. This may sometimes involve a reassessment of the offender's motives. If we recognize that the wrong was motivated by a misplaced paternalism, a concern for our good, albeit a misguided concern, we see the conduct as well as the actor in a more forgivable light. If one's reassessment leads one to conclude that the act was not really a wrong, or that the offender was totally not culpable, one does not forgive. There is another form that reassessments of the wrong might take. Over time, we might realize that the wrong has had beneficial consequences for us, even though unintended by the wrongdoer. A boss's mistreatment might have led one to find a better job; a lover's betrayal might have led to a more compatible relationship. The recognition of such unintended benefits enables us to see the wrong in a different light, and to feel more magnanimous toward what happened since we are not as deeply injured by it any more, and it might lead us to reassess and overcome our negative feelings toward the wrongdoer. Reasons for forgiveness may be based on a reassessment of *our emotional response to being wronged*. We might retrospectively conclude that we overreacted to a minor wrong, and the overreaction might itself constitute a reason for now letting the grievance go. We might be moved to forgive by the recognition that we have held a grudge too long, and because we do not wish to become the sort of morally self-righteous person we would be, if we could not forgive. Holding on to resentments for long periods may well strike us as a character defect in ourselves, an excessive preoccupation with our wrongs, a form of moral narcissism we wish to avoid.[6]

My account suggests that we might have a *variety* of morally appropriate reasons for forgiving a wrongdoer. I do not subscribe to the view that repentance on the part of the wrongdoer constitutes the only morally acceptable reason for forgiving her, or that forgiveness amounts to condoning the wrongdoer in the absence of repentance.[7] Many of my examples make no reference to the wrongdoer's repentance, but the agents are not involved in condonation, since they do not change their judgment that the offender acted wrongly, or retract the judgment that negative feelings toward her were once appropriate. Nor am I inclined to believe that forgiving others on the basis of reasons other than their repentance is incompatible with self-respect. The agents in my examples show sensitivity and discernment with regard to a variety of reasons for reassessing their negative feelings toward an offender, none of which seem necessarily tied to servility or a lack of self-respect. Requiring repentance as a precondition for being able to forgive the wrongdoer in a manner compatible with self-respect is not only harsh and misguided, but stingily insensitive to the rich variety of moral grounds life may provide us for reassessing our negative feelings toward those who wrong us. On the other hand, I am not committed to the view that we must always strive to forgive those who wrong us. Recognizing a variety of morally appropriate reasons for forgiving another does not rule out the possibility of cases where none of the reasons for forgiving, of the sort I have described, in fact obtain. Neither am I attracted to the view that wrongdoers have a *right* to be forgiven, even in cases where their repentance and reformed conduct provide the injured party with reasons for reassessing her negative feelings toward the wrongdoer. Failure to forgive, in such cases, should be criticized on the grounds that it indicates insufficient moral discernment and responsiveness, rather than on the grounds that failure to forgive violates a right of the wrongdoer.

5. Forgiveness and Reconciliation

How do I see the nature of the connection between forgiveness and reconciliation? The short answer is that I see it as much more *contingent* than it is often taken to be. While I believe forgiveness often precedes and helps to bring about reconciliation, I do not see forgiveness as *essential* for reconciliation, nor do I see reconciliation as a *necessary* element of forgiveness. Reconciliation, as I understand it, follows upon a breach in an existing valued relationship, a breach that was due to one person being wronged by the other. The breach need not involve a physical separation, but might be constituted by emotional distancing or hostility, an experienced sense of disconnection. When reconciliation occurs, roughly the same sort of valued relationship, or else a different but nonetheless valued relationship is restored between the two parties. By a valued relationship, I mean one that is valued for more than its conveniences, or for purely prudential reasons. The other person, and the ties to that person must also be objects of value. Thus two lovers would be engaging in reconciliation, if following a breach due to one wronging the other, they re-establish their relationship as lovers, or else break as lovers but decide they still wish to be friends. Reconciliation is not a necessary element of forgiveness because we can forgive total strangers who wrong us. There is no question of reconciliation here, since there was no significant prior relationship that was breached. Another reason is that even when we are not averse to a reconciliation after we have forgiven, other factors may impede an actual reconciliation. The wrongdoer may have disappeared from the orbit of our life, swallowed up by death or distance. Actual reconciliation with a former lover might cause what seems like unnecessary tension in a current relationship. While all forgiveness may involve some degree of moral re-acceptance of the wrongdoer, the re-acceptance does not always constitute reconciliation in its full-blooded sense, where an intrinsically valued relationship is restored. That forgiveness is not necessary for reconciliation may strike us as even more counter-intuitive than the claim that reconciliation is not a necessary element of forgiveness. However, I believe it to be true.

Resentment at being wronged might be a serious obstacle to some intimate relationships, but it is not *always* so. It seems characteristic of intimate relationships that minor wrongs can cause minor breaches, and remain resented and unforgiven, even though there is genuine reconciliation, where the relationship is restored and valued by both parties. Relationships between spouses and lovers often vividly demonstrate that resentment and love are compatible. In such cases, it may well be that love secures the reconciliation, despite the existence of resentment. I am further convinced that in many close relationships, minor resentments are part of the grain of the relationship, part of its complex history, and in some strange way a part of what keeps people interested in and involved with each other. Reconciliation in the aftermath of wrongdoing may take yet another form, where resentment is overcome, but where one prefers to characterize what happens as an instance of *resignation* or *acceptance*, rather than as forgiveness. Imagine a woman whose lover is respectful of her rights, not abusive, and values his connection to her, but fails to meet some of her arguably reasonable expectations. He fails to give her much attentive love, is often distracted when he is with her, fails to be warm or discerning in his responses to her presence and her qualities, and is seldom emotionally indulgent. Let us assume they both acknowledge these expectations to be reasonable, but that he never seems able to sustain his efforts in these directions for long. The woman may well feel hurt and resentful for a time, leading to a breach in the relationship. On reflection, she may come to accept that she cares about him despite his limitations, changes her expectations, and restores and values the relationship to him, and no longer resents his failures. This resigned acceptance might lead both to resentment being overcome, and to reconciliation, but it is not a case of forgiveness, since such a resigned acceptance of lowered expectations are not part of forgiveness. Though temperamentally disinclined to such resignation, I must admit that such resigned acceptance might have moral value in *some* cases, and that reconciliation based on such resignation need not *always* be regarded with contempt.

Such examples make me reluctant to suggest too close a link between forgiveness and reconciliation, or to make reconciliation the primary reason we should value forgiveness. I see its primary value as residing in its being an important facet of our capacities for moral reassessments of our feelings, and of our abilities to bring our feelings into line with the reassessments. I do not wish to imply that all acts of forgiveness are unproblematically virtuous or praiseworthy. Our acts of forgiveness may warrant moral criticism if our reassessments are overly hasty, or partial or misguided. I merely wish to set out the sorts of reasons that would constitute reasons for forgiveness, and result in a morally praiseworthy change of feelings, other things being equal. Negative feelings, such as resentment, are often appropriate reactions to being wronged. But reasons for reassessing the appropriateness of continuing with these feelings often develop. Strong negative feelings make it difficult to recognize the existence of reasons or forgiveness, and are sometimes difficult to overcome even in the light of such reasons. Moral agents thus deserve credit for retaining their sensitivity to the presence of these reasons, and for striving to bring their feelings into line with reassessments. Sometimes our negative feelings simply yield when we recognize reasons for no longer feeling them. At other times, our feelings persist despite reasons for change, and we have to work at getting our feelings to change in the light of our reasons.

Forgiveness is also of value to offenders, not only because it may foster reconciliation, but because the capacity in others to forgive gives them reason to strive to be worthy of reassessment. The recognition that our subsequent conduct and responses can provide those we have wronged with reasons to feel differently toward us could foster the repentance and apology that are morally appropriate when we wrong others. It strikes me as curious that we only pick out *some* forms of moral reassessments of our feelings, and name and identify them as virtues. We often continue to love others despite the existence of moral reasons not to do so, and sometimes change our feelings in the light of reassessment based on such reasons. However, we do not seem to have a virtue term for a moral reassessment and change, where ceasing to love is concerned. I am puzzled by such gaps in our moral vocabulary. I suspect that this particular gap is due to a sentimental assessment of an emotion like anger as generally a bad thing, and an emotion like love as generally a good thing. I am unsympathetic to this view, for it seems to me that both emotions can be morally valuable when appropriate, and morally problematic when misplaced. I am inclined to believe that we should have a general moral concern about the appropriateness of our feelings, and not let our assessments of them be handicapped by absences or deficiencies in our moral vocabulary.

Notes

1. Jeffrie G. Murphy and Jean Hampton, *Forgiveness and Mercy* (New York: bridge University Press, 1988), p. 16.

2. For a discussion of forms of moral anger, see Paul Hughes, "Moral Anger and the Concept of Forgiveness," unpublished manuscript, pp. 3-6.

3. I thus disagree with Norvin Richards's analysis in "Forgiveness," *Ethics*, 99 (October 1988), pp. 77-97.

4. See Jeffrie G. Murphy and Jean Hampton, *Forgiveness and Mercy*, pp. 23-24.

5. Murphy says, "my ceasing to resent will not constitute forgiveness unless it is done for a moral reason. Forgiveness is not the overcoming of resentment *simpliciter*, it is rather this: to forego resentment on moral ground," *ibid.*

6. Thus, I agree with Howard McGary that one might have what he calls "self-pertaining reasons" for forgiveness. See his "Forgiveness," *American Philosophical Quarterly*, 26:4 (October 1989), p. 26.

7. I thus disagree with Joram Graf Haber's contention that "In the absence of repentance forgiveness amounts to little more than condonation," in his *Forgiveness* (Savage, Md.: Rowman and Littlefield, 1991), p. 90. I will not undertake to distinguish forgiveness from other things with which it is often confused—justification, excuse, pardon and mercy—since others have done a good job articulating these distinctions. For some of these distinctions, see Murphy and Hampton, *Forgiveness and Mercy*, and Haber, *Forgiveness*.

Fifteen

THE PHOTOGRAPH ON MY MIND

Robert Ginsberg

In moments of distress, I look up from my work and notice a photograph that many years ago I put up on the wall of my mind. It is a picture by William Vandivert of *Life,* made at a Berlin prison within hours of its liberation in April 1945 by American troops. A bitter liberation it was, for the German soldiers decided to kill their captives and flee before the arrival of the liberators.

The photo is of a man. He is dead. A prisoner, he had partially burrowed under the wooden wall or door. The Nazis had put the torch to the building, and the nameless person had tried his best to escape the flames and the captors. The oxygen was consumed. With his last breath he struggled for life—and failed.

This much of the story we can read in the picture. The man appears not to have been burned to death, nor was he bayonetted or shot in trying to escape. His chance to escape was real. He almost made it. Had he been stronger, he might have dug faster, further, and then squeezed his body through. No matter if he broke nails and fingers, or ribs and legs in the process. Life was at stake and freedom within grasp. His hands clawed at the earth. As children, we have all moved earth with our hands. Each of us should be strong enough to dig our way to safety.

But we cannot fault this man for not being stronger after living in a Nazi prison. I have always imagined his setting as a concentration camp with all the dehumanization attendant upon such a realm, though as a prison in Berlin it had to be much milder. Yet the prison realm too may have been designed to disable the humanity of its inmates. Systematic crippling of health, strength, and will may well have been part of the life intended for him there.

The regret, "If only he had more strength!", gives way, as I contemplate the picture in my mind, to the thought, "how admirable that he had this much strength left." For his body did not give up in the last moments. He did as much as a body can to save his life. The hard-packed earth was too much for him. The readiness was there. After what may have been months of cold, malnutrition, illness, and exhaustion, the man gave himself entirely to the physical exertion of lifesaving. Could I have done as much?

"If only there had been a little more time," I think, continuing the narrative of the photo. If the flames had not spread so quickly and robbed the air of its life-giving properties, if the Germans had been slower in their preparations, if the Americans had been quicker in their advance, if.... We are always ready to ask the world for a little more time to avert the death of someone for whom we care. After the fact, everyone can easily see how a few more moments spent in the right way would have prevented someone's regrettable death. Every few moments in our lives, even when we are asleep, are potentially those moments necessary to make the slight change that saves us. This might be the very moment for me—or you.

Yet while we are caught up in living, we rarely can tell which moments are decisive and how we should use them. Am I wasting my time, while my life is at risk, in pursuing these reflections on an image that takes me away from my work? What really is my work? What is it worth to my life? How shall I live this moment?

The prisoner may have been threatened by death each moment in prison. That threat may have been built into the life intended for prisoners. Yet did not this victim dream each moment of survival? Did he not keep alive, over the months, the hope of life? His final actions testify to his unhesitating resolve to seize the moment on behalf of life. Would I be so bold and deft when my time comes?

The soul of the man is visible in his visage. The configuration of the corpse speaks for him as well. The eyes are shut tight, the nostrils flared, the mouth clenched closed, the cheeks still pocketing the last breath, the hand clenched as if bringing in more air, the fingers waiting for the spark of life.

He did not die fighting the flames, giving up the effort to crawl toward freedom. He did not give his last breath to cursing his killers. He did not cry out to the world, lamenting injustice. He did not sit quietly, composing his soul in prayer or images of love. All these last acts would be appropriate, but the chance to preserve life took precedence over them.

He did not give up living so as to make a final gesture toward life. He continued to live, under maximum exertion, until he died. Would I have been able to do the same thing at the end?

Given the organization of Nazi prisons, we must marvel at this man's choice of life. He should have felt crushed; he should have fallen into panic or despair; he should have made a grand gesture and been content to die. These "shoulds" follow from the logic of the system. But he was not content to die. In the end, imprisonment failed. He did not surrender life.

Yet the man died. He failed to save himself, not because of insufficient strength, or lack of a few more moments, or any indecisiveness about how to act. He was defeated by the world of time and space in its human continuum. "So close, so close, . . . " While the photo makes us probe the chances of the man's survival, death has definitively kept him from success.

We may retell the story in many ways, wishing it to become another photograph: the man had hidden a spoon and used it to dig himself out in time. The prisoners were shot, instead of the prison being burned, and he survived his wounds. The flames consumed the structures, but drafts of air replenished the oxygen in his corner. The Americans sent an advance column that caused the German defenders to flee for their own lives, as happened elsewhere.

So close, yet so far. We try our best in imagination to save the man, but the photo insists that he did not make it. Nor through any fault of his. The world just was not right or ripe for him. The photographer has seen this and shown this to us.

The world was not arranged to provide justice to this victim. Being made to live and die in a Nazi prison camp is unjust. That is the presupposition we keep in mind before we see or recall the picture. The concreteness of the image, the individuality of this person drives deeper the bitterness of injustice. The pale, meager body, spotted with soil and straw, lying strained in a shroud-like garment upon the ground, while we stare from above, deepens our sense of loss. He is helpless, and so it seems are we. Between our gazing eyes and his closed ones stretches the infinite distance between life and death.

He did not fail as person. We the living have failed him and many others in the world. Nothing is left for him but burial. Something childlike adheres to his short hair, dirtied face, and tense expression, as if he had been a boy fighting a fatal fever in his sleep. We have let him down. We go on with our work, with our lives. We sleep and we awaken. We may try to bring justice to the world, but here he is in my mind to remind me that the world failed to help him in his dire need. He is the child that we have lost.

Reminded of him, I do not wonder much about who he was. This does not matter to me, though it mattered everything to him. Whoever he was, it comes out the same way. To be told his name, nationality, sexual preference, or what work he did, what family he had, and what place he took in the world might make him more real to us. The worth of such qualities was likely denied him when he was sent to the prison. Yet, if any of these details were filled in, my identification with this unknown person might be diminished. The photographer has not stopped to provide information about his identity. What strikes the photographer's eye, and what strikes my mind, is that this is a human being, an everyman. He could be you or me.

The hero of the picture could be me. I, like him, am male. I was only about eight years old at the time of his death fifty years ago, and I estimate that I am now about thirty years older than he had been. Yet whenever I consult his picture on my mental wall, I find that both of us are ageless. He could have been killed at any age. And at every age, I can remind myself of him. I am reminded by him that at any moment I could become another him.

In my musings I have become him. Suppose, as in one version of my narrative invention, he was only unconscious and was resuscitated by his liberators. Though weak and gasping, he would have quite a story to tell. The only survivor of a Nazi prison, someone marked for death, he concentrated his life's energy on the single aim of saving himself. Confusion, rapture, exhaustion, doubt, and sorrow would alternate. Long would be his rehabilitation. Nazi prisons and concentration camps are carried within the hearts of those who manage to survive them. Never do they really escape, for to the survivors comes the guilt of having survived.

But the guilt, remorse, and nightmarish memories go into the bundle of life for which he would have successfully struggled. Imagine, instead, the positive life our hero would have led upon his recovery. So many things in life to do. Such a world to take in and to work upon. So much love to be sought and found. Would he have returned to a career or exercised his freedom to start a fresh one? Would he have chosen to be a writer and teacher, as I have? Would he place his experience in the prison at the center of his life's work or would he pursue some other path unconnected with this experience? Would he not enjoy the simple pleasures of life, such as walking in a garden, more than those of us who had not lived a season in hell and escaped by the skin of our teeth? Would not this survivor wish to drink deeply of every form of fulfillment appropriate to a human being? Life, once redeemed, would be treasured for its fullness. Each breath that he took would be priceless.

Such a life could not be dull. Imagine the vivacity of the man, the joyous energy of his activity. He would not waste time. He would be no whiner. He would know that now is the time for living.

But he would not be a self-centered pleasure seeker. He would live with heightened sensitivity to suffering and oppression. He would know from experience that everyone else in the world could become subject to the same situation in which he found himself. In his heart, he would be present with them, just as I have been trying to be present with him. When political prisons and concentration camps are being filled anywhere in the world, he would vigorously work to liberate them, offering just such a saving hand as was extended to him.

Whatever the man's commitments might be in matters of religion, he would be recognized as someone responsive to the sacredness of human life. A pious goodness would spring from the person rather than just a set of doctrines. He would be thought of as blessed, for, unlike most of us whose lives have not been threatened, he would have come back from the edge of dehumanization and pointless death to know the value of human life.

Imagine him walking into a room in which we sit, heavily laden with our disappointments, complaining of our physical ailments, the lack of time, the lack of appreciation for our contributions to the world, the injustice of the world, and the pervasiveness of inhumanity. With infectious exuberance he proclaims:

> As long as you breathe you are alive! As long as you are alive there is hope. Not enough time? Now is the time of your lives! Get up and do something with the world while you can. Don't give up because the world is unjust. Let that injustice be the stimulus for your action in the world. Do not allow inhumanity to triumph because your humanity is tired. Try harder!
>
> Do not count yourself out before you have made every effort. Do not think you have made every effort until you are dead. How can you be disheartened when others suffer so much more? How can you consider yourself weak when you have so much more at your command than others? You should be ashamed of being depressed, considering all that you have.
>
> The history of humanity has ever been a sad story, but we would have had no history if not for those who opposed the odds and acted for the best. You have escaped the fate of millions of victims who suffered on behalf of humanity. You live and are free. Listen to their call within your heart and honor them by your action. Where millions, perhaps billions, failed, you are their second chance.
>
> Therefore choose life. Get up and live. Go out and save the world. Thereby save your soul. The only thing you have to lose is your life. And that you must lose sooner or later. So celebrate life now!

So he would have spoken. He would have gotten us up out of our chairs and back to work, back to the world. He would make me cease my whining; I would laugh off my petty complaints. The soundness of his message is a tonic for depression and despair.

His very example would be the clincher. What are my sufferings compared to his? How can I be so impoverished in hope when reminded of his readiness? How could I go on punishing myself with, "I lack tools, funds, recognition, time, assistance, . . ." when he had enough to save himself for a full life? His survival is the proof of his message.

But he did not survive. He cannot enter this room and give such a speech, though I have been drafting it for him over the decades. He is not at hand to gingerly chastise us for backsliding and to cheerfully encourage us to live fully.

He did not live fully. He tried, but he lost. This is a hero who has been deprived of his adventures. To no one would he tell his story. No one will hear the lesson that he learned. His life was taken away, like millions of others, in silent anonymity. All that he left us are photographs.

Does his absence negate his message? That is the question I must consider as philosopher. If his story has no happy ending, what of mine? If he is lost to the world, who can encourage me? These are the questions I must consider as a human being.

While my imagination plays at making him survive, the photo insists on the inescapable fact of his death. The photo has the illusion of being real. I experienced it primarily not as visual arrangement but as reality encountered. It is no longer a print on a page but an image in my soul. Here is the final injustice of life: a person with enormous potentialities for full human life is unexpectedly and undeservedly turned into a corpse. The loss is irreversible. The victim cannot be compensated for the supreme injustice he has suffered.

The finality of the event is stamped upon the photo of our would-be hero. The warm body lies inert upon the earth. Dead, dead, dead! insists the image, whichever way our revivifying imagination tries to turn. We are too late. He lost the life that should have been his after prison, after the war. For this loss we are inconsolable. We have lost the example that his life would have afforded us afterwards. The photo, it seems, reminds us of our despair.

Each time that I look at it in mind, I see that he did not make it. He could never make the speech to anyone about life being worth living. But though he did not live that life, I have. Though he could not make that speech, I have. I have made it to you on behalf of him and me. I have lived in place of him.

The moment that I met him through the photo, sometime in my youth, probably as a child, for my family subscribed to *Life,* I sensed that I had luckily escaped his fate and that I could lead the life that would have been his. My life, then, has been *our* life. Mine together with his has had a greater chance of fulfillment than his alone would have had.

Had he survived, he would have needed a long recuperation. I have not yet been locked up in political prisons or concentration camps; I have not had to claw my way away from suffocating death. He might have had nothing with which to start over: no family, no home, no job, no money. He would have become a person without a context, whereas I grew up within the stability of loving family, harmonious community, and reliable institutions. I should be ashamed for not doing as well as he might have done. I silence my complaints about the many little things being too hard or not going my way. Would he bother to complain about such matters after what he had gone through? These questions that keep rising up are my lifetime dialogue with his photo.

I have led our life—his and mine—for us, knowing that I have considerable freedom of choice. I may change the direction of my life. I can try to change one career or role or mission for another. No danger in that. I am not a prisoner in life. Freedom is exhilarating. Choice is self-confirming. At times I cannot make up my mind, even about so trivial a matter as what flavor of ice cream to order. I enjoy that perplexity for my sake—and for his sake. Oh, to be alive and to face such difficulties! I laugh and move ahead.

I also seem to share with him the times of bitterness and discouragement, for these bad feelings are part of a fully-rounded human life. After a while, I shrug them off and return to affirmation. For his sake, and mine, I make it a rule never to be depressed more than eight days a week.

I live my life, then, as if it were a miraculous second chance. I am enjoying a life that could have been snuffed out in a moment decades ago. This life I lead has been denied to millions. But what is so special about me? I am no better than those millions; I have no greater right than they do. Only by a quirk were they the victims and I left free: because I was born on this shore rather than the other, because the evil happened then rather than now. In another country and another time. The differences are fortuitous. It could happen here. This year. The unassailable case made by the photo is that any one of us could be lying there, including me.

My Jewishness is a link with the fate of the unknown victim, for had I been in Europe, even as a seven-year old, I would be lying there on the ground, or more probably, lying in a bucket of ashes. You could be looking at my picture, while I would have missed so much of the life that I have had. How absurd to deny my life for being Jewish. Yet I do not make much of my Jewishness. How foolish to be killed because someone else wishes to make much of anyone's Jewishness. Naziism reorganized the world with the Jews as its chosen people—chosen for extermination. The crime did not consist in doing something wrong but in merely being someone undesirable: an ontological condemnation.

My life in America and France has been a safe one in which to be a Jew or not to be a Jew has not been a question of life and death. I have had the privilege of being known as a Jew, if I wished to be so known, but of not being required to identify my Jewishness.

The roots of anti-Semitism may send forth new shoots at any time and any place. The defeat of Nazi Germany did not defeat anti-Semitism. We have witnessed several systematic outbreaks of this form of evil since then. As a Jew, I may have a sensitive ear to listen in the night for the trucks being sent to cart us away. A Jew knows that the world goes after Jews. When the outbreak engulfs me, will I waver in puzzlement and distress or leap forward to save life?

As I muse about the picture, that I am a Jew is not essential. Nor does it matter if my hero were Jewish. He most likely was not. In 1945, Jews in Germany would not have been so lucky as to live in a Berlin prison. But you do not have to be Jewish to suffer absurdly for merely existing. The fiendishness of mass hatred can make Jews of us all.

The suffering of the Jews in the Holocaust is claimed to be unique, since Jews were subjected to systematic dehumanization and planned extermination simply because they were Jews: the ontological accusation. Yet the uniqueness of anyone's undeserved suffering must be made accessible to everyone. The Holocaust has been claimed to be incomprehensible, but we need to grasp what we supposedly cannot fully fathom. If I were not a Jew, would I cease to muse upon the photograph? If I discovered that the prisoner were a Nazi, would I end these reflections? Whoever we are, the world may go after us because of who we are.

The man who lies on the ground in my mind occupies the place of every person: Armenians, Jews, Gypsies, Kurds, Cambodians, Tibetans, Hutus, Tutsis, Amerindians, African-Americans, Bosnians. We can imagine the features in the picture changing with color, gender, or age. Somewhere in the world right now such people may be cautiously moving toward the fences of their concentration camps, condemned to death because of who they are but devoted to life because they are human beings.

We cannot dismiss the case of the man in the picture with, "Oh, he was one of *those*, those unfortunate people. Too bad about them." No, he is one of us. We might all become designated as one of "those unfortunate people." I refuse to be separated from this victim because of a difference in identities. If I differentiate myself from him, and so save my skin, while he unfortunately had to die, others may in turn differentiate themselves from me, saving their skin while I will be the one who has to die. Pastor Martin Niemoeller reminds us of the trap of dividing humanity:

> First they [the Nazis] came for the Jews and I did not speak out—because I was not a Jew. Then they came for the communists and I did not speak out—because I was not a communist. Then they came for the trade unionists and I did not speak out—because I was not a trade unionist. Then they came for me—and there was no one left to speak out for me.[1]

I refuse to allow the Holocaust to remain accessible only to Jews. This kind of unspeakable inhumanity must be spoken of so that it is understood by all humanity. Otherwise it may serve as precedent for treating others.

The photo upon which I muse is a sad image of loss which nonetheless stimulates my moral commitment and my aesthetic life. I have experienced joys in life that the man in the picture missed. They have been deeper joys because I have known that all joys may be wiped away in a moment by an act of monstrous destruction. This knowledge has come to me independently of the photo, but the photo is an apt reminder of it.

Death must come anyway to claim my life of joy. But life is with others. While I am free, part of me dwells in the political prisons and concentration camps now occupied by others. Listen with your inner ear for their cries silenced in the night. Such things are not limited to the past. Around the corner, someone may be building a camp. When you hear the cry, jump up and run forward. This time you may be in time to save someone so hopefully reaching out to life.

The image about which I have been talking is only a photo. Its angled arrangement, concentration on the subject, play of textures, and curious background that includes another body does have art. It is not simply a picture *of* reality, an extension of the eye over distance and time. It is a depiction, an artifact given shape and significance by an intervening human being. The photographer was alive and present at this scene of death. His vision is what we see, although we do not see him. I am grateful for the invisible presence of this man who makes the visible presence of the dead man possible and meaningful. The prisoner may be a corpse upon the ground, but we the living are standing over him. The photographer is the ambassador of our humanity on the site. His work, which attends to the deceased, addresses the living.

The human community is an intersubjectivity in which all viewers of the photograph as well as the photographer are linked with the victim photographed. By the spiraling movement of reflection, I have been exploring these links, which extend to you and me.

Further aesthetic power was given to the photo by its placement with other images on the pages of *Life*. Editors and publishers were also engaged in linkage. Philosophers too may participate in the shared meaning of our humanity by reflection and dialogue.[2] In a world of suffering, injustice, and loneliness, a picture, an artwork, an argument, a speech can be a communicative act that strengthens our common bonds.

My hero died alone, but we are not alone. He died without reaching us, but we have been moved by his reaching out. Fifty years later, I cannot doubt the power of a photograph to move the heart, nor can I doubt the power of an act of hope.

These meditations have only been intermittent. I am not pre-occupied with the picture. I am of a generally cheery temperament. Only on troubled occasions do I find the image as I cast about for something of value to help me carry on. There it is in a protected corner of my mind. Sometimes I see it as if behind the head of someone else who comes to my office or my home with a tale of despair. I keep an inner eye on the photo as I attend to the sufferer. The answer that I usually give is, "Yes, yes, yes, but . . . ," and then follows the message of life that I have formulated so often on behalf of the hero of the photograph. The message is really of my life. I try to set it forth in such a fashion so that the visitors may find a similar message within their hearts. They may then return to living. I have tried to set forth the message in this discussion of an invisible photograph so that you too will be moved and will return to your life with new vision.

All these musings are a sorting out of who I am and who I am to be, using as focal point a picture seen that I imperfectly recollect. The associations and my imaginings tell more about me than about the photo. I am a metaphysical dreamer. The photo invites such dreaming. The picture calls, and I have answered. And I have often called, while the picture has reappeared to answer.

Finally, I am the one lying dead in the photo. The narratives I invent for the other person never succeed in separating his identity from mine. By looking back, I have experienced his death as mine. I have died as if him, yet I have also survived as if for him. I have experienced pointless death, yet I am still alive. Soon I will be dead. I too may be reduced to a photo on the wall or a memory in the mind. So be it. With this retrospective confirmation of my death, I turn back joyfully to life in these few leftover moments.

Notes

1. Martin Niemoeller, quoted in David P. Barash, *Introduction to Peace Studies* (Belmont, Cal.: Wadsworth Publishing Company, 1991), p. 466.

2. I am grateful for the critical responses to my reflections by Dennis Rohatyn, George Bailey, Cynthia Rostankowski, and Thomas Magnell.

Sixteen

THE SCREAMING OF THE LAMBS: PHILOSOPHICAL THEMES IN DEMME'S *SILENCE OF THE LAMBS*

Sander Lee

Audiences have flocked to Jonathan Demme's recent thriller *Silence of the Lambs* based on Thomas Harris's horrifying novel of the same name. Critics have lavishly praised Demme's "delicate, masterful use of suspense" which thrills audiences without showing them scenes of the horrific gore which is described. The primary attraction of this film, however, lies not only in Demme's successful use of the techniques of suspense to create a powerful entertainment, but also in the compelling philosophical themes which the film embodies.

I will compare *Lambs* to the similarly constructed and equally successful Hitchcockian masterpiece *Psycho*. Afterwards, I will engage in a detailed textual analysis of *Lambs* in order to demonstrate evidence for my theses. Finally, I will draw philosophical conclusions regarding the film's ultimate significance. In all the discussions, I assume that the reader is familiar with both films and with the general themes to be found in the philosophies of Nietzsche and Heidegger.

1.

Newsweek praised *Silence of the Lambs* for director Jonathan Demme's use of a "classic Hitchcockian trick: just as the Master of Suspense never showed the knife actually piercing Janet Leigh in the shower scene in *Psycho*, we never see Hannibal so much as nibble somebody's ear."[1] Although this contention is somewhat inaccurate, since we do see Lecter briefly feasting on a policeman's face, it is interesting to expand the comparison between *Lambs* and *Psycho* from the area of technique to the area of content.

When *Psycho* first appeared in 1960, it represented a new height in suspense and terror. Audiences left the theaters shocked and *terrified* at its portrayal of Norman Bates (Anthony Perkins), a seemingly shy, nice young man who secretly transformed himself into his own murdered mother by wearing his mother's clothes and used a butcher knife to kill Marion Crane (Janet Leigh) while she showered in her motel room. *Psycho* established new limits for our shared sense of the horrific as America moved into the 1960s, a decade which presented us with many new national horrors in the form of assassinations, riots, and a bloody unwinable war. *Lambs* presents us with new parameters of sophisticated horror that show us how far we have come since 1960, and in what directions.

In *Lambs*, instead of one *Psycho*, we now are given two, Hannibal Lecter and Buffalo Bill. Bill starves his female victims in order to loosen their skin. He then kills and skins them in order to get material for his dress of female skin with which he psychotically hopes to transform himself into a woman, much as Norman accomplished a similar transformation by wearing his mother's clothes.

Where Norman stuffed birds in flight to symbolically flee his own despised identity, Bill raises rare death-head moths whose cocoons he stuffs down the throats of his victims as a symbolic representation of a similar transformation. Where Norman murdered his mother and preserved her skeleton in his basement, Bill killed the seamstress who taught him his trade and kept her skinned corpse in a bathtub in his seemingly endless cellar. Thus, Norman and Bill are thematically linked as tortured young men of conflicted sexual identity who murder their female victims in a doomed attempt to transform their very nature.

Yet, despite their similarities, Bill is unquestionably a more horrifying, less human specimen than Norman. Indeed, Bill is Norman Bates as he appears after thirty more years of the degeneration of the so-called traditional values and roles which characterized American society until the end of World War II. Where Norman's usual public facade was that of a nice boy who no one would ever suspect of madness, Bill's normal facade, which is only briefly seen in *Lambs*, is transparently suspicious and threatening. We can no longer even pretend to uphold those past and deteriorating values for any sustained length of time.

On the other hand, in *Psycho*, all the women characters exist only within their traditional roles as subordinates to male concerns. Marion Crane begins the film as a weak woman who steals money from her boss in the hope of buying the commitment of her secret lover Sam Loomis (John Gavin). Unsuspecting and self-absorbed, she goes to her horrible death without any understanding of the threat which stalks her in the privacy of her shower. Her sister, Lila Crane (Vera Miles) is more aggressive in her determination to solve her sister's disappearance, but it is only through the help of a man, a now romantically interested Sam Loomis, that Norman is brought into the open.

In *Lambs*, FBI trainee Clarisse Starling (Jodie Foster) may be young and inexperienced, but she is the one who outwits her opponents and kills Bill while her more seasoned male superior is leading an army of male agents on a wild goose chase into an unoccupied house. In the 1990s, we are being told, women, although perhaps still not as experienced as their male professional counterpoints, now have the ability, the intellect, and the stamina to do the same jobs even better than the men.

Even the female victim in the film, the kidnapped daughter of a *woman* senator, another symbol of the newly emerging power of women, is not the passive unsuspecting target of the past. This victim refuses to cooperate with her kidnapper, yelling obscenities at him and hatching plots to engage in her own kidnap of his prized dog in order to bargain for her release. Even as she is being rescued by another woman, she continues to scream her demands for freedom and a participatory role in the process of catching her captor.

Women in *Lambs* have taken over the former, traditionally male, qualities of quick-wittedness and fearless grit, while the men have become the ones who are weak because of their sexual confusion and misplaced values.

The only positive male role model in *Lambs* is the film's most terrifying monster and the most frightening harbinger of the new decade into which we move. In *Psycho*, the male psychiatrist is the reassuring presence who appears at the end of the film to explain Norman's madness, while allowing the audience to leave the theater believing that there are still highly trained and intelligent medical men who can understand and perhaps even treat the Normans among us.

In *Lambs*, however, the brilliant psychiatrist who understands and explains the psycho to us is now himself a psycho, a twisted man who combines sensitivity with cannibalism, and who is the only male capable of creating a mature relationship with an intelligent assertive woman like Clarisse. How far have our notions of positive male qualities degenerated if we now find ourselves rooting for the likes of Hannibal the Cannibal in his quest for freedom and revenge against his enemies. The film ends with the sight of a plucky Hannibal strolling down a Caribbean street in search of his former keeper who he plans to eat for his supper. While *Lambs*'s portrayal of the new and more powerful roles available to women in our society is clearly superior to that of *Psycho*, its vision of our shared societal confusion over proper male attitudes and values issues a challenge to all men to resolve our neuroses over the changes in sexual roles during the last thirty years and join with women in creating more positive and mature human relationships.

2.

Let us now turn to a more detailed textual analysis of *Silence of the Lambs* in order to further demonstrate the validity of my theses. Demme clearly intends that the viewer should pay close attention to the details of the film. Dr. Hannibal Lecter leads Clarisse Starling to Bill's identity through an elaborate series of hints and clues. His anagrams range from the useful as in "Hester Mofet" which transforms to "the rest of me," to the purposely misleading "Louis Fraet" which transforms to "iron sulfate," otherwise known as fool's gold.

Often, Starling, and we, are encouraged to see what is around us. A Nazi propaganda poster in Bill's basement shows a man's face with a band covering his eyes and the slogan, "America, open your eyes." Some of these visual details are merely amusing as in the showing of the magazine *Bon Appetit* on Lecter's table in his cell in Memphis just before he dines on a policeman's face. Yet others are more interesting. In the same sequence of shots we are shown Lecter's drawing of Clarisse's agonized face surrounded by crosses marking the graves of the sheep and the road leading to escape.

In the very first scene of the film, even before the credits, we see Starling running through foggy woods at the FBI's training facility in Quantico, Virginia. Because we come to the film with certain expectations, we are immediately anxious, fearing for her safety even before we know who she is.

The casting of Jodie Foster in this role is appropriate. In addition to being a fine actress, we are also aware that she herself has been the victim of the obsessive fantasies of a lunatic, William Hinckley. Thus, in our collective imaginations, she, like Starling, has powerful psychological motives for doggedly pursuing such criminals. As she leaves the training course, she passes a series of signs tacked to a tree, supposedly to encourage trainees to greater effort. Yet would the FBI really post signs which say, in descending order, "Hurt, Agony, Pain, Love?" We cannot help but be reminded of this when we see the word "Love" written on Bill's hand.

In the FBI building we are immediately made aware of Starling's unusual status as a female trainee, as well as male doubts concerning her abilities. Throughout the film, she is constantly being stared at by male law enforcement officials in ways that suggest that they are evaluating her both in terms of her qualifications for her job and her sexual attractiveness. Demme, however, lets us know again and again that not only is she much more qualified than any male presented to us, including Lecter, in addition, she has no interest in the male appraisals of her appearance.

Lecter himself makes specific mention of Clarisse's familiarity and, by inference, that of *all* women, with the experience of being stared at. Further, Lecter is correct when he tells Starling that she is primarily motivated by ambition. What she wants most in the world is advancement. That she deserves to be advanced is clear. She enters an elevator in the FBI building which is filled with strong young men all dressed in uniform red shirts, yet when the elevator opens to let her out, she is the only one left. None of the others can measure up to her, and none of them will rise as high.

The primary reason for her superiority lies in her understanding of the fundamental tool necessary to catch Bill. That tool is empathy. To catch Bill, she must come to understand him, she must come to think as he thinks. This is a theme that permeates the novels of Thomas Harris on whose work the film is based. In his earlier book, *The Red Dragon*, which was filmed by director Michael Mann under the title *Manhunter*, a male FBI agent seeks Lecter's help in tracking down a serial killer. In that film, however, the danger lies in the possibility that the agent will himself become such a psychopath. Lecter warns him that he is so good at thinking like a killer because he has the potential to become one himself. At the end of *Manhunter*, when the agent returns to his wife and children after successfully catching his prey, we are filled with foreboding that he will snap one day and turn on them as his victims.

We have no such fears concerning Clarisse Starling, however. Demme suggests that because of her gender, she is able to use her intelligence and imagination to fly into the minds of Lecter and Bill without becoming trapped there as a man might.

Jack Crawford, her superior, is presented as a traditional male authority figure, well-trained in the behavioral sciences, and professional in his demeanor. He remembers Starling from his course at the University of Virginia in which she grilled him on the Bureau's civil rights record under Hoover and he remembers thinking she deserved an A, but Starling reminds him that she actually received an A-. He has a newspaper story on Bill's exploits on his bulletin board from a tacky tabloid called the *National Inquisitor*. The headline, "Bill Skins Fifth," sounds more like the lead for a football story than a murder investigation.

Throughout the film, Crawford asks Starling for her insights into Bill's character yet he never shares his own. Crawford's only success in the film is his decision to have Starling interview Lecter and become involved in the case. At no point does he demonstrate any inkling of the empathy or understanding required to solve the case. His biggest problem, like that of all the honest male law enforcement officials we meet, is his belief that traditional analytical male procedures will solve the case.

Because of his lack of humanity, we are told at one point that his nickname is "the ghoul." Crawford pretends that he is not sexist when he excludes Starling from a conference with the West Virginia police, yet he has no response when Starling tells him that his actions matter: "the other cops look to you to see how to act, it matters." Like Lecter, we in the audience speculate on Crawford's sexual interest in Starling, yet it is clear that she only wants a professional relationship, and as the dominant personality, this is what she gets. In the film's conclusion, she offers her hand to Crawford, and he shakes it, walking away as Starling goes to talk to Lecter on the phone. Our last image of Crawford shows him, as always, going in the wrong direction when important things are happening.

When Crawford tells Starling that Lecter tortured Miggs into swallowing his tongue, Starling replies by saying; "I don't know how to feel about this." Crawford responds: "You don't have to feel any way about it, Lecter just did it to amuse himself." Here Crawford shows that he does not have a clue how to use Lecter to catch Bill. Starling knows that it is through her feelings that she will come to understand both Lecter and Bill. Further, she even comes to understand that in this process she must reveal herself emotionally to Lecter who demands a *quid pro quo* from her soul for each tidbit of information which he imparts.

At bottom, Lecter is still a brilliant psychiatrist, evidence that when an intelligent, sensitive man engages in empathetic relationships with others, he runs the serious risk of madness. The suggestion here is that in our society, smart, intuitive men will always be somehow flawed. This point is subtly reinforced by the physical appearance of Dr. Pilcher, the bug specialist to whom Starling turns for information about the moth cocoon. The only other doctor and highly intelligent, sensitive man, in the movie, his most obvious characteristic is the fact that he is cross-eyed. Like Lecter, he is also eccentric, although we and Starling hope that his eccentricities are of a less frightening nature than those of Lecter.

When we first meet Pilcher, he is playing a board game using live bugs as pieces. We are quickly informed that his assistant, a man with a normal appearance, is not worth our attention, since "he doesn't have a Ph.D." Pilcher immediately makes a pass at Starling. At this point in the film, we assume that she would not be interested in such a strange and relatively unattractive man, yet we see at the end of the film that she has invited him and his assistant to her graduation and is drinking and laughing with them when she is called to the phone. Thus, bright, intelligent, and strange men like Pilcher, who wear their hearts on their sleeves, are our models for successful men in this film, as opposed to handsome, masculine and emotionally repressed traditional males like Crawford. We cannot help but wonder how Pilcher and Lecter would have gotten along.

That society is at fault for creating monsters like Lecter and Bill is clearly believed by them both. Lecter tells Starling in his cell in Baltimore that "Bill wasn't born a criminal, he was made into one." Later, when his captive complains of her pain, Bill screams at her: "You know nothing about pain." Whether Starling or Demme in part share this view is not completely clear, yet we shall see that they unquestionably believe that Lecter and Bill did have some choice in the matter of becoming monsters.

As has been already suggested, Lecter is drawn to psychic confessions like a moth to a fly, his appetite for signs of vulnerability is even greater than his desire for eating flesh. Indeed, only by sharing such secrets does anyone truly become a person to Lecter.

Recognizing that, in our society, women seem to have a greater potential than men for sharing their intimate psychological insights, Lecter attempts to pry such secrets from Senator Ruth Martin, the mother of Bill's latest kidnap victim. However, Lecter's need to begin his relationships with a show of brutal and vulgar insight when he asks, "Did you breast-feed your daughter?" repels the Senator completely. In her anguish over her daughter's safety she is unable to recognize Lecter's comments as an offer to do business rather than an attempt to cause meaningless suffering. Thus, she can only respond by telling the guards "to get that animal out of here."

Starling, on the other hand, is sure that Lecter will never hurt her. Lecter tells her that "discourtesy is unspeakably ugly to me," although he refers to discourtesy only within the narrow universe of those he acknowledges as persons. After Lecter escapes, Starling reassures her colleague Ardelia Mapp that Lecter will not attack her because he would consider it impolite. It is Mapp, a black woman, who helps Starling decipher Lecter's final clues. She is the only other FBI employee to understand Starling's methods and it is she who is presented as the hope of the future when she signals success to Starling in the graduation scene. Mapp's presence and insight confirm that, in this film, we are being told that women really do have an ability to see into things which transcend the ability of men. It is not simply that Clarisse Starling is an outstanding individual, Starling is but one example of a new generation of women.

In the climatic scene of the film, Lecter learns Starling's deepest secret and reciprocates by revealing the answer to the mystery of Bill's identity. Here we see their relationship in all of its fullness. When Starling tells Lecter that she came to see him because she wanted to, Lecter responds only half jokingly: "People will say we are in love." Lecter responds to Starling with a genuine respect and affection which is no longer threatening.

Lecter is now her psychiatrist, her mentor, her father, and, most of all, her teacher. He begins by stating first principles and tells her to read Marcus Aurelius. Simplicity is the key. Why does Bill kill? Because he covets. What do we covet? Do we look for things to covet? No, we covet what we see!

Here he sounds like a combination of Socrates, Sherlock Holmes, and Freud. When he insists that she repay him by telling him about running away from the farm in Montana, she anxiously tells him that there is no time for that now. "But we don't reckon time the same way, do we Clarisse? This is all the time you will ever have," he responds. Thus, Starling must reveal the secret of her being to Lecter in her story of the lambs and the key to her passion.

The link created between Starling and Lecter by telling the story is so great that, even as she is being dragged away from his cell by the guards, she is certain that he will maintain his part in their agreement by revealing Bill's secret to her. At that moment, she has so much faith in his sense of honor, that she does not hesitate to break away from the guards and take the file on Bill from Lecter through the bars, even though she obviously knows that he could grab her and overpower her so quickly that she would become a hostage before the guards could get to her.

Lecter is so moved by the moment that he affectionately strokes her finger as he says goodbye. We cannot begin to imagine the last time that Lecter has shown honest affection for another person.

3.

Nietzschean themes permeate *Lambs*. In this film, most men are ignorant sheep, mindlessly following the rules and procedures that have been laid down for them. They live their lives in a slave morality in which they feel nothing but anger and resentment toward those who try to break out of the mold of traditional values. A few people, however, possess sufficient courage to express their will to power in an attempt to fulfill their intuitive creative energies. Such people are free spirits attempting to walk the tightrope of Zarathustra to a superior evolutionary stage, Nietzsche's *Übermensch*.

This transformation requires the recognition that rationality and discipline, Nietzsche's Apollonian qualities, are only of value when they are put completely at the service of the passionate, creative elements of our character, what Nietzsche called Dionysian qualities.

However, the risk of attempting this type of a transformation is that we will fall into an inhuman madness in which we develop an insatiable hunger for power and dominance over others. Such Faustian figures as Lecter and Bill have descended into their own private hells in which their intelligence and sensitivity is placed at the service of perverted desires for control over others. Bill equates beauty with power and covets both in the transformational mystic powers of the death-head moths and female human beings.

This distortion of Nietzschean values leads Bill to an admiration for the usual ideology of failed Nietzscheans, Nazism. In Bill's personal hell, his basement, we see that his blanket is covered with swastikas and he has a Nazi poster with a swastika on his wall.

In his appreciation of the finer qualities of life, classical music, philosophy, art, and gourmet food, Hannibal Lecter revels in the pursuits of the *Übermensch*. He has become so successful in dominating himself and the world around him that he can open a pair of handcuffs behind his back with a small piece of a pen. Indeed, like some Hindu mystic, he is able to simulate the physical symptoms of a *grand mal* seizure while retaining his ability to attack without warning only a few seconds later.

Yet, in his hunger for the flesh of seemingly lesser people, he betrays his own massive insecurities and his literal need to overcome others. He is more than intelligent enough to know that if he could have controlled his penchant for live human flesh and continued to present at least the outward appearance of sanity, very little could have been denied him. As we know from Starling's newspaper research, Lecter was honored with tributes and prizes before his fall. His inability to control his desires even when he knew the cost of indulging them demonstrates his failure to perform the transformation he sought.

Starling, however, is in the process of achieving a more successful transformation. Like Lecter, she strives to develop her intellect only to use it as a tool for serving her deeper feelings and intuitions. Yet the primary difference between her, Lecter, and Bill is that her attitude toward the world's sheep is one of caring and concern. Just as Heidegger transformed Nietzsche's notion of a will to power into the fundamental, ontological existential structure of caring, Starling's deepest impulse is to use her abilities to save life's victims instead of creating new ones. She seeks to quiet the screaming of the lambs, a task which can never be totally completed, because new victims are created every day. In her, we rediscover the traditional view that a caring moral hero will always overcome the Faustian evil genius.

In the film's climax, Bill appears to have the advantage over Starling because, with his night glasses, he can see into the darkness which blinds her. Yet, in the end, Bill continues to be blinded by his own uncontrollable desires. Even at the point of killing Starling, he is so overcome by his desire for her that he cannot resist delaying while he teasingly moves his hand in the air around her.

That pause, and his foolish mistake of assuming that because she cannot see him she will not hear the cocking of his gun, leads to his destruction and the simultaneous shattering of the window which lets in light where before there was only darkness. Where Bill's technology gives him an advantage in the area of the physical senses, Clarisse Starling's additional moral sensitivity will inevitably always give her the final victory.

For this reason, Hannibal Lecter, in his newfound freedom, is anxious to avoid a direct confrontation with Starling in the future. But, of course, Starling, and we, know that her concern for the lambs must lead her to challenge and overcome Lecter in the inevitable sequel to the film.

Note

1. David Ansen, reviewer, *"The Silence of the Lambs"* (motion picture review). *Newsweek*, 117 (18 February 1991), p. 64.

Seventeen

LET'S DANCE WITH WOLVES!

H. P. P. (Hennie) Lötter

1. Introduction

Throughout history people have disliked, rejected, dominated, oppressed, and even killed one another solely because of characteristics that made one group of people different from another. People have often done morally repugnant things to others because they have a different skin color, worship an unknown God, or worship in an unfamiliar way, or because they speak a strange language, practice uncommon habits, and have a way of going about everyday activities that are perceived as weird.

Even today persistent political conflicts result from clashes between groups constituted on the basis of ethnic, cultural, racial, or religious characteristics. Some of them, described by Galston as "the most violent, destructive, and intractable political conflicts" of our time, occur between groups that are part of the same political order.[1]

Many countries in the world today can be referred to as *radically pluralistic* societies. A radically pluralistic society can be defined as a society characterized by a heterogeneous population, in terms of race, ethnicity, culture, language, sexual orientation, religion, and conceptions of the good. This is characteristic of the *postmodern political condition* which, according to Heller and Fehér, is premised on the acceptance of "the plurality of cultures and discourses."[2] Radically pluralistic societies find it difficult to be just and fair to all their members in such a way that the various groups are reasonably satisfied. To safeguard a radically pluralistic society from the potentially destructive conflicts that arise so easily is complex. What can be done so that considerations of justice and fairness regulate all the various kinds of conflict possible within a radically pluralistic society, and to prevent the conflicts from overturning considerations of justice?

Liberal democratic societies seem to have found some kind of *modus vivendi* for people with varying characteristics of otherness and difference who share a specific country, by making use of constitutionally guaranteed individual rights, a fully democratic political system, and the rule of law. However, despite their effectiveness in ensuring basic, just, political institutions in which all the inhabitants can participate, problems of ethnic, racial, religious, and cultural conflict still occur, even in the most progressive liberal democracies. Are the values underlying liberal democracies adequate to help people cope with the conflicts? Could the application of liberal values to institutions, as well as to interpersonal and intergroup relations, lead to a better society for all minority groups, regardless of the characteristics on which they are based?

2. A Neglected Issue

Little attention has been given in contemporary liberal political philosophy to issues of justice and fairness that are involved in conflicts of pluralism, otherness and difference, except for conflicts based on moral and religious pluralism. It may be held that no matters of justice and fairness are involved in conflicts of pluralism, difference, and otherness. This view can hardly be defended in the light of the central role, John Rawls accords to the problem of religious pluralism in his discussion of the principle of religious toleration.[3] Rawls holds that this principle underlies the "fact of pluralism," which is reinforced by democratic institutions that encourage a variety of views. According to Rawls, moral and religious pluralism is a permanent feature of modern democracies. It requires that a workable conception of justice must allow "for a diversity of general and comprehensive doctrines, and for the plurality of conflicting, and indeed incommensurable, conceptions of the meaning, value and purpose of human life."[4]

However, one could just as well ask whether racial, ethnic, linguistic, sexual, and other kinds of pluralism do not also place specific requirements on a workable conception of justice. Do they not require that a workable conception of justice must allow for a diversity of cultural lifestyles, a plurality of languages, a variety of habits, and more effective representation of minorities at all levels of government? Is it not a further requirement that there should be room for the *identity* of the groups, as well as the *interaction* between members of the groups, which makes gradual transformation of the groups possible?[5]

I will show that liberal values can be a help to resolve specific conflicts of pluralistic societies. To show how this is possible, I will first attempt to redefine liberalism in order to get hold of the essential liberal values. Next I will attempt to point out how the values can be put to work in pluralistic societies. Finally, I will try to judge the worth of the proposed values for the resolution of conflicts of pluralism. I will illustrate my arguments by discussing the film *Dances with Wolves*.

3. Why *Dances with Wolves?*

Kevin Costner's *Dances with Wolves* makes a deep emotional impact. The film shows that the bloody frontier confrontations between white settlers and indigenous people *could* have been different, not only in the United States of America, but everywhere else as well. Violence, murder, conquest and domination were *not* the *only* options available for handling the contacts between members of different cultural, ethnic, racial and religious groups. The film also presents viewers with a more balanced view of American Indians, where there are some "good guys," the Sioux tribe, and some "bad guys," the Pawnee tribe. What it does magnificently is to show Indians as *ordinary human beings,* just like any one else.

But there is another reason for the strong impact of *Dances with Wolves*. The film exemplifies the kinds of values that could make a significant difference in our ability to resolve the ethnic, racial, cultural, and religious conflicts of otherness and difference, that are so characteristic of many contemporary societies.

What kinds of values are available to citizens of contemporary liberal democracies in situations where conflicts of otherness are experienced? This question is important, as the values must help people to cope with situations similar to John Dunbar's, in *Dances with Wolves*. Dunbar had one of the sharpest experiences of otherness and difference, when he met members of the Sioux Indian tribe. He differed from them with respect to race, religion, language, and culture. The significance that cultural differences might have on human relationships becomes clear when we note that we are unlike other animals, in that we do not merely live in nature, but continually change.[6] The production of consumables, the manufacturing of tools, the education of children, complex behavioral patterns with respect to sex, parliamentary gatherings, and intellectual activities of science, philosophy, and art can be considered to be products of culture. So too can the design, construction, and maintenance of societal institutions.[7]

Will Kymlicka argues that people are bound to their cultural community.[8] A person cannot just be transplanted from one culture to another, nor can a person's upbringing be easily erased. According to Kymlicka, cultural membership is a constitutive part of personal identity. Charles Taylor's definition of personal identity bears on this. According to Taylor: "my identity is defined by the commitments and identifications which provide the frame or horizon within which I can try to determine from case to case what is good, or valuable, or what ought to be done, or what I endorse or oppose."[9] People may see their identity in terms of some moral or spiritual commitment, or they may define it partly by reference to the nation or tradition to which they belong. People are very strongly attached to a spiritual view or cultural background, which provides "the frame within which they can determine where they stand on questions of what is good, or worthwhile, or admirable, or of value."[10] John Dunbar's cultural background was far removed from the Sioux Indian culture creating a vast difference between him and the Indians.

6. Liberal Values

Like Ronald Dworkin and Rawls I contend that the central values underlying political liberalism, are contained in the principle of equal consideration of interests and equal respect for all people in the design and administration of a society.[11] But what does this principle mean? And in what ways is it exemplified in the encounters between John Dunbar and the Sioux Indians?

Equal respect for every person means that some things are due to a person just for being a person, regardless of desert, merit, moral, cultural, or religious views and lifestyle. In an important sense, all people are equally worthy of having the vote, owning personal property, or getting married. People may be deprived of these things only if they lack necessary capacities for possessing them.

Equal respect thus implies that a person may not inflict bodily injury on anyone without having sufficient reasons for doing so. In *Dances with Wolves* the adult males of the Sioux Indian tribe had to decide whether they would kill John Dunbar, a white American soldier. Wind in My Hair strongly proposed this, but it was resisted by Kicking Bird who gained the support of the governing council. He wanted to determine whether they had sufficient reason to do so. In contrast, members of the Pawnee Indian tribe killed the unarmed white transport driver for an unacceptable reason: they had nothing to show for their expedition. Furthermore, equal respect implies that people should be allowed to develop their own views of the good and to govern themselves according to it, subject to certain limitations. Equal respect and autonomy go together. Finally, the principle of equal respect implies that everyone should be represented in any procedure that is to determine the principles of social and political justice for their society.

Equal consideration of interests presupposes that people have certain interests that they care about and want to have protected. Equal consideration of interests implies that everyone's case must be considered. This seems to be at least part of the motivation of the Sioux governing council for trying to befriend John Dunbar. The other part of their motivation was their self-interest in finding out how many more whites were on their way.

Equal consideration of interests also means treating like cases alike, and unlike cases differently. Where there are relevant differences between cases, different treatment is justified. This implies that conflicts of interest must be decided impartially, although it does not specify the reasons that are to be accepted in cases of conflict.

The principle of equal respect and equal consideration of interests should not be made into two separate principles. The two aspects of the principle should be taken into account simultaneously and should limit each other in the design and administration of societal institutions. The requirement that the two parts of this principle should limit each other reinforces the impression that the principle has a fuzzy and open-ended character. The lack of determinateness is not a drawback. Taken by itself the principle does specify that people must be treated, at least sometimes, as equals just because they are people. It specifies further that the interests of everyone should be considered equally. This rules out many ways of structuring a society.

However, if the principle of equal consideration of interests and equal respect is combined with existing liberal institutions and extended to the interpersonal relations between members of a radically pluralistic society, then it can improve the quality of life in the society. But members of the society must internalize the principle so that it becomes a fundamental part of their conceptions of the good. The principle and its concomitant liberal values must become a part of their ethos. The importance is expressed by Jürgen Habermas when he says: "Reziproke Verbindlichkeiten entstehen nur aus intersubjektiv geteilten Überzeugungen."[12]

If this is done, then a moral and political space is created in which voices of previously excluded people can be heard to express their otherness and difference. This seems to be the only way in which tolerance of major human differences can be combined with the requirement of people living together in a radically pluralistic society.[13]

Elite individuals committed to liberal values can exert a beneficial influence on institutions. What the Sioux Indians would do about the presence of John Dunbar was decided by their governing council in which all mature male members were granted equal respect. Kicking Bird, with the support of the chief, Ten Bears, convinced everyone that they should treat John Dunbar according to liberal values. Within the Sioux Indian tribe, Kicking Bird's moral approach was far more influential than the more warrior-like style of Wind in My Hair who characterized himself as "someone who feels anger first." But Wind in My Hair accepts the authority of the governing council, as well as the leadership of Ten Bears and Kicking Bird. Even so, at the first official meeting between Dunbar and a delegation sent by the governing council, Wind in My Hair was quickly irritated by Dunbar's attempts to ask about the presence of buffalo. He describes Dunbar's attempt with the words "he has lost his mind," whereas Kicking Bird's attitude gets the following comments from Dunbar in his diary: "He is patient, inquisitive and eager to communicate." The behavior by Kicking Bird is the result of the internalization of the principle of equal consideration of interests and equal respect.

5. Dialogue

Once the principle of equal concern and respect is accepted as the foundation for conduct at an institutional level, *dialogue* becomes the only accepted means of communication for the resolution of disputes and conflicts, except in certain extreme cases where restricted forms of violence may be the only way out. In *Dances with Wolves* there are two examples of refusals to engage in dialogue. In one example, Wind in My Hair proposes that Dunbar ought to be killed, because he was not Sioux and therefore less of a human being. His racial and cultural prejudice is clear. His refusal is unjustified, as he has not even tried to understand the otherness of Dunbar. In the other example, Dunbar refuses to speak to his white American captors who treat him with violence and refuse to take what he says about the Sioux Indians seriously. His refusal is motivated on moral grounds, for the soldiers defy the rules of dialogue.

The role of dialogue in a radically pluralistic society can be explained by defining the concept of dialogue and pointing out the functions that it can have in interpersonal, intergroup, and institutional conflicts. A dialogue is a form of human communication in which two or more people exchange views on a certain matter in such a manner that each person has a reasonable opportunity to make a case with supporting arguments while others listen and make use of similar opportunities. Participants may cooperate to find mutual understanding, on the matter being discussed.

Examples of dialogue can be found in the Sioux Indian governing council meetings and in Dunbar's conversations with Kicking Bird and Ten Bears. The governing council shows that a dialogue can often end inconclusively and can sometimes stretch over many meetings. At the end of the first council meeting, the Sioux Indians did not reach a final decision, although there was consensus that Dunbar would not be killed immediately. When Ten Bears remarks that it is difficult to know what to do, continued dialogue about the matter is called for.

Genuine dialogue can only take place if specific prerequisites are fulfilled. One is that people should be willing to become participants, prepared to discuss any matter that is raised by others. Participants should also regard each other as worth listening to, in earnest. Another prerequisite is that participants must be willing to have their arguments criticized and corrected by others. These prerequisites indicate that genuine dialogue presupposes the acceptance of principles of justice. The acceptance of something like the principle of equal consideration of interests and equal respect for every participant in a dialogue underlies the prerequisites. This shows the strong link between central liberal values and dialogue as a means of communication. It does not, however, seem necessary that all prerequisites should be present at the start of a dialogue. Often participation in dialogue is a learning experience. However, gradual learning which leads to the full presence of all prerequisites, is essential.

Dialogue can help to explore mutuality. By examining all sides, people view conflict in a new light.[14] Treating fellow members of a society in this way can lead to the development of affiliation and affection because strangers are transformed into neighbors through empathy and shared interests. In this way, an artificial kinship, may arise.[15]

Something like this has happened to Dunbar's relationship with the Sioux Indians. The perceptions about the Indians current in the world he came from were mostly negative. Dunbar himself was part of an occupying army that fought against the Indians and his decision to ask for placement at a frontier post suggested that he was an Indian fighter. The man who transported him to his outpost described the Indians as "beggars and thieves." In a sense, Dunbar's first encounter with the wolf can be seen as a metaphor for the way in which he handled his encounters with the Indians. When he first saw the wolf, he picked up his gun to protect himself. However, he does not shoot without reason, and he first determines whether the wolf means him any harm. When he finds it not to be threatening, he lets it be, as he feels that the wolf is now his only company besides his horse. He handled his encounters with the Sioux Indians in the same way and gradually befriended them. They changed from being apparently hostile strangers to becoming his neighbors and his friends.

This kind of dialogue is not possible if people cannot speak a common language. Dunbar's determined efforts to learn the Sioux language and Kicking Bird's mastery of English suggest that learning to speak the language of strangers might be expressive of the principle of equal consideration of interests and equal respect. Only people who are dominating and oppressing can insist that all communication should take place in their own tongue.

Besides stimulating communal ties, participation in dialogue reinforces the autonomy of the participants, because they evaluate their views and modify them if they deem this necessary.[16] This aspect of the functioning of dialogue can reinforce cultural, ethnic, religious, and gender identities and create the possibility for genuine interaction between members of groups.

In *Dances with Wolves* there are telling examples of the maintenance of identity, as interaction, and transformation. Dunbar is a typical Westerner in his manner of keeping a diary and recording all his experiences and his observations of nature. He never loses it and the importance he attaches to his diary leads to his capture, since he feels that he has to collect it from his outpost before he can join the tribe in moving to another abode. However, Dunbar also illustrates the effects of interaction when his views on the justification of war eventually coincide with the views of his new friends. His attempted suicide at the beginning of the story reflects the deeply negative experience he had of the moral justification for the Civil War. However, after taking part in the Sioux battle against the Pawnee, he remarks: "I knew for the first time who I really was." He can identify with their moral justification for engaging in war.

As the prerequisites of dialogue leave room for all people to "vent their grievances or frustration or opposition" about any matter, even the views of minorities ought to be expressed.[17] If dissenting minorities cannot succeed in convincing others, dialogue still provides them with the opportunity to give "public status to their strongly held convictions."[18]

Finally, dialogue leads to the reconceptualization of values, principles, and interests so that new visions of the future may emerge. One of the most interesting relationships in *Dances with Wolves* is between John Dunbar and Wind in My Hair. Initially, Wind in My Hair is extremely hostile to Dunbar. He shows his hostility by proposing that Dunbar be killed, by trying to steal his horse, and by his impatience with the slow communication between Dunbar and the Sioux Indians. However, his attitude is overruled by the more humane attitude of the dominant members of the Sioux governing council, and eventually he and Dunbar become good friends. When one of the Sioux Indians gets into a confrontation with Dunbar about his lost hat, Wind in My Hair resolves the dispute. The farewell of Dunbar and his wife at the end of the story is very emotional, as is Wind in My Hair's greeting from afar, when he shouts to Dunbar, "Do you see that I am your friend?" Living with other people, according to the principle of equal consideration of interests and equal respect, and communicating by means of dialogue can transform strangers into friends.

For the participants in a dialogue and its audience, dialogue is an education. Different participants are knowledgeable to differing degrees on various subjects, and exchanges between them, broaden everyone's outlook. Participants obviously receive training by learning from their mistakes and successes. They learn to identify issues, weigh evidence and arguments, express preferences, and acquire rhetorical skills.[19]

6. The Possibility of Consensus

What kind of results could a radically pluralistic society obtain if it based itself on liberal values? Is it possible to attain any form of *consensus* which could lead to harmony between the members of a radically pluralistic society? The concept of consensus requires that members of a group agree with one another with respect to a relation with a certain kind of object. As subjects they can have a relation with objects such as other persons, groups, beliefs, values, and institutions. They have an intellectual relation, in which they agree with the objects and sometimes become attached to them.[20]

Does it make any sense to be concerned with consensus in contemporary societies while numerous voices have called attention to the "overwhelming fact of modern life," the "breakdown of moral and political consensus?"[21] I believe that it does, if consensus on the justice of basic social and political institutions is distinguished from consensus on other kinds of issues such as morality, religion and culture. If this is done, then a concern with consensus on justice becomes a concern with the central practical question of modernity: "What kind of principles can secure allegiance to a form of social order in which individuals who are pursuing diverse conceptions of the good can live together without the disruptions of rebellion and internal war?"[22] Conceptions of the good take in moral values and cultural values. Together they form a comprehensive ideal of the good life.

A limited complex consensus *is* possible within contemporary radically pluralistic societies. In a complex consensus, agreement is accompanied by large areas of dissent. The idea of complex *consensus* suggests that forms of agreement exist between members of a political community about the value of meaningful activities which form part of social practices that do not violate the principle of equal consideration of interests and equal respect.

In *Dances with Wolves* an unarticulated consensus between Dunbar and the Sioux Indians plays a very important role in shaping their relationship in a positive direction. Dunbar is a nature lover, as can be seen in his relation with his horse and the wolf, his fascination with the landscape, and his great interest in the buffalo. Besides sharing his interest in buffalo, the Sioux Indians also experienced the same kind of moral revulsion at the sight of the needless slaughtering of buffalo by white hunters. The Sioux Indians kill almost as many buffalo as the white hunters, but they use all the meat and hides to supply themselves with food and clothes throughout the winter.

In complex *consensus* it is possible to transform injustice into justice where of agreement between members of a political community on such matters is lacking. Initial disagreement can be transformed into some form of consensus. Thus, in cases of strong dissent in a society, the function of a comprehensive theory of justice should be to serve as a "pact of reconciliation" between conflicting groups.[23] The principles of a theory of justice must protect the fundamental interests of everyone in a society.[24]

The idea of reaching *complex* consensus in a radically pluralistic society takes in the complexity of human societies, consisting of social practices that may be organized by disparate, underlying principles. Members of different groups often do not attach the same value to the same social practices. The idea of *complex* consensus also draws attention to the fact that consensus may not be reached on all political issues. A state of consensus "does not *always* imply uniformity of beliefs, goals, interests or expectations."[25] For example, it is not to be expected that members of a morally pluralistic political community would fully agree with one another about the morality of abortion. The dissent in most societies today is not always bad.

But we can reasonably expect consensus on the institutional framework required for people to hold diverging views without fear of persecution. Hanna Pitkin argues that disagreement is almost always present in political discourse before, during, and even after "deliberation on what is to be done."[26] Full elimination of dissent is not the aim, but the avoidance of dissent "so severe that it leads to dissociation."[27]

We must aim for consensus on the principles of justice underlying the basic political framework, as it provides a forum where everyone can be represented and differences of opinion can be settled according to widely acceptable procedures. Publicly shared goods based on common principles of justice, which could include "constitutions, laws, public institutions, decision-making bodies, general frameworks within which social institutions, economic or other in character operate," secure the socio-political conditions of the good life for all members of a society.[28]

The idea of *complex* consensus finally includes John Rawls's idea of an overlapping consensus that could support a theory of justice.[29] In a morally pluralistic political community it is impossible that any "general and comprehensive doctrine can assume the role of a publicly acceptable basis of political justice," unless some people are forced to accept one.[30] As an alternative, Rawls suggests the formulation of a theory of justice that would gain support from a variety of comprehensive moral doctrines. A liberal conception of justice with its limited scope, "together with the looseness of our comprehensive doctrines allows leeway for it to gain an initial allegiance to itself and thereby to shape those doctrines accordingly as conflicts arise, a process that takes place gradually over generations."[31] The same applies to most other doctrines expressive of otherness and difference.

7. Conclusion

I have shown that liberal values can help to resolve various forms of conflict between groups of people in contemporary societies. Living according to liberal values can enable people to enjoy the company of other people who are different and to appreciate whatever is worthwhile in their views of life. I have also shown that it is possible to attain consensus on the basic institutions and practices of a society. This kind of consensus, coupled with the internalization of the principle of equal respect and equal consideration of interests, can lead to a peaceful, radically pluralistic society. Transforming prejudice, hostility and conflict into friendship and appreciation should make anyone feel like dancing joyously with wolves!

Notes

1. William A. Galston, *Justice and the Human Good* (Chicago: The University of Chicago Press, 1980), p. 122.

2. Agnes Heller and Ferenc Fehér, *The Postmodern Political Condition* (Cambridge, Mass.: Polity Press, 1988), p. 5.

3. John Rawls, "The Idea of an Overlapping Consensus," *Oxford Journal of Legal Studies*, 7 (1987), p. 4.

4. *Ibid.*

5. Cf. Jennifer Roback, "Plural but Equal: Groups Identity and Voluntary Integration," *Social Philosophy and Policy*, 8 (1991), pp. 60-81.

6. C. A. Van Peursen, *Cultuur in Stroomversnelling* (Amsterdam/Brussels: Elsevier, 1976), p. 10.

7. Michael Landmann, *Filosofische Antropologie* (Utrecht/Antwerp: Uitgeverij Het Spectrum, 1966), p. 186.

8. Will Kymlicka, *Liberalism, Community and Culture* (Oxford: Oxford University Press, 1991), p. 175.

9. Charles Taylor, *Sources of the Self: The Making of the Modern Identity* (Cambridge, England: Cambridge University Press, 1989), p. 27.

10. *Ibid.*

11. See Ronald Dworkin, *Taking Rights Seriously* (London: Gerald Duckworth & Company, 1978), p. 180. Also see John Rawls, "A Kantian Conception of Equality," John Rajchman and Cornel West, eds., *Post-Analytic Philosophy* (New York: Columbia University Press, 1985), p. 202.

12. Jürgen Habermas, "Erlauterungen zum Begriff des kommunikativen *Handelns*" in Jürgen Habermas, *Vorstudien und Erganzungen zur Theorie des Kommunikativen Handeln* (Frankfurt am Main: Suhrkamp Verlag, 1984), p. 574.

13. Thomas McCarthy, "The Politics of the Ineffable: Derrida's Deconstructionism," in M. Kelly, *Hermeneutics and Critical Theory in Ethics and Politics* (Cambridge, Mass. & London: The MIT Press, 1990), p. 185.

14. Benjamin R. Barber, *Strong Democracy: Participatory Politics for a New Age* (Berkeley: University of California Press, 1984), p. 185.

15. *Ibid.*, p. 189.

16. *Ibid.*, p. 190.

17. *Ibid.*, p. 192.

18. *Ibid.*

19. Carl Cohen, *Democracy* (Athens, Ga.: University of Georgia Press, 1971), p. 18.

20. P. H. Partridge, *Consent and Consensus* (London: Macmillan, 1971), pp. 79-80.

21. Richard J. Bernstein, "One Step Forward, Two Steps Backward: Richard Rorty on Liberal Democracy and Philosophy," *Political Theory*, 15 (1987), p. 552.

22. Alasdair MacIntyre, *Whose Justice? Which Rationality?* (London: Duckworth, 1988), p. 210.

23. John Rawls, *A Theory of Justice* (Oxford: Oxford University Press, 1973), p. 221.

24. John Rawls, "A Kantian Conception of Equality," in John Rajchman and Cornel West, eds., *Post-Analytic Philosophy*, p. 207.

25. P. H. Partridge, *Consent and Consensus* (London: Macmillan, 1971), p. 108.

26. Hanna Fenichel Pitkin, *Wittgenstein and Justice: On the Significance of Ludwig Wittgenstein for Social and Political Thought* (Berkeley: University of California Press), p. 208.

27. *Ibid.*

28. Heller and Fehér, *The Postmodern Political Condition*, p. 81.

29. John Rawls, "Justice as Fairness: Political not Metaphysical," *Philosophy and Public Affairs*, 14 (1985), pp. 246-247.

30. John Rawls, "The Idea of an Overlapping Consensus," *Oxford Journal of Legal Studies*, 7 (1987), p. 6.

31. *Ibid.*

Eighteen

WHAT IS WRONG WITH PROSTITUTION?

Joseph Kupfer

In a thoughtful and provocative article, Janet Radcliffe-Richards argues that there is nothing immoral about prostitution itself.[1] It is wrong in our society only because women are oppressed by men and male-dominated institutions. Prostitution is but another, albeit dramatic, instance of this patriarchal oppression. In a culture where women and men were equals, prostitution would be perfectly all right. To make her point, Radcliffe-Richards compares prostitutes to musicians. She sees nothing obviously worse about selling services to produce sexual pleasure in another than in selling services to produce aesthetic pleasure in others. In what follows I shall offer reflections on what might indeed be morally wrong with prostitution irrespective of female oppression.

1.

Prostitution is degrading and demonstrates a lack of self-respect. It fails to show proper regard for our sense of self or our value. To pursue this idea, we might compare the way prostitution is degrading to other kinds of disrespect for self. Thomas Hill differentiates two forms of lack of self-respect, each devolving upon a different dimension of the self. In each form individuals are not true to themselves by failing to value a capacity integral to autonomous living. The first form Hill describes is Kantian in nature: individuals do not respect themselves as members of Kant's Kingdom of Ends. This may occur when someone tolerates violations of individual rights, "acting as if his rights were nonexistent or insignificant."[2]

In reconsidering self-respect, Hill notes another form of disrespect for self which occurs when we do not live up to our own standards.[3] This is different from not appreciating our objective moral rights because we have failed to honor our personal code. This is still based in autonomy insofar as it involves the *product* of self-legislation: the standards we give ourselves to live by. When suffering this form of self-degradation, individuals are not true to the way of life they have legislated for themselves. For whatever reason, they have not made the effort to become the sort of people to which they once aspired. Although he briefly discusses the lack of self-respect of both the prostitute and the artist, Hill confines his remarks to his theme of failing to live up to our own standards, and does not examine either apart from such failure.

This form of disrespect falls within the more general category of failure at self-definition. Setting standards by which to live is a way of choosing for ourselves who we will become. When we fail to act in accord with those standards, then, we fail to respect our own self-creative efforts. Prostitution resembles it by failing to honor the capacity of sex for self-definition. In not living up to our own standards, we fail to fulfill the commitment of prior self-legislation. Prostitutes, on the other hand, forfeit their ongoing powers of self-definition. Their forfeiture is two tiered. One is highly individual, involving capacities for intimacy. The other is more generic, turning as it does on the determination of gender identity.

When a woman prostitutes herself, she is not true to her natural self; she fails to appreciate adequately capacities and abilities that constitute people as non-moral individuals. When she degrades herself in this way, moreover, she is also abandoning a portion of her power to define herself, to exercise autonomy over herself in self-creative activity. This is because the sexual capacities she does not appreciate are important to self-definition. It is something like a loss of aspiration, a settling for less than people can naturally make of themselves. This may involve a failure to live up to personal standards, but it need not. How then might prostitution demonstrate a lack of self-respect in this way?

2.

Radcliffe-Richards's own musician analogy is helpful, especially since we sometimes speak of musicians as prostituting themselves. When gifted people capable of creative or good work forgo their opportunity in order merely to please or make money, we talk of them as prostituting themselves. They have sold out. They have sold themselves out and in the process sold out their art by short-changing it.

We need to say "merely to please or make money" because there is nothing wrong in pleasing or making money provided the people are at the same time being true to their art and thereby themselves. Being true to themselves has to do with what the musicians could have made of themselves *qua* musicians at least. Pursuing art commensurate with talent is likely to develop non-musical dimensions of an individual. The risk of genuine failure and the discipline required in meeting such a challenge, for instance, typically bring with them non-musical growth.

Is this relevant to the prostitute's selling out? I suspect that there is no art of pleasing sexually. As Socrates maintains in the *Gorgias*, it seems to be more of a knack. Like cooking or makeup, it aims merely to please and must vary its routines to suit particular clients and their individual tastes. Even if there were an art appropriate to sexuality, it would not be a question of the prostitute failing to do her best by the art. If there is something degrading and lacking in self-respect in prostitution, then, it will be there regardless of the level of craftsmanship prostitutes bring to their performance. Where the musician can sell out by taking money for hack work, the prostitute almost always degrades herself whenever she sells her sex. This means that the prostitute's failure stems from a relation to something other than her art or talent.

What is lacking in the prostitute's sexual behavior is affection for her partner and the desire to share herself through sexual interaction. This shows lack of self-respect by undervaluing a basic human capacity, intimate communion. This is the capacity for communication and unity with another at the deepest level. Sexuality is especially suited for expressing emotion and deepening intimacy. Selling short this capacity degrades our power to shape who we will become. Intimate relations are an important domain of self-definition. Who we share ourselves with helps to determine who and what we will become. Choosing our intimates is also choosing ourselves.

Intimate relations help to individualize us. We are intimate with someone we are close to as we are with no one else by expressing values, emotions, and beliefs in particular ways. People we are close to elicit intimate responses from us, as we in turn evoke intimate responses from them. When it is a mode of intimate communion, sexual interaction plays a crucial role in defining us as individuals. To forfeit the role of sex in intimacy, as prostitutes do, is to forfeit a sphere of self-determination.

Insofar as this is a live option, heralded in our society, to chronically neglect the chance to engage our capacity for intimacy is to show ourselves disrespect. It is tantamount to saying that our capacity for intimate, caring sex is not important. Sex has to be widely recognized in the culture as a mode of intimate communion for prostitution to exhibit lack of self-respect. We cannot show ourselves disrespect by degrading a capacity if we do not realize that it exists as such. For example, we would not be responsible for failing to develop our scientific abilities if there were no notion of science in our culture.

Sexuality promotes intimate communion by involving self-exposure, regardless of the presence of affection. In sexual interaction, we allow another access to our person. For women, this access typically includes entrance. At the same time, the other person's body is necessarily permeating our senses: touching, smelling, seeing, hearing, even tasting. Unlike words or meals, sex is more than a means for intimacy. It necessarily involves such proximity, exposure, and inundation of the other person that non-intimacy is naturally experienced as an absence or loss.

This is not the case with other facets of life that may be merely used for communication of tender emotions. Lack of intimacy in non-sexual spheres such as eating is not usually experienced as a deprivation because not especially conducive to intimacy. Engaging in such activities in solitude instead of with others would, however, neglect our capacity for socializing. We would find chronic solitary meal-taking lamentable because our culture places value on eating as a social function.

As Robert Solomon observes, sex is not just a medium for intimacy, it "breeds" intimacy, encouraging the exchange of ideas as well as bodily sensations.[4] Physical closeness, self-exposure, and an inevitable feeling of vulnerability, all conspire to make us want to share other aspects of ourselves. We want to share what is important and what further exposes us. We are spurred to deepen the physical closeness with personal involvement. This is because our bodies are not simply instruments or material for us to manipulate.

As Solomon observes, "Sexuality is not a specific desire so much as it is part of our basic bodily being—the way we comport ourselves, the way we move and the way we feel as well as the way we sense ourselves with others."[5] We experience the other in terms of our bodies. We also experience ourselves in terms of our bodily involvement with the other. When we present ourselves sexually to and for another, we invite mutual exploration and redefinition. Sex is a fundamental embodiment and expression of ourselves.

It might be objected that a prostitute could still be capable of intimacy in general and intimate sex in particular, just as a prostituting musician could still be able to compose or play creatively. In non-prostituting circumstances, then, both could be realizing their respective capacities for self-definition. To what extent either suffers a diminution in capacity is, of course, an empirical question. Human nature being what it is, prostituting behavior is likely to persist and bring about some loss.

Nevertheless, prostitutes and musicians squander their capacities for self-definition. Even if some capacity for good music or intimate experience is left over, a significant portion of their selves is expended cheaply. They show a lack of self-respect and proclaim the relative unimportance of their powers of self-creation. How much can they value themselves when they waste the very capacities for determining who they are? Something like this gnaws at the Jeff Bridges character, a talented pianist playing schlock, in the film *The Fabulous Baker Boys*.

A man who devotes his intimacy and sexuality to a woman who is married and maintains an intimate, sexual relationship with her husband similarly demeans himself. Unlike the prostitute, he may realize his capacity for intimate communion, but he nonetheless holds it cheaply. He treats himself as though he deserves no more than a part-time love, while his lover is entitled to this relationship in addition to another. He is content with too little relative to his lover and perhaps absolutely as well. Prostitution is not simply loveless sex or sex with strangers. It is a way of life that commits someone to chronic loveless sex, usually with strangers. If Solomon is correct, and sex breeds intimacy, then what must the prostitute's experience be like?

Because sex so naturally instigates intimacy, when we have sex with someone toward whom we feel cold or alien, we have to check our urge to share and disclose ourselves. Our inhibition will tend to be experienced as a restriction on our selves. Even without a system of patriarchal oppression, the structure of prostitution frustrates a basic dimension of sexuality. And with it, a significant sphere of our power to define who we are and what we will become is abandoned. No wonder research indicates that prostitutes employ techniques to distance themselves from their bodies during sex.[6] At the very least, this keeps the promptings of intimacy at bay, but its consequences may be more far-reaching.

As a mode of intimate communion, sexual relations help to individualize us. At the opposite pole, sex also defines us in terms of gender. When we do things sexual, we define ourselves importantly as men or women. Carole Pateman elaborates on the significance of sexual embodiment for prostitution in the following way:

> Human bodies and selves are also sexually differentiated . . . masculinity and femininity are sexual identities; the self is not completely subsumed in its sexuality, but identity is inseparable from the sexual construction of the self . . . .
> Workers of all kinds may be more or less "bound up in their work," but the integral connection between sexuality and sense of the self means that, for self-protection, a prostitute must distance herself from her sexual use.[7]

Because our gender identity is importantly implicated in our sexuality, selling ourselves sexually threatens to compromise our sense of gender. Sex in prostitution may or may not contribute to our gender identity. Either way, we demean ourselves. If the prostitute's sexual behavior does shape her gender identity, then it does so shallowly, on the physical plane alone, since it is devoid of intimacy. In this case, her sense of gender is uninformed by her personality or preferences.

Alternatively, the prostitute may feel somewhat disembodied during sex. By keeping her psychical distance she may keep sex from intruding on her gender identity. But this fails to integrate her body in how she defines herself as a woman. This yields a seriously truncated sense of femininity. Either way, the prostitute shows a lack of self-respect by subjecting herself to an attenuated process of gender identification.

Sexuality has the potential to encompass our selfhood in its extremes of generality and particularity. As ingredient to our gender identification, it forms us as men and women. As mode of intimate communion, it individualizes us. In prostitution, we forgo our power to define ourselves in both dimensions. However, prostitution does more than just neglect our capacity for autonomous self-creation, it also gives control of it to another.

3.

Imagine being paid to be intimate with someone in *non-sexual* ways. This would involve listening to the other person reveal deep aspirations, fears, and secrets. We, in turn, would share our innermost thoughts, emotions and concerns, or simulacra of them. Who our intimates are would then be determined extrinsically and arbitrarily by who has the money to pay for our personality. To sell our intimacy, therefore, would be to give short shrift to our own preferences and affections. In genuine intimacy, on the other hand, we choose to share ourselves with another on the basis of who we are and what we value in another. Self-determined choice attests to our self-regard. We are worth determining who we share ourselves with and how our capacity for intimacy is employed. Moreover, we are worth determining who we will become as a result of such sharing.

The prostitute relinquishes to another a sphere of her power to define herself as a woman and an individual. She does not merely neglect to employ her sexuality to shape her identity. She gives to someone else control over this particular capacity of self-definition. It will, within limits, be employed according to the wishes and interests of others. Prostitution necessarily involves permitting this capacity of self-definition to be controlled from without and arbitrarily. Ceding its control, in turn, risks *actually* being defined by clients and pimp.

Whether or not a prostitute is in fact redefined by her sexual activity is contingent. It depends on such variables as the prostitute's ability to distance herself from her body, the client, and the entire situation. By necessarily yielding control over an identity-forming capacity, the prostitute always runs the contingent risk of actually being defined extrinsically and arbitrarily. Relinquishing a hold on an identity-forming capacity is demeaning. It undervalues our selves by taking too lightly the forces which can shape us. It would be like allowing any crackpot scientist to experiment with our brain. No change *might* result, but even so, we would have been careless with our person and thereby failed to show proper self-regard.

This can be seen by returning to the musician analogy. Musicians also yield their power to define themselves musically if they prostitute themselves and their music. They permit their talent to be directed extrinsically, from without. Whether this will result in identities actually being redefined by others is also contingent. But musicians do not simply neglect to define themselves by means of their musical talent, as would be the case if they turned their backs on music altogether. They hand over this particular mode of self-definition to suit the tastes of others.

4.

Hill provides a justification for exceptions of behavior that would typically be degrading but is not because of certain conditions. I think this wise and applicable to prostitution also. It helps us see that prostitution can be a degrading practice and still be non-degrading in certain situations.

As Hill notes: "The Uncle Tom . . . is not servile . . . if he shuffles and bows to keep the Klan from killing his children."[8] There can be reasons which justify what would otherwise be demeaning behavior. The black man knows his rights and places the lives of those he loves above the importance of asserting them. We might say that coercive circumstances can alter the moral character of what would otherwise be self-denigrating behavior.

People bereft of dignified options are not blameworthy for doing what they need to do in order to survive. We risk being self-righteous if we condemn struggling musicians for squandering their talent and prostitutes for relinquishing their capacities for self-creation. We might do better to blame the world for forcing compromising choice on them. When individuals in such straits do not give in, but remain true to their art or capacity for intimacy, they go beyond proper self-regard. They exhibit something on the order of nobility. But we should not condemn people made of less stern stuff for selling their talent or sexual favors to save their lives, or those of their loved ones.

Notes

1. Janet Radcliffe-Richards, "Sex: A Feminist Perspective," in *Morality and Moral Controversies*, John Arthur, ed. (Englewood Cliffs, N.J.: Prentice-Hall, 1986), pp. 84-92.

2. Thomas Hill, "Servility and Self-Respect," in *Today's Moral Problems*, Richard Wasserstrom, ed. (New York: Macmillan, 1975), pp. 137-152.

3. Thomas Hill, "Self-Respect Reconsidered," in *Respect for Persons*, in Tulane Studies in Philosophy, Vol. 31, Hugh Green, ed. (New Orleans: Tulane University, 1982), pp. 129-139.

4. Robert Solomon, *About Love* (New York: Simon and Schuster, 1988), p. 212.

5. *Ibid.*, p. 195

6. Carole Pateman, *The Sexual Contract* (Stanford, Cal.: Stanford University Press, 1988), p. 207.

7. *Ibid.*, pp. 206-207.

8. Hill, "Servility and Self-Respect," in *Respect for Persons*, p. 145.

Nineteen

CAN LOVE RESOLVE THE PROBLEM OF MARRIAGE?

Predrag Cicovacki

There is only one proof for the presence of love: the depth of the relationship, and the alivenessand strength in each person concerned; this is the fruit by which love is recognized.
—Erich Fromm

There is something peculiar and puzzling in our attitude toward marriage. We commonly understand marriage to be an intimate and lasting relationship of two mature persons. This already indicates that we regard marriage as a valuable ideal, as something that is worth cultivating and preserving. And yet, marriage as an institution is in a severe crisis; the divorce rate is alarmingly high. Married partners do not see any more what exactly is the bond which is supposed to keep them together. We are not sure any more why marriage is an ideal and why, if at all, it is worth cultivating and preserving.

I will focus on this conflict. The heart of the conflict lies in the tension between two essential aspects of marriage, its intimacy and its constancy. This tension creates the problem of marriage. Marriage is a truly good relationship only when intimacy and constancy are present. But this does not happen very often. What, then, can resolve the problem? The traditional ways of arranging and regulating marriage do not help here, since they focus almost exclusively on only one of its dimensions, its constancy. A deeply rooted belief in our culture is that marriage should be based on love. Can love, then, resolve the problem of marriage? Love, as we usually understand it, does not untangle it.

We put too much emphasis on the physical aspect of love and on the intimacy of marriage.

But this does not show that love cannot resolve the problem of marriage. Love should be understood with an emphasis on its spiritual aspect. More precisely, love should be understood as the factor that can lead toward the resolution of the major spiritual problem, the problem of becoming a fully developed human being. So understood, love can create a new dimension of the marriage relationship, its depth. It is the depth of the relationship which leads to intimacy and constancy of marriage.

1. The Problem of Marriage

The ideal of marriage is deeply rooted in our spiritual heritage. Our predecessors have celebrated the *hieros gamos*, the "sacral marriage" in which Heaven and Earth, or the *yang* and the *yin*, have been joined together. Marriage is a union in which the spiritual identity of the separated duad is realized and recognized.[1] The unity is represented by a ring, which itself is a symbol of perfection and completeness. In the magic circle of the ring the dualism of the *yang* and the *yin* is balanced and united into a new quality.

Even as a union of two persons, marriage is seen as a noble ideal. Marriage is a lasting and intimate relationship of a man and a woman. Our predecessors believed that what God joins together is one forever and cannot be sundered by man or any other force. Marriage is the relationship in which I open my innermost being to my spouse, and my spouse opens her innermost being to me. We cross the boundaries of our individual egos and become one.

Marriage is still seen by many as an ideal worth cultivating and preserving. It is a relationship to which we make commitment, the commitment to share our experience, our aspirations, our dreams. It is a commitment to share our lives, and this is why the failure of marriage is perceived as the personal failures of the parties involved.[2]

The ideal of marriage is, however, different from real marriage. Real life sometimes reflects the ideal, but more often it shows another side of marriage as well. As Willard Gaylin correctly observes, "enough crimes have been committed in its name; as an institution [marriage] has housed its share of misery as well as security and bliss."[3] In the name of marriage and behind its veil many abuses and mistreatments have been committed. The marriage partner has often been treated as a possession, not as a mature person with his or her own will and rights.

This dark side of marriage has also been clearly recognized. With an increased awareness of it, and with more relaxed legal regulations and procedures, breaking a bad or an unsuccessful marriage has become a common experience. As a matter of fact, the divorce rate is so high that we cannot but wonder if the marriage partners really and seriously attempt to resolve their problems before they ask for a divorce. The divorce rate is so high that we cannot but wonder if marriage is still perceived as a noble ideal.

Marriage as an institution is in crisis. Marriage as a lasting and intimate relationship of two mature persons is in crisis. There should be no illusion that more than one factor is contributing to these crises. Nonetheless, I would like to focus on a particular factor, the significance of which has not been sufficiently recognized.

I have in mind a tension between the two essential features of the marriage relationship, its constancy and its intimacy. A reflective reader will easily recognize an initial tension between these two aspects of marriage. If the emphasis is on its constancy, if marriage has to last until death, it can do so regardless of the level or degree of intimacy. I might live forever in the same house with somebody who is a complete stranger to me, even with a person I happen to dislike or hate. Living together for a long period may not develop any intimacy. But if the emphasis is on intimacy, which is often understood as an intensive emotion toward another person, this is something that can change with time. Intimacy need not be constant and lasting.

The tension between constancy and intimacy is at the heart of the present crisis of marriage. This tension creates the problem of marriage. Many of us firmly believe that if there is a single factor that can resolve the problem, it can only be a genuine love. But what is a genuine love? What kind of love is it? And how can it bring together and balance constancy and intimacy?

2. Romantic Love and Marriage

We have a high esteem for the value of love. Richard Taylor expresses this beautifully by saying that "[i]t is doubtful whether anything in the world is so completely good as genuine love and affection."[4] We are also deeply convinced that marriage should always be based on love; any other reason for marriage is unacceptable.[5] Can love then resolve the problem of marriage? Or, more precisely, how should love be understood if it is to resolve the problem of marriage?

Romantic love may appear to offer the resolution for the problem of marriage. Romantic love is love generated and guided by passion. It reminds us of Aristophanes's mythical account of *Eros* in Plato's *Symposium*.[6] Gods have split the original human beings into two halves and love consists in longing for the lost half. When the lost half is found, the original unity is restored, and this state is a state of bliss. In romantic love, similarly, there is another person for everyone, someone who is a perfect match. This is the only person I can truly love, and the only person who can truly love me. The perfect mate is somewhere in the world waiting for us; we have to find our perfect match, marry him or her, and live happily forever.

If this is really so, romantic love would be able to bring both of the essential aspects of marriage together and resolve the problem of marriage. However, several things are unsatisfactory about this conception of romantic love. Hardly any mature person lives with an illusion of the perfect match, or the lost half, waiting to be found. What we have to find are people with whom we can get along and be close to. Then we eventually have to find one of the people for whom we care more than for others, whom we like or love more than others, and whom we would like to marry.

According to the idea of romantic love, with the act of marriage we seem to reach a certain destination, or succeed in achieving a certain goal. But this simply is not the case. The act of marriage is more properly regarded as the beginning of a journey together that will have its ups and downs. It is only the beginning of the journey in which the partners are yet to find a fruitful and creative balance between their aspirations and needs.

There is yet another aspect of the idea of romantic love that has been predominant in this century. This is the primary orientation of the ideal of romantic love on physical or bodily love. As in Aristophanes's tale, the identity with our lost half is predominantly physical or bodily. Even though, if found, the identity is recognized spiritually, it is primarily based on the physical concerns of the body. It may be based on a sexual drive, a sexual desire, or a passion. Any of them can make the relationship very intimate. The identity can further strengthen the feeling of unity and lead to the development of various spiritual affinities between the partners as well. But the development of such spiritual affinities is dependent on, and secondary both temporally and in importance, to the establishment of the physical affinities.

This conception of romantic love, which puts emphasis on the physical aspect of love, is widely accepted, even among those who do not accept two other features of romantic love, the idea of the perfect match and the idea that marriage is a goal. In this century this conception has found its support, if not in Freud himself, then at least in the widespread interest in vulgarized Freudianism.[7] The connection is established through the following two ideas. The first is that, no matter how genuine and disinterested love for another person can appear to be, in the last analysis it always represents a sexual love.

It always represents a drive of a blind energy directed toward sex libido. If so, love is essentially an irrational phenomenon.

The second idea is that culture, and with it all the social norms that regulate sexual behavior, is seen as something that suppresses the natural instinctual impulses, thereby creating a suitable ground for various mental disorders. This realization was an important factor that contributed to breaking all the taboos of the Victorian moral codes. They were replaced with norms of an almost universal permissiveness with respect to the manifestations of our passions. Perhaps the last act in this drama was the so-called sexual revolution of the sixties and the seventies.

I shall leave it to others to conclude whether this revolution has led us to something more progressive, or to decadence. I shall focus on the relevance of this conception of love for marriage and consider the implication of the idea that, as Joseph Campbell puts it, love is stronger than marriage and morality.[8] In our assumption that love is the only proper reason for marriage we focus on the positive aspect of love. Love leads to marriage. Love creates marriage. But there is another part of the story too: love can break and destroy marriage. One of the partners can fall in love with a third person, despite the marriage. But we do not have to go that far. Perhaps our ring, the reminder of our commitment, can make our will stronger than our passion. Love does not have to create a new physical attraction in order to break marriage. It is enough that love gradually dies and that one partner does not perceive the other as physically attractive any more. Unless their love is grounded in something deeper, the loss of physical attraction can lead to the loss of spiritual attraction and affiliation as well. If so, marriage is in danger, since the principal reason for its existence is not present any more.

Unlike many external factors of the past that aimed at the stability and constancy of a relationship, romantic love puts emphasis on the other relevant aspect of marriage, its intimacy. Understood as primarily based on physical desire and attraction, romantic love can indeed create an intimate relationship. It can bring about the development of the spiritual attraction, and thereby contribute to the constancy of the relationship. However, romantic love can fail to create any genuine spiritual relationship. It can also fail to promote a lasting relationship.

All of this suggests that romantic love is an unstable basis for marriage. For one thing, it involves an unrealistic conception of marriage. Perhaps even more importantly, because of the lack of any role of the spiritual element in it, romantic love cannot offer any adequate account of the nature of love. Romantic love is concerned with finding the proper object of love and falling in love. It assumes that everything that comes after is simple. But it is not. Being in love is very different from falling in love. Understanding what it is to be in love is important for understanding the role that love should play in marriage. In order to understand that role, let us consider the traditional understanding of love, with its emphasis on the spiritual element in love, and see if the spiritual element of love can bring together the two essential components of marriage, its constancy and intimacy.

3. *Eros, Philia, Agape,* and *Amor*

There are four major traditional ways of understanding love in Western civilization: *eros, philia, agape,* and *amor*. The uniqueness of *amor* is that, unlike the other three conceptions, it treats love as a person-to-person relationship; *amor* is essentially an individual relationship.[9] It is precisely this aspect of *amor* that is appealing for us today. Its origin can be traced back to the end of the eleventh century. It is related to the poetry of the troubadours that appeared in southwest France and quickly spread over Europe. Champions of *amor* that we know of are Abelard and Heloise, as well as Tristan and Isolde. They are champions of love not oriented to the body or intellect alone; *amor* is love that addresses itself primarily to the soul.

Two interesting things about *amor* deserve to be mentioned here. First, *amor* was almost always directed against the institution of marriage. Marriage is an obstacle in the way of *amor*; it is the marriage of the lovers that creates tensions and trials for the lovers until they are finally and inseparably united in death. Second, the major motive of *amor* for the troubadours is the personal experience and the sublimation of the soul. The troubadours repeatedly insist that *amor* ennobles and deifies the souls of the lover and the beloved.

Eros is initially described as a deity of procreation and the god of sexual desire. *Eros* is claimed to be the youngest and the oldest of the gods who govern the world. On a personal plane, *eros* is described as an uncontrolled state of divine possession or *enthousiasmos*. As a possession of an unchained passion by a demonic being, it is often compared to a mental disease or madness. *Eros* is love that longs for procreation or beauty, whether physical or spiritual. *Eros* longs for immortality.

There is no uniform understanding of the nature and the value of *eros* and erotic love. A popular Freudian interpretation puts emphasis on *eros* as a blind drive directed toward sexuality, or as a passive emotional attachment. But there is a long tradition of the understanding of *eros* in a more positive, edifying, and creative sense as well. For Heraclitus and Empedocles *eros* was the generative principle of the universe, something that was not opposed to *logos*, but to strife. Plato saw *eros* as the ground for all moral and spiritual progress.[10] More recently *eros* has been understood by Henry Bergson as *élan vital*, a life force or energy.[11] The blind life energy can be directed toward something negative and destructive, or toward something positive and creative. In that sense, *eros* can help us develop our individual and human potentials.

Philia is love that characterizes friendship. For Socrates *philia* and *eros* are nearly the same. True friendship aims primarily at the spiritual improvement of the beloved, and this is the goal of *Eros* as well.[12] It was Aristotle who made a significant difference between *philia* and *eros*. He devoted a considerable part of the *Nicomachean Ethics* to the consideration of friendship, its sources, motives, and importance.[13] Aristotle argued, for instance, that perfect friendship between good men is based on character, while spurious friendship aims at pleasure and utility. Modern philosophers have preserved a high esteem for friendship. Kant, for instance, defines it as "the union of two persons through equal and mutual love and respect."[14]

Agape is the conception of love that is essentially Christian. Christianity gives little or no importance to sexual or sentimental love. *Agape* is not a passive affection or emotion, but an active attitude toward others. *Agape* means compassion, suffering with, or sharing suffering.[15] *Agape* is the opening and awakening of the heart. *Agape* is "the awakening of the heart from bestial self-interest to humanity," and in this respect it is "the beginning of humanity, the birth of spiritual man out of the animal man."[16] *Agape* is a disinterested and non-personal relationship; it is the love for God, neighbors, and even enemies.

What is the relevance of all of these conceptions for the proper understanding of love and marriage? One important realization that we get from these considerations is that in the past love was understood to be primarily spiritual, or to lead toward spiritual development. This does not imply the rejection of the physical aspect of love. They can exist parallel to each other, and spiritual development can lead the development of physical intimacy and unity. But it is important that the spiritual aspect of love is not, in terms of its significance, secondary to the physical aspect of love.

Another important realization is that love, and especially love in marriage, does not have to be identified with any one of these conceptions. Our full understanding of the role of love in marriage can benefit if we try to combine some aspects of all four conceptions into one. Let us outline a comprehensive conception of love in marriage. Marriage partners should treat each other with all the due respect, care, and responsibility for their humanity. They should have an active attitude of giving, rather than receiving. In this respect *agape* is relevant for love in marriage. Married partners should certainly be friends and have a warm and special attitude of support and interest that we reserve for our real friends. We respect and love our friends not only for their humanity, but for who they individually are. Hence, *philia* is also relevant for love in marriage. Moreover, marriage for us has the uniqueness and the degree of intimacy and openness that goes beyond friendship. It is the relationship in which we attempt to achieve the balance of the *yang* and the *yin*. Love in marriage has to involve the person-to-person relationship emphasized in *amor*. Finally, living together and attempting to achieve the balance requires *eros*, our vital force and energy. We need our *eros* if we are longing for physical and spiritual procreation.

4. The Problem of Becoming Human

One of the crucial mistakes of the conception of romantic love is that it treats marriage as a completion of the search for the perfect mate. As we have already noticed, there are two problems with this view, insofar as it has to provide an adequate account of love in marriage. First, it focuses on falling in love rather than on being in love. Second, it overlooks that marriage is essentially a dynamic process rather than a static state of affairs. In order to understand what being in love means, we have to understand the dynamism of this process. And in order to understand the dynamism of this process, its motivations and its goals, we have to understand what precedes the process and leads to it. We must have at least a rough understanding of the key moments of childhood, and early adolescence and youth.

With every passing year we tend to idealize and develop nostalgic memories of our childhood. The days of our youth were times of happiness and sweet and careless life. Or so it may seem. Childhood, indeed, may be idyllic and happy. And yet there is something about it that should not fully deceive a mature person. The happiness of childhood was something that was simply there and that we did not have to deserve. As mature persons we can hope to achieve fulfillment and happiness only if we struggle for and deserve it.

The period of adolescence and youth, roughly the period between fifteen and twenty-five, appears to be free and full of adventures and excitements. Yet this is among the most difficult periods in our lives. In that period we cease to be children, but are not mature either. Unconditional love, protection, and guidance are denied to us; but they are not replaced by any other love, protection, or guidance.

The key problem of adolescence and youth is the problem of developing into a fully grown human being. Two important and most difficult aspects of this problem deal with unrelatedness, or separateness, and self-development.[17]

Since society and the family do not normally perform rituals of initiation any more, we find ourselves suddenly in an isolated and lost land. We are separated from our mothers and fathers, and we are not fully members of society. The whole world is turning around. We do not know what is happening, where we are, or, most importantly, who we are. The only thing we realize is that in the chaos of the world we are on our own.

The problem of self-development is no less important than the problem of separateness. A young person ought to wonder: Who am I? What do I stand for? What are my potentials? What am I capable of? It should be clear that this is not the problem of developing into a successful professional. A profession will be a more or less important part of someone's overall personality. But a profession is never a person's whole being. The ideal of self-development is the ideal of a fully developed humanity and individuality. It consists in a completeness, not in performing a few activities. Again, the ideal is not the development of intellect or body alone, but of the complete and whole being.

The problems of separateness and self-development are among the deepest problems of human existence. Our instincts and drives do not help us much here. We are not as thoroughly instinctually determined as animals. We have the advantage and burden of freedom. We are free to choose how to attempt to satisfy our needs and desires, to attempt to resolve our deepest problems. The problem with our freedom is that choices are not made for us by others; we have to make them. The responsibility is ultimately ours.

The problems of separateness and self-development are permanent problems of human existence. Simply living with somebody does not by itself solve the problem of separateness. We can live with somebody and find the relationship fruitful and creative at one time, but cold and unproductive at another. We can live with somebody and yet, truly speaking, be unrelated to that person and lack a genuine interest for that person. The relatedness to another person has to be re-established time and again. Our self-development poses a similar problem. It certainly does not stop with our formal education, as some people may believe. Almost every day brings a new challenge that has to be resolved.

The problems of separateness and self-development are two aspects of a more general problem of becoming human. This is exclusively a spiritual problem, the biggest we can face.

5. The Depth of Love and the Problem of Marriage

Everyone brings the problems of separateness and self-development to marriage. It is pretty clear how love and marriage are relevant to the problem of separateness. Through love I relate to my marriage partner. Through my genuine respect, care, interest, and support I renew my relatedness to my partner. But it is also through my being able to open my innermost self to share my joys and my sorrows that I overcome my separateness and establish a genuine relationship with the other person. This is why marriage is not a union that is given and established with the act of marriage once and forever. It is more like a union of the *yang* and the *yin* which has always to achieve its balance anew.

Even when the marriage partners attempt to relate to each other with love, life will not always go smoothly. It is unrealistic and naive to expect otherwise. Each partner has to adapt completely to another person; it is natural to assume that one of them will adapt more quickly than the other. But even after the period of adaptation new and unexpected problems will arise.[18] The partners have to be aware that to love each other does not mean living without problems. They also have to be prepared to deal with the problems. This means much more than simply being tolerant to make the partner feel better. To genuinely relate to the partner requires a readiness to deal with the problems with full responsibility. It requires a readiness to understand what the problems are really about, as well as a willingness to resolve them. This is why a relatedness to another person can never be taken for granted.

Let us turn now to the problem of self-development. This problem is closely tied to the problem of separateness. I relate myself to another person through my whole personality. My ways of relating myself are based on my character; they display my choices and preferences, my aspirations and potentials. As important as it is that I give myself with love, what I can offer matters no less. The more I grow, the better I can give of myself to the relationship.

The other direction is equally important. A somewhat neglected aspect of love is that love, more than anything else, can stimulate and bring about learning, growth, and self-development. Even when marriage partners deeply love each other, living together does not mean living without problems. It is, of course, always possible to ignore them and behave as if they do not exist. It is also possible to find superficial solutions to the problems. But if the marriage partners are truly relating to each other, they will try to penetrate to the roots of the problems and resolve them.

This way of dealing with problems means openly facing the crisis and accepting the challenge. Serious problems do not have ready-made recipes for solution. Finding the right solutions requires a struggle. As Jung puts it: "there is no birth of consciousness without pain."[19] We, of course, do not always find the right solutions. However, when we approach our problems openly and love motivates us to resolve them, there is a hope that we shall find the right solutions. Nietzsche assures us that "the deepest insights spring from love alone."[20] It is, then, through love that we learn. Love truly transforms us and helps us grow.

If love is the condition of our growth and self-development, then our growth and self-development are possible only through a relationship with other people, especially with those whom we love. As Goethe emphasized: "We learn only from those we love."[21] Through our attempts to overcome our separateness and relate ourselves to the others, we grow and fully develop ourselves. Trying to relate and develop ourselves are but two aspects of the attempt to become human beings in the full sense of the term.

In the end, then, can love resolve the problem of marriage? Can love bring together the two essential elements of marriage, its constancy and its intimacy? I believe that now we have a ground for a positive answer to these questions. When in the marriage relationship we attempt to deal with the problems of separateness and self-development through love and with love, the relationship gets a new dimension of depth. Marriage, insofar as it is an attempt to deal with these two basic problems of human existence through love and with love, is a deep relationship. It has to be deep because it requires openness and a willingness of both sides to deal with the problems that occur in a way that will go to their roots.

If love can establish a relationship which is deep, then love can indeed solve the problem of marriage. The depth of the relationship, achieved through love, can lead toward the intimacy and the constancy of the relationship. A deep relationship cannot but be intimate; that much is clear. But the depth can bring about the constancy as well; it is not easy to find a person with whom we can attempt to deal with the problems of separateness and self-development. Marriage based on love will provide a permanent ground to deal with these problems. Marriage based on love is a ground for an intimate and lasting relationship of the partners. Such marriage is a genuine ground for an authentic life, a life worth living.[22]

Notes

1. For the idea of *hieros gamos* see Joseph Campbell, *The Mythic Image* (Princeton: Princeton University Press, 1974), pp. 38, 82, 154, 479. For the idea that marriage is the union in which the spiritual identity is recognized, see Campbell, *The Power of Myth* (New York: Doubleday, 1988), pp. 5-8, 147, 235-236, 250-251.

2. This has been pointed out by Willard Gaylin; see his *On Being and Becoming Human* (New York: Penguin, 1990), p. 228.

3. *Ibid.*, p. 229.

4. Richard Taylor, *Having Affairs* (Buffalo: Prometheus Books, 1982), p. 105. For Taylor's fuller account of the nature of love, see his *Good and Evil: A New Direction* (New York: Macmillan, 1970), chs. 15-18, pp. 205-268.

5. The idea that marriage should be based on love was introduced in the eighteenth century and has become dominant since the middle of the nineteenth century. See Denis de Rougemont, "Love," in *Dictionary of the History of Ideas* (New York: Charles Scribner's Sons, 1973), vol. 3, pp. 103-104.

6. Plato, *Symposium*, 190b-193e.

7. Pointed out by de Rougemont, "Love," pp. 105-106. For Freud's theory of love and sexuality see his "Three Essays on Sexuality," in *The Standard Edition of the Complete Psychological Works of Sigmund Freud*, ed. J. Strachey (London: Hogarth Press, 1953), vol. 7, pp. 150ff. See also his account of love in "Civilization and Its Discontents," vol. 21.

8. Campbell, *The Power of Myth*, p. 254.

9. My account of *amor* is mostly based on de Rougemont, "Love," pp. 97-103, and Campbell, *The Masks of God: Creative Mythology* (New York: The Viking Press, 1968), chs. 2, 4, and 6. See also his *The Power of Myth*, pp. 233-234, 238, 242. Some philosophers incorrectly identify *amor* with *eros*, and ascribe to *eros* a person-to-person relationship which *Eros* did not have. *Cf.* Alan Soble's "An Introduction to the Philosophy of Love," in *Eros, Agape, and Philia*, ed. Alan Soble (New York: Paragon House, 1989), pp. xxii-xxiv.

10. Plato, *Symposium*, 199e-212c, esp. 200c, 201c, 203e, 206e-207a, 208de, 211c.

11. This has been pointed out by Gaylin, *On Being and Becoming Human*, p. 213. Campbell has a similar account of *Eros*.

12. *Cf.* Plato's *Lysis*, 216cff. See also Gerasimos Santas, *Plato and Freud–Two Theories of Love* (New York: Basil Blackwell, 1988), ch. 4, pp. 81-96.

13. *Cf.* Aristotle, *Nicomachean Ethics*, Books 8-9, 1155l-1172a.

14. Immanuel Kant, *On Duties of Virtue to Others*, trans. Mary Gregor (Philadelphia: University of Pennsylvania Press, 1964), p. 160.

15. *Cf.* Campbell, *The Power of Myth*, pp. 139, 143-144, 201, 233-234, 245-246.

16. *Ibid.*, p. 219.

17. The significance of this problem is understood better by psychoanalysts than by philosophers. See, for instance, Erich Fromm's classic *The Art of Loving* (New

York: Harper & Row, 1956), esp. pp. 8ff, and Jung's "Marriage as a Psychological Relationship," in *The Collected Works of Carl Gustav Jung*, eds. Sir Herbert Read et al. (New York: Pantheon Books, 1953), vol. 17, pp. 187-201, and "The Stages of Life," vol. 8, pp. 387-403.

18. This important point has been argued for by Carl Gustav Jung, "Marriage as a Psychological Relationship," pp. 194ff, and Erich Fromm, *The Art of Loving*, pp. 79ff.

19. Jung, "Marriage as a Psychological Relationship," p. 193.

20. *Cf.* Paul Friedländer, *Plato: An Introduction* (Princeton: Princeton University Press, 1973), p. 50.

21. *Ibid.*

22. I am grateful to Hilde Hein and Christopher Lucier Green for their comments on an earlier draft of this essay.

CONTRIBUTORS

William Aiken is Professor of Philosophy at Chatham College. He has worked on topics in applied ethics and social philosophy. He is co-editor of *World Hunger and Morality* (Prentice-Hall, 1996). Among his articles in these areas are "Human Rights in an Ecological Era" and "Value Conflicts in Agriculture."

Predrag Cicovacki is Assistant Professor of Philosophy at The College of the Holy Cross. He has interests in Kant, epistemology, and value theory. His recent articles include, "Kant on the Nature of Truth," "Kant and Philosophical Anthropology," and "Locke on Mathematical Knowledge."

Carlo Filice is Associate Professor of Philosophy at The State University of New York College at Geneseo. His interests lie in the philosophy of mind and all areas of ethics. Two of his articles are "Pacifism: A Philosophical Exploration," *Journal of Philosophical Research* (1992), and "Non-Substantial Streams of Consciousness and Free Actions," *International Studies in Philosophy* (1988).

Robert K. Fullinwider is Senior Research Scholar at The Institute for Philosophy and Public Policy at the University of Maryland. He has worked extensively in political theory, moral learning, and multicultural education. He is editor of *Public Education in a Multicultural Society* (Cambridge University Press, 1996). Among his recent articles is "Citizenship, Individualism, and Democratic Politics," *Ethics* (1995).

Robert Ginsberg is Professor of Philosophy at The Pennsylvania State University, Delaware County Campus. He has interests in aesthetics, social philosophy, and all areas of value inquiry. He is Executive Editor of the Value Inquiry Book Series and was Executive Editor of the *Journal of Value Inquiry* from 1991 through 1995. He is also a Past President of the American Society for Value Inquiry. He is the author of *Welcome to Philosophy!* (Freeman, Cooper, 1977) and editor of *The Philosopher as Writer: The Eighteenth Century* (Susquehanna University Press, 1987).

Joram Graf Haber is Distinguished Teaching Professor at Bergen Community College. He has broad interests in all areas of ethics and social philosophy. He is the author of *Forgiveness* (Rowman and Littlefield, 1991). He is editor or co-editor of several texts, including *Ethics for Today and Tomorrow* (Jones and Bartlett, 1997), a companion to a video series he conducted, *Ethics in the 90s* (Jones and Bartlett, 1996). Two of his recent articles are "Should Physicians Assist the Reaper?" and "The Moral Obligations of Lawyers."

Jonathan Jacobs is Associate Professor of Philosophy at Colgate University and a Life Member of Clare Hall, Cambridge University. His interests lie in ethics, moral psychology, and metaphysics. He is the author of *Practical Realism and Moral Psychology* (Georgetown University Press, 1995) and "Why Is Virtue Naturally Pleasing?", *Review of Metaphysics* (1995).

James S. Kelly is Associate Professor of Philosophy at Miami University, Ohio. He has interests in the metaphysics of the humanities and ethics. His articles include "Semantic Presence," "Wide and Narrow Interdisciplinarity," and "On Neutralizing Introspection—The Data of Sensuous Awareness."

Joseph Kupfer is Professor of Philosophy at Iowa State University. He has interests in ethics and aesthetics. He is the author of *Autonomy and Social Interaction* (SUNY Press, 1990). Two of his recent articles are "Romantic Love" and "Swift Things are Beautiful."

Julian Lamont is a Postdoctoral Research Fellow, Queensland University of Technology, Australia. His interests lie in economics, as well as political philosophy and ethics. He is one of the founders of the International Economics and Philosophy Society. His recent articles include "The Concept of Desert in Distributive Justice," *Philosophical Quarterly* (1994), and "Incentive-Income, Deserved-Income, and Economic Rents."

Sander Lee is Professor of Philosophy at Keene State College. He has interests in aesthetics, as well as ethics and social philosophy. He is President of the Society for the Philosophic Study of the Contemporary Visual Arts, a Past President of the American Society for Value Inquiry, and a Past President of the International Society for Value Inquiry. He is the editor of *Inquiries into Values* (Mellen, 1988) and the author of *Woody Allen's Angst: Philosophical Commentaries on His Serious Films* (McFarland, 1996).

H. P. P. (Hennie) Lötter is Associate Professor in the Department of Philosophy, Rand Afrikaans University. His interests lie primarily in political philosophy and the philosophy of science. He is the author of *Justice for an Unjust Society* (Rodopi, 1993). One of his recent articles is "A Postmodern Philosophy of Science?", *South African Journal of Philosophy* (1994).

Thomas Magnell is Associate Professor of Philosophy at Drew University. He has interests in epistemology and the philosophy of mind, as well as ethics and all areas of value inquiry. He is the editor of A. J. Ayer's *Metaphysics and Common Sense* (Jones and Bartlett, 1994). He is the Editor-in-Chief of the *Journal of Value Inquiry* and the Executive Director of the Conference on

Value Inquiry. He is also a Past President of the American Society for Value Inquiry. His recent articles include the two-part "Evaluations as Assessments," "Present Concerns and Future Interests," and "Fundamental and Technical Methods of Ethics."

Joseph Margolis is Laura H. Carnell Professor of Philosophy at Temple University. He has worked extensively on problems in contemporary Anglo-American and Continental European philosophy, often with a focus on the philosophy of the human sciences and metaphysics. He is the author of many books and articles and the editor of several texts. His more recent books include *Historied Thought, Constructed World* (University of California Press, 1995), *Interpretation Radical but Not Unruly: The New Puzzle of the Arts and History* (University of California Press, 1995), and *The Flux of History and the Flux of Science* (University of California Press, 1993).

Don E. Marietta, Jr. is Adelaide R. Snyder Distinguished Professor of Ethics and Professor of Philosophy at Florida Atlantic University. He has particular interests in the application of phenomenology to issues in ethics and value theory. He is the author of *For People and the Planet: Holism and Humanism in Environmental Ethics* (Temple University Press, 1994).

Uma Narayan is Assistant Professor of Philosophy at Vassar College. She has interests in social philosophy, ethics, the philosophy of law, and feminist philosophy. Her recent articles include "Male-Order Brides: Immigrant Women, Domestic Violence and Immigration Law," *Hypatia* (1995), and "Appropriate Responses and Preventive Benefits: Justifying Censure and Hard Treatment in Criminal Punishment," *Oxford Journal of Legal Studies* (1993).

Roger Paden is Associate Professor of Philosophy at George Mason University. His interests lie in social and political philosophy and ethics. Some of his recent articles are "Hobbesian Deliberators," *Hobbes Studies*, and "Welfare Policy and Moral Depravity of the Poor," *Public Affairs Quarterly*.

Tom Regan is Professor of Philosophy at North Carolina State University. He has worked extensively on problems in applied ethics, much of it concerning the rights of non-human animals. He has interests also in meta-ethics and the philosophy of G. E. Moore. He is a Past President of the American Society for Value Inquiry and the author of several books and many articles, as well as the editor or co-editor of a number of texts. His books include *The Case for Animal Rights* (University of California Press, 1983); *The Thee Generation: Reflections on the Coming Revolution* (Temple University Press, 1991); and

Bloomsbury's Prophet: G. E. Moore and the Development of His Moral Philosophy (Temple University Press, 1986).

James B. Wilbur III was Professor of Philosophy at The State University of New York College at Geneseo. He founded the *Journal of Value Inquiry* and served as its Executive Editor from 1967 through 1990. He founded the Conference on Value Inquiry and directed its first nineteen conferences. He was also a Past President of the American Society for Value Inquiry. He was the author of *The Moral Foundations of Business Practice* (University Press of America, 1992) and the editor or co-editor of several other books, including *The Worlds of the Early Greek Philosophers* (Prometheus Books, 1979); *The Worlds of Plato and Aristotle* (Prometheus Books, 1979); and *The Worlds of Hume and Kant* (Prometheus Books, 1982).

INDEX

absolutism, 4, 57, 141, 146, 149, 151, 152
academic freedom, 101, 102
Adams, E.M., 89, 92
adversarial contexts, 112
advocacy, 1, 3, 94-97, 99, 100, 102, 105-109, 111-117
aesthetics, 7, 58, 84, 235, 236
agape, 5, 226, 227, 232
Aiken, William, 3, 105, 115, 117, 235
American Medical Association, 103
American Philosophical Association, 102, 113
amor, 5, 226, 228, 232
animal rights, 70, 81, 95-99, 102, 103, 237
animal rights movement, 97-99
Anscombe, G.E.M., 82, 148, 152
Apollonian, 196
applied ethics, 2, 9, 94, 235, 237
applied values, 7
Aristotle, 21, 22, 32-35, 40, 41, 43, 63, 69, 71, 73, 74, 78, 82, 114-116, 121, 125, 130, 138, 140, 227, 232, 238
Arnheim, Rudolf, 49, 58
Aurelius, Marcus, 196
autonomous, 77, 85, 213, 218
autonomy, 2, 5, 71, 75, 77-81, 203, 206, 214, 236

Bassen, Paul, 165, 166
Bellah, Robert, 91
benefit, 4, 9, 19, 34, 38, 98, 99, 147, 155-165, 227
benefiting, 1, 4, 155, 156, 158, 162, 166
Bennett, Jonathan, 143, 146-150, 152
Bentham, Jeremy, 33, 34, 43, 69, 119, 120, 128
Brink, David, 132, 133, 139
Broadie, Surat, 134, 140
Butchvarov, Panayot, 74, 78, 82

Callahan, Sidney, 87, 92
Campbell, Joseph, 225, 231, 232
Castell, Alburey, 62, 67

Cicovacki, Predrag, 5, 221, 235
citizens, 96, 107, 113, 114, 126, 201
concentration camps, 182, 184, 186, 187
conceptual system, 11, 16
Conference on Value Inquiry, 1, 9, 237, 238
consciousness, 47-50, 64, 70-72, 74-81, 86, 103, 124, 125, 230, 235
consensus, 5, 16, 87, 205, 207-211
consequentialism, 4, 31, 141, 145, 147, 150-152
convention, 130, 134-136, 138, 140

de Rougemont, Denis, 232
death, 4, 5, 55, 103, 142, 149, 150, 153, 160, 161, 166, 176, 179-188, 190, 191, 197, 223, 226
Demme, Jonathan, 192, 193, 195
depression, 183
Dewey, John, 64
Dionysian, 196
disciplinary value inquiry, 1, 7-12, 17
Donagan, Alan, 151, 152

economics, 7, 8, 236
emotions, 3, 73, 86-90, 100, 107, 108, 115, 134, 135, 169, 170, 178, 215, 216, 218
empathy, 87, 92, 193, 205
end-value, 52-54, 56
epistemic encounters, 89, 90
epistemic powers, 85, 91
equal respect, 5, 202-207, 209
equality, 4, 12, 144-149, 152, 210, 211
eros, 5, 224, 226-228, 232
ethics, 1, 2, 4, 7, 9-12, 15-19, 21, 23, 35, 41, 42, 45, 55, 58, 59, 62, 81, 82, 85, 91, 93, 94, 97, 98, 100, 101, 115, 121, 129, 130, 132, 134, 139, 140, 151, 178, 210, 227, 232, 235-237
evaluation, 12, 51, 52, 56, 57, 83, 121, 125, 134, 135, 169, 170, 173
evaluative assessments, 11, 16, 17
evaluative concepts, 11, 12

existence, 4, 38, 50, 58, 65, 78, 79, 84, 87, 89, 102, 125, 155, 163, 164, 176, 177, 225, 229, 231

feelings, 4, 64, 70, 73, 75, 86, 87, 106, 132, 134, 169-175, 177, 178, 185, 194, 197
feminism, 85, 86, 91
Filice, Carlo, 2, 69, 235
Foot, Philippa, 143, 151
forgiveness, 1, 4, 169-178, 235
Frankena, William, 82
freedom, 62, 63, 65, 66, 101, 102, 135, 151, 179, 180, 182, 184, 185, 191, 198, 229
Freud, Sigmund, 196, 224, 232
Fromm, Erich, 221, 233
Fullinwider, Robert K., 3, 111, 235
future people, 155, 156, 164-166

Gaylin, Willard, 222, 231, 232
gender, 119, 186, 193, 206, 214, 217, 218
Ginsberg, Robert, 5, 179, 235
Giroux, Henry, 83, 91
Gleik, James, 66
God, 62, 63, 119, 151, 162, 199, 222, 226, 227, 232
Goethe, Johann Wolfgang, 231
good, 1, 12-18, 33, 35, 37, 44, 52, 54-57, 62-64, 71-74, 81, 82, 89, 94, 103, 105, 106, 108, 111-114, 120, 123, 130, 131, 133-140, 143-145, 149, 152, 153, 158, 159, 162, 163, 170, 174, 177, 178, 193, 199, 202, 203, 206-209, 215, 217, 221, 223, 227, 232
goodness, 1, 12-15, 17, 18, 23, 74, 85, 112, 132, 134, 182
Goodwin, Frederick K., 98, 99, 103
grievance, 171, 173, 174
Grisez, Germain, 144, 145, 151

Haber, Joram Graf, 4, 141, 178, 235
Harding, Sandra, 85, 91
Hare, R.M., 18, 37

Harman, Gilbert, 130, 139
Harris, Thomas, 193
Heidegger, Martin, 189, 197
Hill, Thomas, 92, 103, 213, 214, 219, 220
history, 7, 19, 22, 45, 57, 66, 84, 93, 95, 125, 126, 174, 176, 183, 199, 232, 237
Hobbes, 18, 109, 128, 237
Hobbesian, 13
Hoffman, Martin, 87, 92
Holocaust, 186
Homo economicus, 3, 119-123, 125-127
hope, 9, 28, 98, 111, 180, 183, 187, 191, 194, 195, 228, 230
Hull, Richard T., 18, 67
human life, 4, 69, 134-136, 140, 141, 144, 147, 149, 152, 182-185, 200
Hume, 8, 40, 238
Husserl, Edmund, 48

identity, 3, 62, 70, 122-125, 127, 128, 172, 181, 188, 190, 192, 195, 200, 202, 206, 209, 210, 214, 217-219, 222, 224, 231
immortality, 62, 63, 226
incomparability, 4, 144
independent value, 2, 52-56
individualism, 62, 84, 120, 127, 235
infinite value, 146-149
intellectuals, 111, 113, 114
inter-disciplinary value inquiry, 1, 9-11, 17
intimacy, 1, 5, 214-218, 220-223, 225-227, 231
intimate communion, 215-218
intrinsic value, 2, 53, 69-72, 74, 76-81
intuitionism, 130

Jacobs, Jonathan, 4, 129, 236
Jaggar, Alison, 86, 87, 90, 91
Jewishness, 185
Jung, Carl Gustav, 230, 233
justice, 13-15, 30, 43, 75, 78, 92, 116, 132, 133, 138, 181, 199, 200, 203, 205, 207-211, 236

Kant, Immanuel, 14, 18, 21, 22, 27, 28, 31, 35, 40, 41, 62-64, 69, 71, 73, 74, 94, 146, 227, 232, 235, 238
Kelly, J.S., 2, 83, 92, 236
Kupfer, Joseph, 5, 213, 236

Lamont, Julian, 4, 155, 236
Lee, Sander, 5, 189, 236
legitimation, 22, 23, 25, 27, 31, 34, 38, 41
Lewis, C.I., 62, 82
liberal values, 5, 200-205, 207, 209
liberty, 12, 162
life, 4, 13, 19, 20, 24, 28, 31-41, 43-45, 53-56, 58, 69-71, 73, 78, 83, 86, 89, 94, 96, 98, 103, 111, 122-124, 134-136, 138, 140-142, 144-149, 151, 152, 156, 157, 159-163, 173-176, 179-188, 197, 200, 203, 207-209, 214, 216, 217, 222, 226, 228, 230, 231, 233, 236
literature, 7, 41, 101, 143, 150
logical positivism, 101
Lötter, H.P.P. (Hennie), 5, 199
love, 1, 5, 69, 164, 170, 171, 174, 176, 177, 180, 182, 192, 195, 217, 220-232

MacIntyre, Alasdair, 14, 18, 22, 28, 119-121, 127, 210
Mackie, J.L., 2, 21, 23-27, 29, 30, 32, 35, 37, 39, 41, 42, 85, 91
Magnell, Thomas, 1, 7, 18, 167, 188, 236
Margolis, Joseph, 2, 19, 44, 237
Marietta, Jr., Don E., 2, 47, 58, 237
marriage, 5, 40, 81, 221-232
meta-ethical, 2, 94, 100
meta-ethical philosophy, 94
meta-ethics, 129, 237
metaphysics, 2, 21, 27, 29, 31, 33, 61, 65, 66, 92, 166, 236, 237
Mill, J.S., 69, 71-73, 81, 131, 132, 139
Moore, A.W., 152

Moore, G.E., 36, 40, 44, 85, 93, 94, 102, 103, 131, 237, 238
moral concern, 1, 12-15, 18, 65, 178
moral conflict, 14
moral dilemma, 14
moral facts, 85, 129, 130, 132, 133
moral goodness, 1, 12-15, 17, 18, 23
moral objectivity, 19, 21, 23, 27, 30, 32, 36
moral philosophy, 1, 7-10, 15, 19, 23, 33, 41-43, 100, 151, 152, 238
moral realism, 21, 34-36, 40, 44, 132, 139, 140
moral reassessments, 177
morally good, 12-17, 131, 133
Murphy, Jeffrie, 170, 172, 178

Nagel, Thomas, 2, 19-25, 27-35, 37, 41-43, 81, 85, 91
naturalism, 4, 23, 61, 66, 84, 85, 129-134, 137, 139
naturalistic realism, 4, 129, 130, 137, 139
Narayan, Uma, 4, 169, 237
Nazism, 197
Nielsen, Kai, 142, 151
Niemoeller, Martin, 186, 188
Nietzsche, Friedrich, 189, 196, 230
normative, 1-4, 9-12, 15-17, 20, 21, 24-26, 28, 30, 31, 56, 84, 85, 88-90, 95-97, 100-102, 105-109, 129, 130, 132, 134, 135, 138, 173
normative advocacy, 3, 100, 105-109
normative reality, 3, 85, 90

objective, 1, 2, 10, 15, 20, 21, 23-32, 40-42, 47, 50, 51, 53, 54, 57-59, 65, 75-77, 84-87, 89, 99, 101, 120, 132-136, 214
objectivity, 2, 20, 22, 25, 26, 28, 31-34, 36, 37, 47, 50-53, 55, 57, 85, 86, 134, 137
obligation, 13, 15, 18, 23, 26, 32, 38, 56, 102, 156, 163-166
one-sidedness, 112

242 INDEX

oppression, 182, 213, 217

Paden, Roger, 3, 119, 237
Parfit, Derek, 3, 4, 122, 123, 128, 151, 155, 157-163, 165-167
partisan, 22, 31, 32, 105, 107-109
Pateman, Carole, 217, 220
persuasive argument, 108, 115
phenomenology, 47, 48, 57, 58, 72, 237
philia, 226, 227, 232
philosophy, 1-4, 7-10, 15, 19-21, 23, 33, 41-45, 61, 62, 66, 67, 92, 94-97, 100-102, 105, 111, 114, 116, 117, 119, 151, 152, 165-167, 197, 200, 201, 209-211, 220, 232, 235-238
Plato, 3, 48, 58, 69, 71, 78, 116, 117, 126-128, 226, 232, 233, 238
pleasure, 2, 30, 33, 69-75, 79, 99, 131, 138, 182, 213, 227
pluralistic, 5, 107, 199-201, 203, 204, 207-209
political advocacy, 3, 96, 105, 107-109, 114, 116
politics, 83, 86, 91, 114, 116, 210
Popper-Lynkeus, Josef, 152
population policy, 155, 163
postmodern, 2, 83, 91, 199, 209, 211, 236
practical cognition, 133, 137
practical realism, 129, 131, 138, 236
practical reason, 20, 21, 28, 30, 61-63, 67, 130-133, 135, 136, 138, 139
practice, 1, 2, 19, 29, 61-67, 100, 105-108, 120, 121, 124, 137, 138, 199, 219, 238
Principia Ethica, 93, 103
prison, 5, 96, 179-182, 184, 185
prudence, 2, 3, 122, 123, 125-127
public servants, 111, 113, 114

quasi-intrinsic value, 2, 69

rational decision theory, 7
rationality, 35, 71, 72, 75-81, 122, 135, 196, 210

Rawls, John, 22, 28, 29, 43, 200, 202, 209-211
reasonable expectations, 176
reasons, 1, 4, 12, 15, 22, 28-30, 34, 41, 48, 55-57, 66, 72, 87, 88, 90, 96-99, 105, 114, 122, 128, 137, 155, 163, 165, 166, 172-177, 202, 203, 219
reconciliation, 4, 169, 175-177
Regan, Tom, 3, 70, 81, 93, 101, 105, 109, 114-116, 237
relationship, 21, 66, 67, 150, 172-177, 191, 194, 195, 205, 207, 217, 221-233
repentance, 173, 175, 177, 178
resentment, 137, 172, 173, 176-178, 196
resignation, 176, 177
rhetoric, 99, 106, 114, 115
rightness, 13, 15, 18, 65
rights, 66, 70, 81, 95-99, 102, 103, 113, 142, 171, 172, 176, 193, 200, 210, 214, 219, 222, 235, 237
romantic love, 5, 223-225, 228
Ross, W. D., 14, 18, 74, 75, 82
Russell, Bertrand, 84, 91, 95

Sartre, Jean-Paul, 18
Scheffler, Samuel, 142, 145, 146, 150-152
Schlick, Moritz, 18
scholars, 48, 100, 111, 113-115
second-tier, 22, 23, 25, 28, 32, 34-38
self, 5, 13, 18, 22, 25, 39, 55, 62-64, 67, 77, 85, 92, 98, 106, 121-128, 135, 139, 156, 169, 172, 174, 175, 182, 185, 191, 203, 210, 213-220, 227-231
self-creative, 214
self-definition, 214-216, 218, 219
self-determination, 215
self-development, 5, 121, 228-231
self-interest, 64, 122, 125, 203
self-respect, 5, 213-218, 220
semantic content, 87-90
senses, 7, 91, 95, 100, 126, 198, 216
sentience, 2, 69, 71, 75-81
separateness, 228-231

sexuality, 215-218, 226, 232
Shaw, Russell, 144, 145, 151
Shaw, William, 151
slave morality, 196
Smith, Adam, 8, 64
Smith, Dorothy, 85
Snow, C.P., 104
Soble, Alan, 232
social scientists, 8
Socrates, 196, 215, 227
Solomon, Robert, 216, 217, 220
strong evaluator, 121, 122, 125
subjective, 20, 21, 29-32, 38, 40, 41, 47-51, 58, 59, 76, 77, 84, 85, 101, 120, 135
Sullivan, Louis, 91, 99
supererogatory, 13
supervenience, 44, 132, 133

Taurek, John, 144, 151
Taylor, Charles, 120, 121, 125, 127, 128, 140, 202, 210
Taylor, Richard, 34-38, 40, 44, 223, 232
teleological, 10, 120, 121
theoretical reason, 28, 61, 62, 67, 133
third-tier, 19, 22-24, 28, 29, 31, 32, 34, 36-38, 41, 42
Thoreau, H.D., 141
Tooley, Michael, 66
Two Cultures, 99, 104
Two-State Requirement, 157-162

Übermensch, 196, 197

value, 1-12, 17, 18, 23, 24, 28, 30, 35, 36, 38, 47, 50-58, 61, 67, 69-72, 74-81, 83, 84, 86-91, 101, 105, 112, 120, 121, 125, 129, 130, 132-134, 141-152, 174, 176, 177, 183, 187, 196, 200, 202, 207, 208, 213, 216-218, 223, 226, 235-238
value experiences, 3, 87, 89-91
value inquiry, 1, 2, 5, 7-12, 17, 18, 47, 58, 61, 67, 235-238
value requiredness, 89
valuing, 51, 52, 55-57, 135

virtue, 18, 55, 63, 72, 74, 75, 78-81, 113, 115, 119, 121, 125-127, 133, 146, 177, 232, 236

Warren, Mary Anne, 149, 152
Weber, Vin, 99
Whitehead, A.N., 64
Wiggins, David, 2, 23-25, 32-41, 43-45
Wilbur, James B. III, 2, 61, 238
Williams, Bernard, 2, 14, 18, 22, 42, 151, 152
Wittgenstein, Ludwig, 40, 41, 76, 82, 143, 151, 211
wrong, 2, 5, 12, 21, 36, 42, 47, 52, 85, 87-89, 91, 93, 125, 126, 131, 133, 134, 136, 142, 146, 147, 160, 171-177, 185, 194, 213, 215
wrongdoer, 4, 171-176
wrongdoing, 170, 176

VIBS

The **Value Inquiry Book Series** is co-sponsored by:

American Maritain Association
American Society for Value Inquiry
Association for Personalist Studies
Association for Process Philosophy of Education
Center for East European Dialogue and Development, Rochester Institute of Technology
Centre for Cultural Research, Aarhus University
College of Education and Allied Professions, Bowling Green State University
Concerned Philosophers for Peace
Conference of Philosophical Societies
International Academy of Philosophy of the Principality of Liechtenstein
International Society for Universalism
International Society for Value Inquiry
Natural Law Society
Philosophical Society of Finland
Philosophy Seminar, University of Mainz
R.S. Hartman Institute for Formal and Applied Axiology
Society for Iberian and Latin-American Thought
Society for the Philosophic Study of Genocide and the Holocaust
Yves R. Simon Institute.

Titles Published

1. Noel Balzer, *The Human Being as a Logical Thinker.*

2. Archie J. Bahm, *Axiology: The Science of Values.*

3. H. P. P. (Hennie) Lötter, *Justice for an Unjust Society.*

4. H. G. Callaway, *Context for Meaning and Analysis: A Critical Study in the Philosophy of Language.*

5. Benjamin S. Llamzon, *A Humane Case for Moral Intuition.*

6. James R. Watson, *Between Auschwitz and Tradition: Postmodern Reflections on the Task of Thinking.* A volume in **Holocaust and Genocide Studies.**

7. Robert S. Hartman, *Freedom to Live: The Robert Hartman Story,* edited by Arthur R. Ellis. A volume in **Hartman Institute Axiology Studies.**

8. Archie J. Bahm, *Ethics: The Science of Oughtness.*

9. George David Miller, *An Idiosyncratic Ethics; Or, the Lauramachean Ethics.*

10. Joseph P. DeMarco, *A Coherence Theory in Ethics.*

11. Frank G. Forrest, *Valuemetrics: The Science of Personal and Professional Ethics.* A volume in **Hartman Institute Axiology Studies.**

12. William Gerber, *The Meaning of Life: Insights of the World's Great Thinkers.*

13. Richard T. Hull, Editor, *A Quarter Century of Value Inquiry: Presidential Addresses of the American Society for Value Inquiry.* A volume in **Histories and Addresses of Philosophical Societies.**

14. William Gerber, *Nuggets of Wisdom from Great Jewish Thinkers: From Biblical Times to the Present.*

15. Sidney Axinn, *The Logic of Hope: Extensions of Kant's View of Religion.*

16. Messay Kebede, *Meaning and Development.*

17. Amihud Gilead, *The Platonic Odyssey: A Philosophical-Literary Inquiry into the Phaedo.*

18. Necip Fikri Alican, *Mill's Principle of Utility: A Defense of John Stuart Mill's Notorious Proof.* A volume in **Universal Justice.**

19. Michael H. Mitias, Editor, *Philosophy and Architecture.*

20. Roger T. Simonds, *Rational Individualism: The Perennial Philosophy of Legal Interpretation.* A volume in **Natural Law Studies.**

21. William Pencak, *The Conflict of Law and Justice in the Icelandic Sagas.*

22. Samuel M. Natale and Brian M. Rothschild, Editors, *Values, Work, Education: The Meanings of Work.*

23. N. Georgopoulos and Michael Heim, Editors, *Being Human in the Ultimate: Studies in the Thought of John M. Anderson.*

24. Robert Wesson and Patricia A. Williams, Editors, *Evolution and Human Values.*

25. Wim J. van der Steen, *Facts, Values, and Methodology: A New Approach to Ethics.*

26. Avi Sagi and Daniel Statman, *Religion and Morality.*

27. Albert William Levi, *The High Road of Humanity: The Seven Ethical Ages of Western Man,* edited by Donald Phillip Verene and Molly Black Verene.

28. Samuel M. Natale and Brian M. Rothschild, Editors, *Work Values: Education, Organization, and Religious Concerns.*

29. Laurence F. Bove and Laura Duhan Kaplan, Editors, *From the Eye of the Storm: Regional Conflicts and the Philosophy of Peace.* A volume in **Philosophy of Peace.**

30. Robin Attfield, *Value, Obligation, and Meta-Ethics.*

31. William Gerber, *The Deepest Questions You Can Ask About God: As Answered by the World's Great Thinkers.*

32. Daniel Statman, *Moral Dilemmas.*

33. Rem B. Edwards, Editor, *Formal Axiology and Its Critics.* A volume in **Hartman Institute Axiology Studies.**

34. George David Miller and Conrad P. Pritscher, *On Education and Values: In Praise of Pariahs and Nomads.* A volume in **Philosophy of Education.**

35. Paul S. Penner, *Altruistic Behavior: An Inquiry into Motivation.*

36. Corbin Fowler, *Morality for Moderns.*

37. Giambattista Vico, *The Art of Rhetoric (Institutiones Oratoriae,* 1711-1741), from the definitive Latin text and notes, Italian commentary and introduction by Giuliano Crifò, translated and edited by Giorgio A. Pinton and Arthur W. Shippee. A volume in **Values in Italian Philosophy.**

38. W. H. Werkmeister, *Martin Heidegger on the Way,* edited by Richard T. Hull. A volume in **Werkmeister Studies.**

39. Phillip Stambovsky, *Myth and the Limits of Reason.*

40. Samantha Brennan, Tracy Isaacs, and Michael Milde, Editors, *A Question of Values: New Canadian Perspectives in Ethics and Political Philosophy.*

41. Peter A. Redpath, *Cartesian Nightmare: An Introduction to Transcendental Sophistry.* A volume in **Studies in the History of Western Philosophy.**

42. Clark Butler, *History as the Story of Freedom: Philosophy in Intercultural Context,* with Responses by sixteen scholars.

43. Dennis Rohatyn, *Philosophy History Sophistry.*

44. Leon Shaskolsky Sheleff, *Social Cohesion and Legal Coercion: A Critique of Weber, Durkheim, and Marx.*

45. Alan Soble, Editor, *Sex, Love, and Friendship: Studies of the Society for the Philosophy of Sex and Love, 1977-1992*. A volume in **Histories and Addresses of Philosophical Societies.**

46. Peter A. Redpath, *Wisdom's Odyssey: From Philosophy to Transcendental Sophistry*. A volume in **Studies in the History of Western Philosophy.**

47. Albert A. Anderson, *Universal Justice: A Dialectical Approach*. A volume in **Universal Justice.**

48. Pio Colonnello, *The Philosophy of José Gaos*. Translated from Italian by Peter Cocozzella. Edited by Myra Moss. Introduction by Giovanni Gullace. A volume in **Values in Italian Philosophy.**

49. Laura Duhan Kaplan and Laurence F. Bove, Editors, *Philosophical Perspectives on Power and Domination: Theories and Practices*. A volume in **Philosophy of Peace.**

50. Gregory F. Mellema, *Collective Responsibility*.

51. Josef Seifert, *What Is Life? The Originality, Irreducibility, and Value of Life*. A volume in **Central-European Value Studies.**

52. William Gerber, *Anatomy of What We Value Most*.

53. Armando Molina, *Our Ways: Values and Character*, edited by Rem B. Edwards. A volume in **Hartman Institute Axiology Studies.**

54. Kathleen J. Wininger, *Nietzsche's Reclamation of Philosophy*. A volume in **Central-European Value Studies.**

55. Thomas Magnell, Editor, *Explorations of Value*.